ANCIENT POLITICAL
THOUGHT

ANCIENT POLITICAL
THOUGHT
A Reader

edited by Richard N. Bosley and Martin M. Tweedale

broadview press

Library and Archives Canada Cataloguing in Publication

　　　Ancient political thought : a reader / edited by Richard N. Bosley and Martin M. Tweedale.

Includes bibliographical references and index.
ISBN 978-1-55111-811-6 (pbk.)

　　　1. Political science—Greece—History. 2. Political science—Rome—History. I. Bosley, Richard, editor of compilation II. Tweedale, Martin, 1937-, editor of compilation

JC51.A53 2013　　　　　　320.0938　　　　　　C2013-905872-9

Broadview Press is an independent, international publishing house, incorporated in 1985.

We welcome comments and suggestions regarding any aspect of our publications—please feel free to contact us at the addresses below or at broadview@broadviewpress.com.

North America
PO Box 1243, Peterborough, Ontario, Canada K9J 7H5
2215 Kenmore Ave., Buffalo, New York, USA 14207
Tel: (705) 743-8990; Fax: (705) 743-8353
email: customerservice@broadviewpress.com

UK, Europe, Central Asia, Middle East, Africa, India, and Southeast Asia
Eurospan Group, 3 Henrietta St., London WC2E 8LU, United Kingdom
Tel: 44 (0) 1767 604972; Fax: 44 (0) 1767 601640
email: eurospan@turpin-distribution.com

Australia and New Zealand
NewSouth Books
c/o TL Distribution, 15-23 Helles Ave., Moorebank, NSW, Australia 2170
Tel: (02) 8778 9999; Fax: (02) 8778 9944
email: orders@tldistribution.com.au

www.broadviewpress.com

Copy-edited by Robert M. Martin

Broadview Press acknowledges the financial support of the Government of Canada through the Canada Book Fund for our publishing activities.

This book is printed on paper containing 50% post-consumer fibre.

PRINTED IN CANADA

Contents

INTRODUCTION

Greek philosophy is distinguished in all areas by a desire to come up with explanatory accounts (*logoi*) of phenomena that appeal to what we think makes sense rather than to fantastic myths and fables. In the areas of ethics and politics this means that the philosophers of the ancient world sought to justify certain ways of life and ways of organizing society by arguments that ultimately appeal to what seem to most to be reasonable goals to seek, and not by reference to decrees of the gods or advice from past legendary heroes. The philosophical undertaking in the area of politics assumes that at least a good deal of political and social order is something people themselves can consciously control and make sense of; otherwise asking what sort of order it makes sense to have would seem a useless endeavour. That assumption can certainly be challenged, but it is one that the modern West generally shares with the mainstream of its ancient progenitor. Consequently, although ancient political thought deals in part with problems peculiar to its own time, it remains thoroughly relevant to our own concerns. Indeed, we often find that our own questions and responses echo ones given by the ancients, and that the ancient versions are often simpler and clearer than their sophisticated modern articulations. It is the hope of the editors that this collection presents readings that illustrate this claim.

Nevertheless, the ancient world was politically and socially very different from our own, and it is necessary to be aware of the peculiarities of that world. The Greeks of ancient times lived in small city states (*poleis*), each of which consisted of a city which controlled and depended on the surrounding agricultural land farmed by its citizens. These city states were never politically united together until they all fell under Macedonian hegemony toward

1

the end of the fourth century BCE. Before the Roman period the largest of these city states was Athens, but even it had no more than 100,000 residents at its peak of power. Probably about half the population was composed of slaves and resident aliens; and of the free and native born, half would have been women, who essentially had no political rights. This means that the adult male citizenry could not have numbered much more than 20,000 when Athens went to war with Sparta in 431.

There was a considerable variety of forms of government represented among the city states. A very common problem was strife between the rich and the poor. When the rich were ascendant the government was oligarchic with strict property qualifications for participation in ruling; when the poor were ascendant the government was democratic to the extent, in Athens at least, of allowing all the adult male citizens participation in the governing assembly and a chance to fill various government offices.

From the sixth century BCE on, the importance of law was recognized, and court proceedings before juries were an important part of civic life. But occasionally someone would amass inordinate power and establish a tyranny in which the tyrant himself usurped the place of law. These tyrannies could be extremely bloody and repressive. (For an example, read the description of Archelaus in Plato's *Gorgias* in section B.4.b.)

After the defeat of the Persians in the first quarter of the fifth century, Athens became an imperial power, and in virtue of its immense navy exercised hegemony over most of the cities on the Aegean Sea. This imperialism brought great wealth to Athens in the form of tributes, and that in turn allowed for the flourishing of the city under the leadership of Pericles. However, in the Peloponnesus Sparta achieved dominance, and the two powers came into conflict. Sparta's army dominated on land, but the Athenians kept the seas for themselves and thus managed to preserve their empire largely intact. Eventually plague and then a disastrous expedition to conquer Syracuse in Sicily led to Athens' gradual collapse and eventual surrender to Sparta in 404. For a while a Spartan-imposed oligarchy ruled in Athens, but soon democracy was reinstated. Sparta itself mismanaged the empire it had conquered and soon fell into decline.

It is in the post-war Athens that Plato wrote his many works and established his school and research centre, the Academy. Aristotle studied there, and then in the late fourth century, when Greece had fallen under Macedonian rule, he established his own school, the Lyceum. The great works of Greek political theory arose, then, after a tumultuous century in which the fortunes of Athens as well as many other city states had risen and fallen in extremely dramatic fashion.

The great problem that exercised the political theorists of the ancient world was how a state could successfully govern itself without falling either into civil strife or into a tyranny that would in effect enslave the people. It was assumed almost universally that some sort of a state, more or less the size of a city, was necessary if humans were to live anything but a barbaric and primitive life. Also assumed was that any such state would involve some sort of division of rulers and ruled, although not excluded was the democratic possibility that citizens would take turns in filling these roles. Perhaps the most important tool thinkers fell back on to avoid both civil strife and tyranny was law. From very early on the Greeks saw law, including written constitutions, as an important stabilizing force in society. Consequently, in the classical period there was much thought given as to what a good constitution should contain, and cities would occasionally call in expert help in designing their constitutions. Much thought was expended too on how much of law was justified by the peculiar circumstances of the state in question and how much by universal principles based in human nature, or even in something divine.

Another common theme is the sharp distinction made between slaves and free citizens. The ancient economy depended heavily on slave labour to free at least some of the citizens from the need to perform the work of obtaining the necessities of life. The menial jobs that most slaves were forced to perform were considered demeaning to a free-born person, and one of the chief concerns was to avoid a form of government which forced servitude on its citizens. A distinction had to be made between ruling over free people and ruling as a master over slaves. The question then is how much power can be given to rulers without incurring the danger of the state turning into a vehicle for the rulers' obtaining that latter sort of domination. Can institutional safeguards be built in to prevent this sort of catastrophe?

Finally, the ancient Mediterranean world until the establishment of the Roman Empire was in a state of constant conflict between the various states and nations; and even after the Romans largely brought an end to this warfare within the borders of the empire, there were still external enemies to be fought and a large military establishment had to be maintained. This constant need to have a fighting force on hand meant that the military class and its leaders were very often allowed to rule, or at least be very influential in ruling, and frequently they simply forced their way to the top of the hierarchy. Military skills and spirit were often what people wanted in their leaders, and the demands of waging war often dominated the civic agenda. Philosophers after Socrates generally tried to moderate this sort of thinking by examining what in fact was a good life for citizens and what the real purposes of a state were. But one has to admit that there is a wide gap between the theories of the philosophers about the political order, on the one hand, and what was actually going on in government and political affairs, on the other, especially after the Roman Empire settled into a pattern of rule by military leaders and the succession to power was often settled by civil war rather than any constitutionally established process.

This gap between reality and philosophy is in large measure due to the widespread acceptance among philosophers from Plato on of something like the ethic that Socrates espouses in those Platonic dialogues which most scholars consider to have been written relatively early. That ethic is on display in the selection from Plato's *Gorgias* given below. For Socrates the good life, the one any sensible person would want to live, was one that was morally virtuous, and especially just. Injustice (which largely equates with what we would call immorality with respect to others) is for the persons who engage in it the worst thing they could inflict on themselves, no matter what supposed benefits it might bring them. Socrates expects to find, and has no qualms about, people seeking a good life for themselves. What goes wrong, on his view, is that they misjudge what makes a good life a good one by thinking that external goods, particularly wealth and ordinary pleasures, are what life is all about. Instead they should concentrate on the health of their souls, i.e., on the faculties that enable them to make good decisions on how to run their lives. In the end, the soul, for Socrates, equates with a person's self, a view which implies a significant separation of the self from the body which the self directs.

As a consequence of this ethic many thinkers construe the good society as one which in some measure, at least, promotes the moral virtue of its citizens through both laws and education. The welfare, then, which governments should be promoting includes factors that are unlikely to be considered in our own day, and the agreement on moral values which the Socratic view promotes is a lot more than either we or ancient societies could approach. Consequently, the Socratic legacy makes much of ancient political thought a challenge to many present day ideas about liberal, pluralist states and relativism with respect to moral values; but challenges of that sort should be taken as invitations to deeper thought about our own assumptions.

A: Presocratics

As early as the first quarter of the sixth century BCE, the Athenians recognized that the ways in which a community was governed could be modified by conscious human design and allowed Solon to devise a set of laws which managed to quell, for a while at least, the class conflict between the few rich and the many poor. But this opposition was to be a continuing and tragic dilemma for the Greek city states throughout the ancient period. The fact that the Athenians would turn to Solon as a person with enough wisdom to fix their laws and government evidences their strong tendency to bring practical thought to bear on such matters, rather than just relying on past tradition, customs, or supposed decrees of the gods. It also shows that laws and government were envisioned as having the purpose of keeping the community together and preserving internal peace. Heraclitus also notes this function of civic law, but he sets it in the context of a "divine" law governing the cosmos, accord with which is somehow requisite for good governance. The stage is thus set for the later debate over whether laws and justice itself are a matter of convention (*nomos*) or nature (*phusis*). The greatest playwright of the period, Aeschylus, recognizes in his play *Eumenides* that at Athens at least there had been a shift away from the view of justice as divine decrees to something humans could stand in judgement on, although it is clear he views this with mixed feelings.

The text from Herodotus shows us that already by mid-fifth century the Greeks recognized three basic forms of government: monarchy, oligarchy, and democracy, i.e., rule by one, rule by a few, and rule by the many. Because the few who rule are so often the rich, the ancients usually thought of oligarchy in a more particular sense: rule by the *wealthy* few; the class conflict between rich and poor then is translated into the form of oligarchy versus democracy, and further into warfare in many cities between the parties espousing these incompatible ways of running civic affairs.

A.1: SOLON

In the early sixth century BCE Solon was called upon to revise the laws of his native Athens in the face of impending civil strife between the poor farmers and the rich ruling families. He proceeded to find some sort of a compromise which gave neither party all it wanted. It is clear, however, that his chief concern is that the poor, in a fit of *hubris*, will unjustly grab for themselves all the wealth of the rich.

(1) POEM 4, LINES 1-10, 26-39[1]

> Our city will never be destroyed by the fate
>> of Zeus or the plans of immortal gods,
> for Pallas Athena our protector, great-spirited daughter
>> of a mighty god, holds her hands over us.
> But the citizens themselves, lured by wealth, want to bring
>> this great city down with their stupidities.
> The common people's leaders have a mind to do injustice,
>> and much grief is about to come from their great arrogance [*hubris*],
> for they do not know how to hold excess in check, nor to give
>> order to the pleasures of their present feast in peace.
> In this way the public evil comes home to each man
>> and the outer doors can no longer hold it back;
> it leaps high over the courtyard wall and finds you
>> anywhere, even if you hide in your inmost bedroom.
> This is what my spirit tells me to teach the Athenians:
>> bad government brings the most evils to a city;

---

1 Translated by Gagarin and Woodruff, pp. 25-26.

while good government makes everything fine and orderly,
and often puts those who are unjust in fetters;
it makes rough things smooth, stops excess, weakens arrogance,
and withers the growing blooms of madness.
It straightens crooked judgements, makes arrogant deeds
turn gentle, puts a stop to divisive factions,
brings to an end the misery of angry quarrels. This is the source
among human beings for all that is orderly and wise.

(2) POEM 5[1]

I gave the common people as much privilege as they needed,
neither taking honor from them nor reaching out for more.
But as for those who had power and were admired for their wealth,
I arranged for them to have nothing unseemly.
And I set up a strong shield around both parties
by not allowing either to defeat the other unjustly.

(3) POEM 34, LINES 1-9[2]

But some came for the purposes of robbery; they had rich hope,
and each of them thought that he would find much prosperity,
and that, although I was chattering gently, I would reveal a harsh mind.
They thought foolish things then, and now, angry at me,
they all look at me aslant, as at an enemy.
That's not right, for with the help of the gods, I accomplished what I said,
and as to the rest, I acted not without reason, nor was it pleasing to me
[to do] anything by force of tyranny, nor for the base to have an equal share of the rich
fatherland with the noble.

DIOGENES LAERTIUS, FROM *LIVES*:
SOLON'S SPEECH TO THE ATHENIANS:[3]

Solon to the Athenians: If you have suffered sadly through your own wickedness, lay not the blame for this upon the gods. For it is you yourselves who gave pledges to your foes and made them great; this

---

1   Translated by Gagarin and Woodruff, p. 26.
2   Translated by Emily Katz Anhalt, p. 106.
3   Diogenes Laertius, *Lives of Eminent Philosophers*, translated by R.D. Hicks (Cambridge, MA and London: Harvard UP and William Heinemann Ltd., 1950), vol. 1, p. 53.

is why you bear the brand of slavery. Every one of you walks in the footsteps of the fox, yet in the mass you have little sense. You look to the speech and fair words of a flatterer, paying no regard to any practical result.

A.2: HERACLITUS

eraclitus (fl. late sixth century BCE) seems to be the first philosopher to claim a dependence of human or civic law on the cosmic
law of the universe. The theme would reappear in much more
developed form among the Stoics.

(1) FRAGMENT 44[1]

The people must fight on behalf of the law as though for the city wall.

(2) FRAGMENT 114[2]

Those who speak with sense must rely on what is common to all, as a city must rely
on its law, and with much greater reliance. For all the laws of humans are nourished
by one law, the divine law; for it has as much power as it wishes and is sufficient for
all and is still left over.

DIOGENES LAERTIUS, FROM *LIVES*: ABOUT HERACLITUS:[3]

He would retire to the temple of Artemis and play at knuckle-bones[4]
with the boys; and when the Ephesians stood round him and looked
on, "Why, you rascals," he said, "are you astonished? Is it not better to
do this than to take part in your civic life?"

---

1 From Diogenes Laertius, *Lives*, IX, 2 translated by Kirk and Raven, p. 211.
2 From Stobaeus, *Anth.* iii, 1, 179, translated by Kirk and Raven, p. 211.
3 *Lives*, translated by Hicks, vol. 2, p. 411.
4 A children's game resembling jacks.

A.3: AESCHYLUS, *EUMENIDES*

Lines 397-995[1]

The "father" of Greek tragedy is traditionally said to have been born in 525/24 BCE. His first dramatic productions were at the Dionysian festival in Athens in 500. He was still young enough to fight against the Persians at Marathon in 490 and he witnessed the defeat of the Persian fleet at Salamis in 480. He is said to have written at least eighty dramatic works during the course of his career, but only some of the later ones survive. He died in Sicily in 456/55. The *Eumenides* is the last of a trilogy of tragedies called the Oresteia. In it Aeschylus tells the oft-told tale of the fortunes of the House of Atreus and its king Agamemnon, who according to the *Iliad* led the Greek expedition against Troy, but brings it to an original end by linking the story to the rise to power and dominance of his native city, Athens.

In the first of the three plays Agamemnon is murdered on his return home from the war by his own wife Clytemnestra, who herself is taking revenge for her husband's sacrifice of their daughter Iphigenia when this was demanded by the goddess Artemis as the price to be paid to end the unfavourable winds that were keeping the Greek fleet from sailing to Troy. In the second play Agamemnon's son, Orestes, is spurred on by Apollo, the prophet deity of Delphi, to take revenge on his mother, and this he does with encouragement from his sister Electra. But because of this matricide Orestes is pursued by the Furies, weird, winged hags who bring deserved anguish on those who have committed gross injustice.

The *Eumenides* (the title, not given to the play by Aeschylus himself, means the "kindly ones" and refers, ironically, to the Furies) brings the

---

1   Translated by Vellacott, pp. 161-80.

story to a conclusion that is almost entirely an addition created by the playwright rather than part of the ancient tale. In it the Furies represent the old tradition of unforgiving justice toward those who kill blood relatives; this tradition is associated with the older gods like Cronus and Gaia who preceded the Olympian gods headed by Zeus.

In this selection from the *Eumenides*, the Furies are out to visit their terrible torments on Orestes for his matricide, and they have not been deterred when Apollo, at the beginning of the play, said he has cleansed Orestes of all his wrongdoing, since the vengeance he wreaked on his mother was just. The dispute ends up decided by a court set up by the goddess Athene,[1] the guardian divinity of Athens, consisting of herself and twelve reputable citizens of the city. That is, Aeschylus would have us believe that the first homicide trial and the origins of the Areopagus (the Athenian high court of appeal), which in Aeschylus's day had long been a fixture in Athenian law.

Aeschylus is here presenting in mythical terms the new dispensation of justice which Athens had enacted, but that presentation does not disparage the old ways, nor does it unambiguously glorify the new. Although the judgement goes narrowly against the Furies, Athene mollifies them by offering them a revered place within the Athenian cults. With this compromise Athens' future prosperity and power are assured.

Our selection opens after Orestes, followed by the chorus of Furies, has reached Athens and is clinging in supplication to the statue of Athene, hoping to get her protection against his pursuers.

Athene enters from her temple.
ATHENE: From far away I hear my name loudly invoked,

       Beside Scamander, where I went in haste to claim
       Land that the Achaean chieftains had allotted me,[2]
       An ample gift chosen from plunder won in war
       And given entire to Theseus' sons to hold forever.
       And quickly, without toil of foot or wing, I came
       Borne on my strident aegis, with the galloping winds
       Harnessed before me.

                This strange company I see

---

1   This is the transliteration for the usual Greek spelling for the goddess's name; we mostly use the Roman spelling, 'Athena'.

2   The reference here is to some land near Troy which was in dispute between Athens and Mytilene at the time the play was produced.

Here in my precincts moves me, not indeed to fear,
But to amazement. Who are you? I speak to all:
This man who clasps my statue as a suppliant,
And you, beings like none I know that earth brings forth,
Either of those seen among gods and goddesses—
Nor yet are you like mortals. But I am unjust;
Reason forbids to slander others unprovoked.

CHORUS: Daughter of Zeus, you shall hear all, and briefly told.
We are the children of primeval Night; we bear
The name of 'Furies' in our home deep under earth.

ATHENE: Your race I know, also your names in common speech.

CHORUS: Maybe. Next you shall hear our office.

ATHENE: Willingly;
Therefore be plain of speech.

CHORUS: We drive out murderers.

ATHENE: And where can such a fugitive find rest and peace?

CHORUS: Only where joy and comfort are not current coin.

ATHENE: And to such end your hue and cry pursues this man?

CHORUS: Yes. He chose to become his mother's murderer.

ATHENE: Was there not some compulsive power whose wrath he feared?

CHORUS: And who has power to goad a man to matricide?

ATHENE: One plea is now presented; two are to be heard.

CHORUS: But he would ask no oath from us, nor swear himself.[1]

ATHENE: You seek the form of justice, more than to be just.

CHORUS: How so? Instruct me; you do not lack subtlety.

ATHENE: Injustice must not win the verdict by mere oaths.

CHORUS: Then try him fairly, and give judgement on the facts.

ATHENE: You grant to me final decision in this case?

CHORUS: We do; we trust your wisdom, and your father's name.

ATHENE: It is your turn to speak, my friend. What will you say?
Your faith in justice sent you to my statue here,
A holy suppliant, like Ixion,[2] at my hearth;
Therefore tell first your country, birth, and history;
Then answer to this charge; and let your speech be plain.

---

1 Normally before a case was tried a magistrate would take oaths from both the plaintiff and the defendant guaranteeing the truth of their pleas.

2 Ixion was the first mortal human to kill one of his own kinfolk. Zeus purified him of the crime. But he attempted to seduce Hera, queen of the gods, and for this he was punished by being bound to an ever-turning wheel for all time.

ORESTES: Divine Athene, first from your last words I will
          Set one great doubt at rest. My hand is not unclean;
          I do not sit polluted at your statue's foot.
          And I will tell you weighty evidence of this.
          To a blood-guilty man the law forbids all speech,
          Till bold-drops from some suckling beast are cast on him
          By one whose office is to purge from homicide.
          Long since, these rituals were all performed for me
          In other temples; beasts were slain, pure water poured.
          That question, then, I thus dispose of. For my birth,
          I am of Argos, and you know my father well,
          For you and he joined league to make the city of Troy
          No city—Agamemnon, leader of the warlike fleet.
          When he came home, he met a shameful death, murdered
          By my black-hearted mother, who enfolded him
          In a cunning snare, which now bears witness to the stroke
          That felled my father as he cleansed the stains of war.
                    When later, after years of exile I came home,
          I killed my mother—I will not deny it—in
          Just retribution for my father, whom I loved.
          For this Apollo equally is answerable;
          He told me of the tortures that would sear my soul
          If I neglected vengeance on the murderers.
          Whether or not I acted rightly is for you
          To judge; I will accept your word, for life or death.
ATHENE: This is too grave a cause for any man to judge;
          Nor, in a case of murder, is it right that I
          Should by my judgement let the wrath of Justice loose;
          The less so, since you came after full cleansing rites
          As a pure suppliant to my temple, and since I
          And Athens grant you sanctuary and welcome you.
          But your accusers' claims are not to be dismissed;
          And, should they fail to win their case, their anger falls
          Like death and terror, blight and poison, on my land.
          Hence my dilemma: to accept, or banish them;
          And either course is peril and perplexity.
          Then, since decision falls to me, I will choose our
          Jurors of homicide, for a perpetual court,

In whom I vest my judgement. Bring your evidence,
Call witnesses, whose oaths shall strengthen Justice's hand.
I'll pick my wisest citizens, and bring them here
Sworn to give sentence with integrity and truth.

Exit Athene, to the city; Orestes retires into the temple.

CHORUS:

Now true and false must change their names,
Old law and justice be reversed,
If new authority put first
The wrongful right this murderer claims.
His act shall now to every man
Commend the easy path of crime;
And parents' blood in after time
Shall gleam on children's hands accurst,
To pay the debt this day began.

The Furies' watchful rage shall sleep,
No anger hunt the guilty soul;
Murder shall flout my lost control;
While neighbours talk of wrongs, and weep,
And ask how flesh can more endure,
Or stem the swelling flood of ill,
Or hope for better times—while still
Each wretch commends some useless cure.

When stunned by hard misfortune,
On us let no man call,
Chanting the old entreaties:
"Come, swift, avenging Furies!
O sword of Justice fall!"
Some parent, struck or slighted,
In loud and vain distress
Often will cry, a stranger
To the new wickedness,
Which soon shall reach and ruin
The house of Righteousness.

For fear, enforcing goodness,
Must somewhere reign enthroned,
And watch men's ways, and teach them,
Through self-inflicted sorrow,
That sin is not condoned.
What man, no longer nursing
Fear at his heart—what city,
Once fear is cast away,
Will bow the knee to Justice
As in an earlier day?

Seek neither licence, where no laws compel,
Nor slavery beneath a tyrant's rod;
Where liberty and rule are balanced well
Success will follow as the gift of god,
Though how he will direct it none can tell.
This truth is apt: the heart's impiety
Begets after its kind the hand's misdeed;
But when the heart is sound, from it proceed
Blessings long prayed for, and prosperity.

This above all I bid you: reverence
Justice's high altar; let no sight of gain
Tempt you to spurn with godless insolence
This sanctity. Cause and effect remain;
From sin flows sorrow. Then let man hold dear
His parents' life and honour, and revere
Each passing guest with welcome and defence.

Wealth and honour will attend
Love of goodness gladly held;
Virtue free and uncompelled
Fears no harsh untimely end.
But the man whose stubborn soul
Steers a rash defiant course
Flouting every law's control—
He in time will furl perforce,

Late repenting, when the blast
Shreds his sail and snaps his mast.

Helpless in the swirling sea,
Struggling hands and anguished cries
Plead with the unheeding skies;
And god smiles to note that he,
Changing folly for despair,
Boasts for fear, will not escape
Shipwreck on the stormy cape;
But, his former blessings thrown
On the reef of justice, there
Perishes unwept, unknown.

Athene returns, bringing with her twelve Athenian citizens. Apollo comes from the temple, leading Orestes.

ATHENE: Summon the city, herald, and proclaim the cause;
  Let the Tyrrhenian trumpet,[1] filled with mortal breath,
  Crack the broad heaven, and shake Athens with its voice.
  And while the council-chamber fills, let citizens
  And jurors all in silence recognize this court
  Which I ordain today in perpetuity,
  That now and always justice may be well discerned.
CHORUS: Divine Apollo, handle what belongs to you.
  Tell us, what right have you to meddle in this case?
APOLLO: I came to answer that in evidence. This man
  Has my protection by the law of suppliants.
  I cleansed him from this murder; I am here to be
  His advocate, since I am answerable for
  The stroke that killed his mother. Pallas, introduce
  This case, and so conduct it as your wisdom prompts.
ATHENE: The case is open. [*To the leader of the chorus*] Since you are the accuser,
  speak.
  The court must first hear a full statement of the charge.

---

1 A trumpet with an especially deep and piercing tone.

CHORUS: Though we are many, few words will suffice. [*To Orestes*] And you
          Answer our questions, point for point. First did you kill
          Your mother?

ORESTES: I cannot deny it. Yes, I did.

CHORUS: Good; the first round is ours.

ORESTES: It is too soon to boast;
          I am not beaten.

CHORUS: You must tell us, none the less,
          How you dispatched her.

ORESTES: With a sword I pierced her heart.

CHORUS: On whose persuasion, whose advice?

ORESTES: Apollo's. He
          Is witness that his oracle commanded me.

CHORUS: The god of prophecy commanded matricide?

ORESTES: Yes; and he has not failed me from that day to this.

CHORUS: If today's vote condemns you, you will change your words.

ORESTES: I trust him. My dead father too will send me help.

CHORUS: Yes, trust the dead now; your hand struck your mother dead.

ORESTES: She was twice guilty, twice condemned.

CHORUS: How so? Instruct
          The court.

ORESTES: She killed her husband, and my father too.

CHORUS: Her death absolved her; you still live.

ORESTES: But why was she
          Not punished by you while she lived?

CHORUS: The man she killed
          Was not of her own blood.

ORESTES: But I am of my mother's?

CHORUS: Vile wretch! Did she not nourish you in her own womb?
          Do you disown your mother's blood, which is your own?

ORESTES: Apollo, now give evidence. Make plain to me
          If I was right to kill her. That I struck the blow
          Is true, I own it. But was murder justified?
          Expound this point, and show me how to plead my cause.

APOLLO: To you, august court of Athene, I will speak
          Justly and truly, as befits a prophet-god.
          I never yet, from my oracular seat, pronounced
          For man, woman, or city any word which Zeus,

The Olympian Father, had not formally prescribed.
I bid you, then, mark first the force of justice here;
But next, even more, regard my father's will. No oath
Can have more force than Zeus, whose name has sanctioned it.

CHORUS: Then Zeus, you say, was author of this oracle
You gave Orestes—that his mother's claims should count
For nothing, till he had avenged his father's death?

APOLLO: Zeus so ordained, and Zeus was right. For their two deaths
Are in no way to be compared. He was a king
Wielding an honoured sceptre by divine command.
A woman killed him: such death might be honourable,
In battle, dealt by an arrow from an Amazon's bow.
But you shall hear, Pallas and you who judge this case,
How Clytemnestra killed her husband. When he came
Home from the war, for the most part successful, and
Performed his ritual cleansing, she stood by his side;
The ritual ended, as he left the silver bath,
She threw on him a robe's interminable folds,
Wrapped, fettered him in an embroidered gown, and struck.
          Such, jurors, was the grim end of this king, whose look
Was majesty, whose word commanded men and fleets.
Such was his wife who killed him—such that none of you,
Who sit to try Orestes, hears her crime unmoved.

CHORUS: Zeus rates a father's death the higher by your account.
Yet Zeus, when his own father Cronos became old,
Bound him with chains. Is there not contradiction here?
Observe this, jurors, on your oath.

APOLLO: Execrable hags,
Outcasts of heaven! Chains may be loosed, with little harm,
And many ways to mend it. But when blood of man
Sinks in the thirsty dust, the life once lost can live
No more. For death alone my father has ordained
No healing spell; all other things his effortless
And sovereign power casts down or raises up at will.

CHORUS: You plead for his acquittal; have you asked yourself
How one who poured out on the ground his mother's blood
Will live henceforth in Argos, in his father's house?
Shall he at public altars share in sacrifice?
Shall holy water lave his hands at tribal feasts?

APOLLO: This too I answer; mark the truth of what I say.

        The mother is not the true parent of the child

        Which is called hers. She is a nurse who tends the growth

        Of young seed planted by its true parent, the male.

        So, if Fate spares the child, she keeps it, as one might

        Keep for some friend a growing plant. And of this truth,

        That father without mother may beget, we have

        Present as proof, the daughter of Olympian Zeus:[1]

        One never nursed in the dark cradle of the womb;

        Yet such a being no god will beget again.

            Pallas, I sent this man to supplicate your hearth;

        He is but one of many gifts my providence

        Will send to make your city and your people great.

        He and his city, Pallas, shall forever be

        Your faithful allies; their posterity shall hold

        This pledge their dear possession for all future years.

ATHENE: Shall I now bid the jurors cast each man his vote

        According to his conscience? Are both pleas complete?

APOLLO: I have shot every shaft I had; and wait to hear

        The jurors' verdict.

ATHENE: [to the chorus] Will this course content you too?

CHORUS: [to the jurors] You have heard them and us. Now, jurors, as you cast

        Your votes, let reverence for your oath guide every heart.

ATHENE: Citizens of Athens! As you now try this first case

        Of bloodshed, hear the constitution of your court.

        From this day forward this judicial council shall

        For Aegeus'[2] race hear every trial of homicide.

        Here shall be their perpetual seat, on Ares' Hill.

        Here, when the Amazon army[3] came to take revenge

        On Theseus, they set up their camp, and fortified

        This place with walls and towers as a new fortress-town

        To attack the old, and sacrificed to Ares; whence

        This rock is named Areopagus. Here, day and night,

---

1 Athene sprang directly out of Zeus's head.
2 Aegeus was really the sea-god Poseidon, after whom the Aegean Sea is named. He was the father of Theseus, the legendary founder of Athens.
3 This legend about the Amazons and their eventual defeat by Theseus came to symbolize the Athenian resistance to the Persians.

Shall Awe, and Fear, Awe's brother, check my citizens
From all misdoing, while they keep my laws unchanged.
If you befoul a shining spring with an impure
And muddy dribble, you will come in vain to drink.
So, do not taint pure laws with new expediency.
Guard well and reverence that form of government
Which will eschew alike licence and slavery;
And from your polity do not wholly banish fear.
For what man living, freed from fear, will still be just?
Hold fast such upright fear of the law's sanctity,
And you will have a bulwark of your city's strength,
A rampart round your soil, such as no other race
Possesses between Scythia and the Peloponnese.
I here establish you a court inviolable,
Holy, and quick to anger, keeping faithful watch
That men may sleep in peace.
                                   I have thus far extended
My exhortation, that Athens may remember it.
Now give your votes in uprightness, and judge this cause
With reverence for your oath. I have no more to say.

During the following dialogue the jurors rise in turn to vote. There are two urns, one of which is "operative", the other "inoperative". Each juror has two pebbles, a black and a white. Into the "operative" urn each drops a white pebble for acquittal or a black one for condemnation; then disposes of the other pebble in the other urn, and returns to his seat.

CHORUS: I too advise you: do not act in scorn of us,
          Your country's visitants, or you will find us harsh.
APOLLO: I bid you fear my oracle and the word of Zeus,
          And not make both unfruitful.
CHORUS: [*to Apollo*]   Deeds of blood are not
          For your protection. Henceforth you will prophesy
          From a polluted shrine.
APOLLO: Then what of Zeus? Did he
          Suffer pollution, when he willed to purify
          His suppliant Ixion, the first murderer?
CHORUS: You argue; but if we should fail to win this case,
          We will infest the land with plagues unspeakable.

APOLLO: You have as little honour amongst elder gods
        As amongst us, the younger. I shall win this case.
CHORUS: This recalls your behaviour in Admetus' house:[1]
        You bribed the Fates to let a mortal live again.
APOLLO: Was it not right to help a man who worshipped me?
        Undoubtedly; besides, Admetus' need was great.
CHORUS: You mocked primeval goddesses with wine, to break
        The ancient dispensation.
APOLLO: Disappointment soon
        Will make you vomit all your poison—harmlessly.
CHORUS: You think your youth may tread my age into the dust.
        When we have heard the verdict will be soon enough
        To launch my anger against Athens. I will wait.
ATHENE: My duty is to give the final vote. When yours
        Are counted, mine goes to uphold Orestes' plea.
        No mother gave me birth. Therefore the father's claim
        And male supremacy in all things, save to give
        Myself in marriage, wins my whole heart's loyalty.
        Therefore a woman's death, who killed her husband, is,
        I judge, outweighed in grievousness by his. And so
        Orestes, if the votes are equal, wins the case.
        Let those appointed bring the urns and count the votes.

Two of the jurors obey her.

ORESTES: O bright Apollo, what verdict will be revealed?
CHORUS: O Mother Night, O Darkness, look on us!
ORESTES: To me
        This moment brings despair and death, or life and hope.
CHORUS: To us increase of honour, or disgrace and loss.
APOLLO: The votes are out. Count scrupulously, citizens;
        Justice is holy; in your division worship her.
        Loss of a single vote is loss of happiness;
        And one vote gained will raise to life a fallen house.[2]

---

1 Apollo was for a time forced to be a servant in the house of Admetus and his wife Alcestis.
    When Apollo found out that Admetus was soon to die, he persuaded the Fates to let him
    live, but only if someone else died in his stead. Alcestis volunteered.
2 He refers to the house of Atreus, Orestes' grandfather. ('House' in this sense means family,

The votes are brought to Athene. The black and white pebbles are equal in number.
Athene adds hers to the white.

ATHENE: Orestes is acquitted of blood-guiltiness.
           The votes are even.

ORESTES: Pallas, Saviour of my house!
      I was an exile; you have brought me home again.
      Hellas can say of me, "He is an Argive, as
      He used to be, and holds his father's house and wealth
      By grace of Pallas and Apollo, and of Zeus
      The Saviour, the Fulfiller." Zeus has shown respect
      For my dead father, seeing my mother's advocates,
      And has delivered me.
                So now, before I turn
      My steps to Argos, hear the oath I make to you,
      Your country, and your people, for all future time:
      No Argive king shall ever against Attica
      Lead his embattled spears. If any may transgress
      This oath of mine, I will myself rise from the grave
      In vengeance, to perplex him with disastrous loss,
      Clogging his marches with ill omens and despair,
      Till all his soldiers curse the day they left their homes.
      But if my oath is kept, and my posterity
      Prove staunch and faithful allies to the Athenian State,
      They shall enjoy my blessing. So, Pallas, farewell;
      Farewell, citizens of Athens! May each struggle bring
      Death to your foes, to you success and victory!

Exeunt Apollo and Orestes.

CHORUS: The old is trampled by the new!
          Curse on you younger gods who override
          The ancient laws and rob me of my due!
          Now to appease the honour you reviled
          Vengeance shall fester till my full heart pours
          Over this land on every side

---

including Atreus and his descendants. The evil deeds of an ancestor bring fated disaster to his
descendants.)

         Anger for insult, poison for my pain—
         Yes, poison from whose killing rain
         A sterile blight shall creep on plant and child
         And pock the earth's face with infectious sores.
         Why should I weep? Hear, Justice, what I do!
         Soon Athens in despair shall rue
         Her rashness and her mockery.
         Daughters of Night and Sorrow, come with me,
         Feed on dishonour, on revenge to be!

ATHENE: Let me entreat you soften your indignant grief.
         Fair trial, fair judgement, ended in an even vote,
         Which brings to you neither dishonour nor defeat.
         Evidence which issued clear as day from Zeus himself,
         Brought by the god who bade Orestes strike the blow,
         Could not but save him from all harmful consequence.
         Then quench your anger; let not indignation rain
         Pestilence on our soil, corroding every seed
         Till the whole land is sterile desert. In return
         I promise you, here in this upright land, a home,
         And bright thrones in a holy cavern, where you shall
         Receive forever homage from our citizens.

CHORUS: The old is trampled by the new!
         Curse on you younger gods who override
         The ancient laws and rob me of my due!
         Now to appease the honour you reviled
         Vengeance shall fester till my full heart pours
         Over this land on every side
         Anger for insult, poison for my pain—
         Yes, poison from whose killing rain
         A sterile blight shall creep on plant and child
         And pock the earth's face with infectious sores.
         Why should I weep? Hear, Justice, what I do!
         Soon Athens in despair shall rue
         Her rashness and her mockery.
         Daughters of Night and Sorrow, come with me,
         Feed on dishonour, on revenge to be!

ATHENE: None has dishonoured you. Why should immortal rage
         Infect the fields of mortal men with pestilence?

You call on Justice: I rely on Zeus. What need
To reason further? I alone among the gods
Know the sealed chamber's keys where Zeus's thunderbolt
Is stored. But force is needless; let persuasion check
The fruit of foolish threats before it falls to spread
Plague and disaster. Calm this black and swelling wrath;
Honour and dignity await you; share with me
A home in Athens. You will applaud my words,
When Attica's wide fields bring you their firstfruit gifts,
When sacrifice for childbirth and for marriage-vows
Is made upon your altars in perpetual right.

CHORUS: O shame and grief, that such a fate
                Should fall to me, whose wisdom grew
                Within me when the world was new!
                Must I accept, beneath the ground,
                A nameless and abhorred estate?
                O ancient Earth, see my disgrace!
                While anguish runs through flesh and bone
                My breathless rage breaks every bound.
                O Night, my mother, hear me groan,
                Outwitted, scorned and overthrown
                By new gods from my ancient place!

ATHENE: Your greater age claims my forbearance, as it gives
      Wisdom far greater than my own; though to me too
      Zeus gave discernment. And I tell you this: if you
      Now make some other land your home, your thoughts will turn
      With deep desire to Athens. For the coming age
      Shall see her glory growing yet more glorious.
      You here possessing an exalted sanctuary
      Beside Erechtheus' temple, shall receive from all,
      Both men and women, honours which no other land
      Could equal. Therefore do not cast upon my fields
      Whetstones of murder, to corrupt our young men's hearts
      And make them mad with passions not infused by wine;
      Nor plant in them the temper of the mutinous cock,
      To set within my city's walls man against man
      With self-destructive boldness, kin defying kin.
      Let war be with the stranger, at the stranger's gate;

There let men fall in love with glory; but at home
Let no cocks fight.

                    Then, goddesses, I offer you
A home in Athens, where the gods most love to live,
Where gifts and honours shall deserve your kind good-will.

CHORUS: O shame and grief, that such a fate
                 Should fall to me, whose wisdom grew
                 Within me when the world was new!
                 Must I accept, beneath the ground,
                 A nameless and abhorred estate?
                 O ancient Earth, see my disgrace!
                 While anguish runs through flesh and bone
                 My breathless rage breaks every bound.
                 O Night, my mother, hear me groan,
                 Outwitted, scorned and overthrown
                 By new gods from my ancient place!

ATHENE: I will not weary in offering you friendly words,
                 You shall not say that you, an elder deity,
                 Were by a younger Power and by these citizens
                 Driven dishonoured, homeless, from this land. But if
                 Holy Persuasion bids your heart respect my words
                 And welcome soothing eloquence, then stay with us!
                 If you refuse, be sure you will have no just cause
                 To turn with spleen and malice on our peopled streets.
                 A great and lasting heritage awaits you here;
                 Thus honour is assured and justice satisfied.

CHORUS: What place, divine Athene, do you offer me?

ATHENE: One free from all regret. Acceptance lies with you.

CHORUS: Say I accept it; what prerogatives are mine?

ATHENE: Such that no house can thrive without your favour sought.

CHORUS: You promise to secure for me this place and power?

ATHENE: I will protect and prosper all who reverence you.

CHORUS: Your word is pledged forever?

ATHENE: Do I need to promise
        What I will not perform?

CHORUS: My anger melts. Your words
        Move me.

ATHENE: In Athens you are in the midst of friends.

CHORUS: What blessings would you have me call upon this land?

ATHENE: Such as bring victory untroubled with regret;

Blessing from earth and sea and sky; blessing that breathes
In wind and sunlight through the land; that beast and field
Enrich my people with unwearied fruitfulness,
And armies of brave sons be born to guard their peace.
Sternly weed out the impious, lest their rankness choke
The flower of goodness. I would not have just men's lives
Troubled with villainy. These blessings *you* must bring;
I will conduct their valiant arms to victory,
And make the name of Athens honoured through the world.

CHORUS: I will consent to share Athene's home,

To bless this fortress of the immortal Powers
Which mighty Zeus and Ares
Chose for their habitation,
The pride and glory of the gods of Greece,
And guardian of their altars.
This prayer I pray for Athens.
Pronounce this prophecy with kind intent:
Fortune shall load her land with healthful gifts
From her rich earth engendered
By the sun's burning brightness.

ATHENE: I will do my part, and win

Blessing for my city's life,
Welcoming within our walls
These implacable and great
Goddesses. Their task it is
To dispose all mortal ways.
He who wins their enmity
Lives accurst, not knowing whence
Falls the wounding lash of life.
Secret guilt his father knew
Hails him to their judgement seat,
Where, for all his loud exclaims,
Death, his angry enemy,
Silent grinds him into dust.

CHORUS: I have yet more to promise. No ill wind

Shall carry blight to make your fruit trees fade;

        No bud destroying canker

        Shall creep across your frontiers,

Nor sterile sickness threaten your supply.

May Pan give twin lambs to your thriving ewes

        In their expected season;

        And may the earth's rich produce

Honour the generous Powers with grateful gifts.

ATHENE: Guardians of our city's wall,

        Hear the blessings they will bring!

        Fate's Avengers wield a power

        Great alike in heaven and hell;

        And their purposes on earth

        They fulfill for all to see,

        Giving, after their deserts,

        Songs to some, to others pain

        In a prospect blind with tears.

CHORUS: I pray that no untimely chance destroy

        Your young men in their pride;

And let each lovely virgin, as a bride,

        Fulfill her life with joy.

For all these gifts, you sovereign gods, we pray,

        And you, our sisters three,

        Dread Fates, whose just decree

Chooses for every man his changeless way,

You who in every household have your place,

        Whose visitations fall

        With just rebuke on all—

Hear us, most honoured of the immortal race!

ATHENE: Now, for the love that you perform

        To this dear land, my heart is warm.

        Holy Persuasion too I bless,

        Who softly strove with harsh denial,

        Till Zeus the Pleader came to trial

        And crowned Persuasion with success.

        Now good shall strive with good; and we

        And they shall share the victory.

CHORUS: Let civil war, insatiate of ill,

        Never in Athens rage;

Let burning wrath, that murder must assuage,

Never take arms to spill,

In this my heritage,

The blood of man till dust has drunk its fill.

Let all together find

Joy in each other;

And each both love and hate with the same mind

As his blood-brother;

For this heals many hurts of humankind.

ATHENE: These gracious words and promised deeds

Adorn the path where wisdom leads.

Great gain for Athens shall arise

From these grim forms and threatening eyes.

Then worship them with friendly heart,

For theirs is friendly. Let your State

Hold justice as her chiefest prize;

And land and city shall be great

And glorious in every part.

FOR DISCUSSION:

Why is justice important for the city?

What do you think is the significance of having Orestes' fate decided by human jurors rather than by the gods themselves?

What is the significance of giving the Furies a respected place in the city precincts?

A.4: HERODOTUS, *HISTORIES* III

B orn between 490 and 480 BCE in Halicarnassus on the southwest coast of Asia Minor, Herodotus is the earliest known Greek author to write in prose. His *Histories* (meaning investigations) are aimed at sorting out the history of Persia prior to its two attempts to conquer Greece in the early fifth century and showing how the conflict with Greece arose. He travelled widely in the domains affected by Persia and in North Africa, collecting stories of their own interactions with the Persians and noticing their customs and how they differed from Greek ways. The result is an invaluable window into the greater world of which Greece was a part in the sixth and fifth centuries.

(1) 37-38[1]

King Cambyses of Persia seems to have gone mad, at least in Herodotus' view, while on an expedition to Egypt. The chief evidence of this was his violation of local customs. This story calls forth from Herodotus the following remark on the power of custom over people's judgments about what is permissible and what is not.

In view of all this, I have no doubt whatever that Cambyses was completely out of his mind; it is the only possible explanation of his assault upon, and mockery of, everything which ancient law and custom have made sacred in Egypt. If anyone, no matter who, were given the opportunity of choosing from amongst all the nations in the world the set of beliefs which he thought best, he would inevitably, after careful consideration of their relative merits, choose that of his own country. Everyone without exception believes his own native customs, and the religion he was brought up in, to be the best; and that being so, it is unlikely that anyone but a madman would mock at such things. There is abundant evidence that this is the universal feeling about the ancient customs

---

1 Translated by de Selincourt, pp. 190-91.

of one's country. One might recall, in particular, an anecdote of Darius.[1] When he was king of Persia, he summoned the Greeks who happened to be present at his court and asked them what they would take to eat the dead bodies of their fathers. They replied that they would not do it for any money in the world. Later, in the presence of the Greeks, and through an interpreter so that they could understand what was said, he asked some Indians, of the tribe called Callatiae, who do in fact eat their parents' dead bodies, what they would take to burn them. They uttered a cry of horror and forbade him to mention such a dreadful thing. One can see by this what custom can do, and Pindar,[2] in my opinion, was right when he called it "king of all".

FOR DISCUSSION:

Is it impossible to criticize reasonably the customs of one's own community, or even prefer different customs one has encountered in some other community?

(2) 79-83[3]

While he was away on the aforementioned campaign in Egypt, back in the Persian capital of Susa Cambyses had his throne usurped by two Magi,[4] one of whom pretended to be Cambyses' brother when, in fact, Cambyses had already had his brother murdered. Cambyses died before he could return to Susa and reclaim his kingdom. The hoax was discovered by a Persian nobleman, Otanes, who with six other conspirators, assassinated the two Magi and exposed the fraud they had perpetrated. The passage below claims to summarize a discussion among the victors soon after the coup as to what form of government to establish. The speakers are Otanes and two of the other confederates, Megabyzus, and Darius, who was later to be the king who attempted to invade Greece and was defeated at Marathon.

Five days later, when the excitement had died down, the conspirators met to discuss the situation in detail. At the meeting certain speeches where made; some of our own countrymen refuse to believe they were actually made at all; nevertheless, they were. The first speaker was Otanes, and his theme was to recommend the establishment in Persia of democratic government.

"I think," he said, "that the time has passed for any one man amongst us to have absolute power. Monarchy is neither pleasant nor good. You know to what lengths

---

1   Persian king (522-486 BCE). He is mentioned also in the next selection.
2   One of the most famous of all Greek poets.
3   Translated by de Selincourt, pp. 209-11.
4   The Magi were Medes rather than Persians, but served as priests and wise men in the Persian government. The coup led to the slaughter of much of the Medean population in the Persian capital.

the pride of power carried Cambyses, and you have personal experience of the effect of the same thing in the conduct of the Magus. How can one fit monarchy into any sound system of ethics, when it allows a man to do whatever he likes without any responsibility or control? Even the best of men raised to such a position would be bound to change for the worse; he could not possibly see things as he used to do. The typical views of a monarch are envy and pride; envy, because it is a natural human weakness, and pride, because excessive wealth and power lead to the delusion that he is something more than a human being. These two vices are the root cause of all wickedness: both lead to acts of savage and unnatural violence. Absolute power ought, by rights, to preclude envy on the principle that the man who possesses it has also at command everything he could wish for; but in fact it is not so, as the behavior of kings to their subjects proves: they are jealous of the best of them merely for continuing to live, and take pleasure in the worst; and no one is readier than a king to listen to tale-bearers. A king, again, is the most inconsistent of men; show him reasonable respect, and he is angry because you do not abase yourself before his majesty; abase yourself, and he hates you for being an obsequious rogue. But the worst of all remains to be said: he breaks up the structure of ancient tradition and law, forces women to serve his pleasure and puts men to death without trial. Contrast with this the rule of the people; first, it has the finest of all names to describe it, 'isonomy',[1] or equality before the law; and, secondly, the people in power do none of the things that monarchs do. Under a government of the people a magistrate is appointed by lot and is held responsible for his conduct in office, and all questions are put up for open debate. For these reasons I propose that we do away with the monarchy and raise the people to power, for the state and people are synonymous terms."

Otanes was followed by Megabyzus, who recommended the principle of oligarchy in the following words: "Insofar as Otanes spoke in favor of abolishing monarchy, I agree with him; but he is wrong in asking us to transfer political power to the people. The masses are a feckless lot; nowhere will you find more ignorance or irresponsibility or violence. It would be an intolerable thing to escape the murderous caprice of a king, only to be caught by the equally wanton brutality of the rabble. A king does at least act consciously and deliberately; but the mob does not. Indeed, how should it when it has never been taught what is right and proper, and has no knowledge of its own about such things? The masses have not a thought in their heads; all they can do is to rush blindly into politics and sweep all before them like a river in flood. As for the people, then, let them govern Persia's enemies, not Persia; and let us ourselves choose a certain number of the best men in the country and give *them* political power. We personally shall be

---

1 From the Greek '*isos*' meaning equal, and '*nomos*' meaning law.

amongst them, and it is only natural to suppose that the best men will produce the best policy."

Darius was the third to speak. "I support," he said, "all Megabyzus' remarks about the masses, but I do not agree with what he said of oligarchy. Take the three forms of government we are considering—democracy, oligarchy, and monarchy—and suppose each of them to be the best of its kind; I maintain that the third is greatly preferable to the other two. One ruler: it is impossible to improve upon that, provided he is the best man for the job. His judgment will be in keeping with his character; his control of the people will be beyond reproach; his measures against enemies and traitors will be kept secret more easily than under other forms of government. In an oligarchy the fact that a number of men are competing for distinction in the public service cannot but lead to violent personal feuds; each of them wants to get to the top, and to see his own proposals carried; so they quarrel. Personal quarrels lead to open dissension, and then to bloodshed; and from that state of affairs the only way out is a return to monarchy—a clear proof that monarchy is best. Again, in a democracy malpractices are bound to occur; in this case, however, corrupt dealings in government services lead not to private feuds but to close personal associations, the men responsible for them putting their heads together and mutually supporting one another. And so it goes on, until somebody or other comes forward as the people's champion and breaks up the cliques which are out for their own interests. This wins him the admiration of the mob, and as a result he soon finds himself entrusted with absolute power; all of which is another proof that the best form of government is monarchy. To sum up: where did we get our freedom from, and who gave it us? Is it the result of democracy, or of oligarchy, or of monarchy? We were set free by one man, and, therefore, I propose that we should preserve that form of government, and further, that we should refrain from changing ancient laws, which have served us well in the past. To do so would lead only to disaster."

These were the three views set out in the three speeches, and the four men who had not spoken voted for the last.

FOR DISCUSSION:

Who of the speakers do you think presents the best case? What considerations do you think they have omitted?

Are there other options for forms of government besides the three mentioned?

B: Classical Period

The classical period witnessed the decline of the Greek city states, and of Athens in particular, first through the disastrous war between Athens and Sparta, and then by gradually succumbing to Macedonian hegemony in the fourth century. It is not surprising then to see a great deal of thought given to exactly how things go wrong in the government of cities and what remedies might be prescribed. There is an interest in utopian schemes, as evidenced by Aristophanes' satirizing of them and Plato's promotion of his own program of political reform. In both Plato and Aristotle the effort is made to bring the ethical thought that had its start with Socrates, as well as theories of the human soul, to bear on the whole question of how states should be governed. What we do not find is any idea that perhaps the whole enterprise of living in city states was a mistake, or that some larger kind of political union, such as emerged with the Macedonian empire, might be required to remedy the ills of the traditional order.

B.1: SOPHOCLES, *ANTIGONE*

ophocles lived from 496 to 406 BCE in Athens and was much revered in his own time both as a poet, writing over 120 plays, and as a statesman, undertaking both military and diplomatic roles. Only seven of the plays, all tragedies, remain extant. His plays won the annual competition at the Great Dionysian Festival in Athens eighteen times. The extant ones all deal with traditional tales handed down centuries before, which Sophocles retells in a way which still has power to grip an audience. The most famous of these plays deal with the story of Oedipus, legendary king of Thebes, and how his insistence on knowing everything about his life led to his own ruin. Sophocles' plays often involve unexpected reversals of fortune arising from over-confidence by someone in their ability to control life.

Sophocles' *Antigone* is set in legendary Thebes, the city Oedipus had come to rule after killing its king, Laius, who was, unknown to him at the time, his own father. Oedipus then married Laius' widow, Jocasta (his mother) and by her had two sons, Polyneices and Eteocles, and two daughters, Ismene and Antigone. After Oedipus' tragic end (recounted in two other plays by Sophocles, *Oedipus the King* and *Oedipus at Colonna*) his two sons were too young to rule and Jocasta's brother, Creon, took power. But eventually the brothers came into conflict over who was to succeed to the throne, and this led to a war in which Polyneices got support from Thebes' enemies, the Argives, and invaded his homeland. In the ensuing battle the brothers kill each other, but the Argives are defeated and Creon left to rule the city. In his anger at Polyneices' treason he forbids any burial for him, or for any of the fallen foe, leaving them as carrion for the dogs and birds. Antigone is so outraged by this show of disrespect for her brother, and for the ancient decrees of the gods regarding the bodies of dead kinfolk, that she goes herself to the field and gives Polyneices a minimal burial in defiance of her uncle's decree. This sets up the conflict between two stubborn personalities, but also between two radically different conceptions of law.

(1) LINES 332-375[1]

In this famous ode Sophocles has the chorus recount the ways in which the human race has tamed the natural environment for its own uses and then gone on to invent law so that men may live in cities. But the poem has an undercurrent of foreboding, a fear, or perhaps presentiment, that all may yet go wrong.

First Stasimon

CHORUS:

[*Strophe a*]

Many wonders, many terrors,
But none more wonderful than the human race
    Or more dangerous.
This creature travels on a winter gale
Across the silver sea,
Shadowed by high-surging waves,
While on Earth, grandest of the gods,
He grinds the deathless, tireless land away,
Turning and turning the plow
From year to year, behind driven horses.

[*Antistrophe a*]

Light-headed birds he catches
And takes them away in legions. Wild beasts
    Also fall prey to him.
And all that is born to live beneath the sea
Is thrashing in his woven nets.
For he is Man, and he is cunning.
He has invented ways to take control
Of beasts that range mountain meadows:
Taken down the shaggy-necked horses,
The tireless mountain bulls,
And put them under yoke.

---

1 Translated by Woodruff, pp. 14-16.

[*Strophe b*]
Language and a mind swift as the wind
        For making plans—
These he has taught himself—
And the character to live in cities under law.
He's learned to take cover from a frost
And escape sharp arrows of sleet.
He has the means to handle every need,
Never steps toward the future without the means.
Except for Death: He's got himself no relief from that,
Though he puts every mind to seeking cures
For plagues that are hopeless.

[*Antistrophe b*]
He has cunning contrivance,
        Skill surpassing hope,
And so he slithers into wickedness sometimes,
Other times into doing good.
If he honours the law of the land
And the oath-bound justice of the gods,
Then his city shall stand high.
But no city for him if he turns shameless out of daring.
He will be no guest of mine,
He will never share my thoughts,
If he goes wrong.

FOR DISCUSSION:

Does the ode imply anything about why we have laws?

(2) LINES 441-525[1]

Brought before her king and uncle by a watchman fearful for his own life, Antigone willingly confesses she has knowingly violated the king's decree, the law he himself has established. But she has scant respect for such a law, especially when it violates laws the gods themselves have established, *unwritten* laws that hold for all time. (This is the earliest known mention of such laws in Greek literature.) Viewed against the idea of law expressed in the choral ode of the previous selec-

---

1   Translated by Woodruff, pp. 18-22.

tion, Antigone's position, in challenging the claim of humanly contrived law to unconditional obedience, recognizes limits on how far human invention and cleverness can proceed before it brings down ruin on its perpetrators.

CREON:

　　　　You there! With your head bowed to the ground—
　　　　Are you guilty? Or do you deny that you did this thing?

ANTIGONE:

　　　　Of course not. I did it. I won't deny anything.

CREON: (to the watchman who has arrested Antigone)

　　　　You're dismissed. Take yourself where you please;
　　　　You're a free man, no serious charge against you.

　　　　　　(to Antigone)

　　　　As for you, tell me—in brief, not at length—
　　　　Did you know that this had been forbidden?

ANTIGONE:

　　　　I knew. I couldn't help knowing. It was everywhere.

CREON:

　　　　And yet you dared to violate these laws?

ANTIGONE:

　　　　What laws? I never heard it was Zeus
　　　　Who made that announcement.
　　　　And it wasn't Justice, either. The gods below
　　　　Didn't lay down this law for human use.
　　　　And I never thought your announcements
　　　　Could give you—a mere human being—
　　　　Power to trample the gods' unfailing,
　　　　Unwritten laws. These laws weren't made now
　　　　Or yesterday. They live for all time,
　　　　And no one knows when they came into the light.
　　　　No man could frighten me into taking on
　　　　The gods' penalty for breaking such a law.
　　　　I'll die in any case, of course I will,
　　　　Whether you announce my execution or not.
　　　　But if I die young, all the better:
　　　　People who live in misery like mine
　　　　Are better dead. So if that's the way
　　　　My life will end, the pain is nothing.

But if I let the corpse—my mother's son—
Lie dead, unburied, that would be agony.
This way no agony for me. But you! You think
I've been a fool? It takes a fool to think that.

CHORUS:

Now we see the girl's as wild by birth as her father.
She has no idea how to bow her head to trouble.

CREON:

Don't forget: The mind that is most rigid
Stumbles soonest; the hardest iron—
Tempered in fire till it is super-strong—
Shatters easily and clatters into shards.
And you can surely break the wildest horse
With a tiny bridle. When the master's watching,
Pride has no place in the life of a slave.
This girl was a complete expert in arrogance
Already, when she broke established law.
And now, arrogantly, she adds insult to injury:
She's boasting and sneering about what she's done!
Listen, if she's not punished for taking the upper hand,
Then I am not a man. *She* would be a man!
I don't care if she is my sister's child—
Or closer yet at my household shrine for Zeus—
She and her sister must pay the full price
And die for their crime.

(*The chorus indicate their surprise that both must die.*)

Yes, I say they have equal guilt,
Conniving, one with the other, for this burial.

Bring her out. I saw her in there a minute ago;
She was raving mad, totally out of her mind.
Often it's feelings of a thief that give him away
Before the crimes he did in darkness come to light.

(*turning to Antigone*)

But how I hate it when she's caught in the act,
And the criminal still glories in her crime.

ANTIGONE:

You've caught me, you can kill me. What more do you want?

CREON:

For me, that's everything. I want no more than that.

ANTIGONE:

Then what are you waiting for? More talk?

Your words disgust me, I hope they always will.

And I'm sure you are disgusted by what I say.

But yet, speaking of glory, what could be more

Glorious than giving my true brother his burial?

All these men would tell you they're rejoicing

Over that, if you hadn't locked their tongues

With fear. But a tyrant says and does

What he pleases. That's his great joy.

CREON:

You are the only one, in all Thebes, who thinks that way.

ANTIGONE:

No. They all see it the same. You've silenced them.

CREON:

Aren't you ashamed to have a mind apart from theirs?

ANTIGONE:

There's no shame in having respect for a brother.

CREON:

Wasn't he your brother, too, the one who died on the other side?

ANTIGONE:

Yes, my blood brother—same mother, same father.

CREON:

When you honour the one, you disgrace the other. Why do it?

ANTIGONE:

The dead will never testify against a burial.

CREON:

Yes, if they were equal. But one of them deserves disgrace.

ANTIGONE:

He wasn't any kind of slave. He was his brother, who died.

CREON:

He was killing and plundering. The other one defended our land.

ANTIGONE:

Even so, Hades longs to have these laws obeyed.

CREON:

But surely not equal treatment for good and bad?

ANTIGONE:

> Who knows? Down below that might be blessed.

CREON:

> An enemy is always an enemy, even in death.

ANTIGONE:

> I cannot side with hatred. My nature sides with love.

CREON:

> Go to Hades, then, and if you have to love, love someone dead.
> As long as I live, I will not be ruled by a woman.

FOR DISCUSSION:

If we dispense with divine decrees, can there be any grounds for defying the decrees of a legitimate authority?

(3) LINES 626-765[1]

Haemon, Creon's son, who is betrothed to Antigone, tries gently to persuade his father to relent, but the older man's stubbornness and fear of being seen as a weak ruler bring on a fit of anger at his own son. Creon, in his rage, supports the principle that rulers and their orders must be obeyed whether right or wrong, and come what may. In the conclusion of the play, not given here, Creon's tyrannical wilfulness brings on the destruction of his whole family and of his own rule at Thebes.

CHORUS:

> Now here is Haemon, the last of your children.
> Is he goaded here by anguish for Antigone,
> Who should have been his bride?
> Does he feel injured beyond measure?
> Cheated out of marriage?

CREON:

> We'll know the answer right away, better than prophets:
> Tell me, son, did you hear the final verdict?
> Against your fiancée? Did you come in anger at your father?
> Or are we still friends, no matter what I do?

HAEMON:

> I am yours, Father. You set me straight,

---

1   Translated by Woodruff, pp. 28-34.

Give me good advice, and I will follow it.
No marriage will weigh more with me,
Than your good opinion.

CREON:

Splendid, my boy! Keep that always in your heart,
And stand behind fatherly advice on all counts.
Why does a man pray that he'll conceive a child,
Keep him at home, and have him listen to what he's told?
It's so the boy will punish his father's enemies
And reward his friends—as his father would.
But some men beget utterly useless offspring:
They have planted nothing but trouble for themselves,
And they're nothing but a joke to their enemies.
Now, then, my boy, don't let pleasure cloud your mind,
Not because of a woman. You know very well:
You'll have a frigid squeeze between the sheets
If you shack up with a hostile woman. I'd rather have
A bleeding wound than a criminal in the family.
So spit her out. And because the girl's against us,
Send her down to marry somebody in Hades.
You know I caught her in the sight of all,
Alone of all our people, in open revolt.
And I will make my word good in Thebes—
By killing her. Who cares if she sings "Zeus!"
And calls him her protector? I must keep my kin in line.
Otherwise, folks outside the family will run wild.
The public knows that a man is just
Only if he is straight with his relatives.

So, if someone goes too far and breaks the law,
Or tries to tell his masters what to do,
He will have nothing but contempt from me.
But when the city takes a leader, you must obey,
Whether his commands are trivial, or right, or wrong.
And I have no doubt that such a man will rule well,
And, later, he will cheerfully be ruled by someone else.
In hard times he will stand firm with his spear
Waiting for orders, a good, law-abiding soldier.

But reject one man ruling another, and that's the worst.
Anarchy tears up a city, divides a home,
Defeats an alliance of spears.
But when people stay in line and obey,
Their lives and everything else are safe.
For this reason, order must be maintained,
And there must be no surrender to a woman.
No! If we fall, better a man should take us down.
Never say a woman bested us!

CHORUS:

Unless old age has stolen my wits away,
Your speech was very wise. That's my belief.

HAEMON:

Father the gods give good sense to every human being,
And that is absolutely the best thing we have.
But if what you said is not correct,
I have no idea how I could make the point.
Still, maybe someone else could work it out.

My natural duty's to look out for you, spot any risk
That someone might find fault with what you say or do.
The common man, you see, lives in terror of your frown;
He'll never dare to speak up in broad daylight
And say anything you would hate to learn.
But I'm the one who hears what's said at night—
How the entire city is grieving over this girl.
No woman has ever had a fate that's so unfair
(They say), when what she did deserves honour and fame.
She saved her very own brother after he died,
Murderously, from being devoured by flesh-eating dogs
And pecked apart by vultures as he lay unburied.
For this, hasn't she earned glory bright as gold?
This sort of talk moves against you, quietly, at night.

And for me, Father, your continued good fortune
Is the best reward that I could ever have.
No child could win a greater prize than his father's fame,

No father could want more than abundant success
From his son.

       And now, don't always cling to the same anger,
Don't keep saying that this, and nothing else, is right.
If a man believes that he alone has a sound mind,
And no one else can speak or think as well as he does,
Then, when people study him, they'll find an empty book.
But a wise man can learn a lot and never be ashamed;
He knows he does not have to be rigid and close-hauled.
You've seen trees tossed by a torrent in a flash flood:
If they bend, they're saved, and every twig survives,
But if they stiffen up, they're washed out from the roots.
It's the same in a boat: if a sailor keeps the footline taut,
If he doesn't give and inch, he'll capsize, and then—
He'll be sailing home with his benches down and his hull to the sky.
So ease off, relax, stop being angry, make a change.
I know I'm younger, but I may still have good ideas;
And *I* say that the oldest idea, and the best,
Is for one man to be born complete, knowing everything.
Otherwise—and it usually does turn out otherwise—
It's good to learn from anyone who speaks well.

CHORUS:

  Sir, you should learn from him, if he is on the mark. And you,
  Haemon, learn from your father. Both sides spoke well.

CREON: (*to the chorus*)

  Do you really think, at our age,
  We should be taught by a boy like him?

HAEMON:

  No. Not if I am in the wrong. I admit I'm young;
  That's why you should look at what I do, not my age.

CREON:

  So "what you do" is show respect for breaking ranks?

HAEMON:

  I'd never urge you to show respect for a criminal.

CREON:

  So you don't think this girl has been infected with crime?

HAEMON:

  No. The people of Thebes deny it, all of them.

CREON:

> So you think the people should tell me what orders to give?

HAEMON:

> Now who's talking like he's wet behind the ears?

CREON:

> So I should rule this country for someone other than myself?

HAEMON:

> A place for one man alone is not a city.

CREON:

> A city belongs to its master. Isn't that the rule?

HAEMON:

> Then go be ruler of a desert, all alone. You'd do it well.

CREON: (*to the chorus*)

> It turns out this boy is fighting for the woman's cause.

HAEMON:

> Only if *you* are a woman. All I care about is you!

CREON:

> This is intolerable! You are accusing your own father.

HAEMON:

> Because I see you going wrong. Because justice matters!

CREON:

> Is that wrong, showing respect for my job as leader?

HAEMON:

> You have no respect at all if you trample on the rights of gods!

CREON:

> What a sick mind you have: You submit to a woman!

HAEMON:

> No. You'll never catch me giving in to what's shameful.

CREON:

> But everything you say, at least, is on her side.

HAEMON:

> And on your side! And mine! And the gods below!

CREON:

> There is no way you'll marry her, not while she's still alive.

HAEMON:

> Then she'll die, and her death will destroy Someone Else.

CREON:

> Is that a threat? Are you brash enough to attack me?

HAEMON:

What threat? All I'm saying is, you haven't thought this through.

CREON:

I'll make you wish you'd never had a thought in your empty head!

HAEMON:

If you weren't my father, I'd say you were out of your mind.

CREON:

Don't beat around the bush. You're a woman's toy, a slave.

HAEMON:

Talk, talk, talk! Why don't you ever want to listen?

CREON:

Really? Listen, you are not going on like this. By all the gods,

One more insult from you, and the fun is over.

(*to attendants*)

Bring out that hated thing. I want her to die right here,

Right now, so her bridegroom can watch the whole thing.

HAEMON:

Not me. Never. No matter what you think.

She is not going to die while I am near her.

And you will never, ever see my face again. Go on,

Be crazy! Perhaps some of your friends will stay by you.

(*Exit Haemon.*)

FOR DISCUSSION:

Why do you think Creon remains so immoveable on the issue of Antigone's fate? Is there any logic to his position?

B.2: THUCYDIDES, *THE HISTORY OF THE PELOPONNESIAN WAR*

B orn to a wealthy Athenian family in the mid-fifth century BCE, Thucydides participated in the Peloponnesian war as an Athenian general, but after being responsible for the loss of the city of Amphibolis in 424, he was exiled and spent the rest of the war in Thrace. He then began writing a history of the conflict and continued this task after the war was over, but never entirely finished it. The resulting work, *History of the Peloponnesian War*, is one of the great classics of its genre and a very severe cautionary tale about the pitfalls of imperialism. He died sometime near the end of the century.

Like Solon, Thucydides was very aware of the way the split between rich and poor could tear society apart, and how easily government could slip into the hands of persons primarily interested in their own private gain. Both oligarchy and democracy suffer, in his mind, from this failing.

(1) BK.II: SELECTIONS FROM THE FUNERAL ORATION DELIVERED BY PERICLES IN HONOR OF THE FALLEN ATHENIAN SOLDIERS[1]

Much of Thucydides' *History* is given over to speeches by some of the main participants in the tragic events of the war. Thucydides has composed these speeches himself, but in them he tries to present the line of thought he remembers the speaker to have put forth. Here Thucydides gives his reader a rendering of the way in which the great Athenian leader Pericles could inspire his people to take pride in their achievements and resolve to bear the costs of war.

---

1 From *History* ii, 37, 40-41, 43, translated by Woodruff, pp. 40-45.

37. We have a form of government that does not try to imitate the laws of our neighboring states. We are more an example to others, than they to us. In name it is called a democracy, because it is managed not for a few people, but for the majority. Still, although we have equality at law for everyone here in private disputes, we do not let our system of rotating public offices undermine our judgment of a candidate's virtue; and no one is held back by poverty or because his reputation is not well-known, as long as he can do good service to the city. We are free and generous not only in our public activities as citizens, but also in our daily lives: there is no suspicion in our dealing with one another, and we are not offended by our neighbor for following his own pleasure. We do not cast on anyone the censorious looks that—though they are no punishment—are nevertheless painful. We live together without taking offense on private matters; and as for public affairs, we respect the law greatly and fear to violate it, since we are obedient to those in office at any time, and also to the laws—especially to those laws that were made to help people who have suffered an injustice, and to the unwritten laws[1] that bring shame on their transgressors by the agreement of all.

40. We are lovers of nobility without ostentation, and lovers of wisdom without any softening of character. We use wealth as an opportunity for action, rather than for boastful speeches. And as for poverty, we think there is no shame in confessing it; what is shameful is doing nothing to escape it. Moreover, the very men who take care of public affairs look after their own at the same time; and even those who are devoted to their own businesses know enough about the city's affairs. For we alone think that a man who does not take part in public affairs is good for nothing, while others only say he is "minding his own business." We are the ones who develop policy, or at least decide what is to be done; for we believe that what spoils action is not speeches, but going into action without first being instructed through speeches. In this too we excel over others: ours is the bravery of people who think through what they will take in hand, and discuss it thoroughly; with other men, ignorance makes them brave and thinking makes them cowards. But the people who most deserve to be judged tough-minded are those who know exactly what terrors or pleasures lie ahead, and are not turned away from danger by that knowledge. Again we are opposite to most men in matters of virtue: we win our friends by doing them favors, rather than by accepting favors from them. A person who does a good turn is a more faithful friend: his goodwill towards the recipient preserves his feeling that he should do more; but the friendship of a person who has to return a good deed is dull and flat, because he knows he will be merely paying a debt, rather than doing a favor, when he shows his

---

1 Probably a reference to religious prohibitions and obligations. See the reference to "unwritten laws" in Sophocles' *Antigone*, in the previous selection.

virtue in return. So that we alone do good to others not after calculating the profit, but fearlessly and in the confidence of our freedom.

41. In sum, I say that our city as a whole is a lesson for Greece, and that each of us presents himself as a self-sufficient individual, disposed to the widest possible diversity of actions, with every grace and great versatility. This is not merely a boast in words for the occasion, but the truth in fact, as the power of this city, which we have obtained by having this character, makes evident....

43. ... When the power of the city seems great to you, consider then that this was purchased by valiant men who knew their duty and kept their honor in battle, by men who were resolved to contribute the most noble gift to their city: even if they should fail in their attempt, at least they would leave their virtue to the city. For in giving their lives for the common good, each man won praise for himself that will never grow old, and the monument that awaits them is the most splendid—not where they are buried, but where their glory is laid up to be remembered forever, whenever the time comes for speech or action. For to famous men, all the earth is a monument, and their virtues are attested not only by inscriptions on stone at home; but an unwritten record of the mind lives on for each of them, even in foreign lands, better than any gravestone.

Try to be like these men, therefore: realize that happiness lies in liberty, and liberty in valor, and do not hold back from the dangers of war. Miserable men, who have no hope of prosperity, do not have a just reason to be generous with their lives; no, it is rather those who face the danger of a complete reversal of fortune for whom defeat would make the biggest difference: they are the ones who should risk their lives. Any man of intelligence will hold that death, when it comes unperceived to a man at full strength and with hope for his country, is not so bitter as miserable defeat for a man grown soft.

FOR DISCUSSION:

Can only the brave be truly free?

(2) BK.II, 65: THUCYDIDES' ASSESSMENT OF PERICLES AS A STATESMAN[1]
Thucydides' admiration for Pericles emerges in this summary of his career, as does also his disdain for lesser men who could only achieve power by flattering the people and who in the end were more interested in their own power than in the good of the state. The passage raises the question of how in a democracy persons of ability and genuine civic concern can achieve leadership.

---

1   From *History* ii, 65, translated by Woodruff, pp. 56-57.

As long as he was at the head of the city in time of peace, he governed it with moderation and guarded it securely; and it was greatest under him. After the war was afoot, it was obvious that he also foresaw what the city could do in this. He lived two years and six months after the war began. And after his death his foresight about the war was even better recognized, for he told them that if they would be quiet and take care of their navy, and not seek to expand the empire during this war or endanger the city itself, they should then have the upper hand. But they did the opposite on all points, and in other things that seemed not to concern the war they managed the state for their private ambition and private gain, to the detriment of themselves and their allies. Whatever succeeded brought honor and profit mostly to private individuals, while whatever went wrong damaged the city in the war.

The reason for Pericles' success was this: he was powerful because of his prestige and his intelligence, and also because he was known to be highly incorruptible. He therefore controlled the people without inhibition, and was not so much led by them, as he led them. He would not humor the people in his speeches so as to get power by improper means, but because of their esteem for him he could risk their anger by opposing them. Therefore, whenever he saw them insolently bold out of season, he would put them into fear with his speeches; and again, when they were afraid without reason, he would raise up their spirits and give them courage. Athens was in name a democracy, but in fact was a government by its first man. But because those who came after were more equal among themselves, with everyone aiming to be the chief, they gave up taking care of the commonwealth in order to please the people.

FOR DISCUSSION:

Is it of the essence of democracy that the leaders try to please the people, or at least a majority of them?

(3) BK.III, 81-84: THE HORRORS OF CIVIL WAR[1]

In 427 the city of Corcyra fell into conflict of a sort familiar to many Greek city-states: war between the wealthy few and the impoverished masses, the former supporting some form of oligarchic government, the latter democracy. A Spartan force arrived first and supported the oligarchic side, but later an Athenian fleet forced the Spartans out and allowed the democrats to seize power. The latter had the assistance of a group of "Messinians",

---

1   From *History* iii, 81.2-84, translated by Woodruff, pp. 89-93.

people who had once been *helots* in the Spartan state, i.e., serfs whom the Spartans kept in semi-slavery, but whom the Athenians had resettled near Corcyra. A horrific slaughter ensued.

81.2 When the people of Corcyra heard that the Athenian ships were approaching and that the Peloponnesians were leaving, they brought in the Messenian soldiers who had been outside the city, and ordered the ships they had manned to come around into the Hyllaic port. While they were going around, the Corcyrean democrats killed all the opposing faction they could lay hands on; and as for the ones they had persuaded to man the ships, they killed them all as they disembarked. And they came to the temple of Hera and persuaded fifty of the oligarchic sympathizers who had taken sanctuary there to submit themselves to a trial; then they condemned them all to death. When they saw what was being done, most of the suppliants—all those who were not induced to stand trial by law—killed one another right there in the temple; some hanged themselves on trees, and everyone made away with himself by what means he could. For the seven days that the Athenian admiral Eurmedon stayed there with his sixty ships, the Corcyreans went on killing as many of their own people as they took to be their enemies. They accused them of subverting the democracy, but some of the victims were killed on account of private hatred, and some by their debtors for the money they had lent them. Every form of death was seen at this time; and (as tends to happen in such cases) there was nothing people would not do, and more: fathers killed their sons; men were dragged out of the temples and then killed hard by; and some who were walled up in the temple of Dionysus died inside it.

82. So cruel was the course of this civil war, and it seemed all the more so because it was among the first of these. Afterwards, virtually all Greece was in upheaval, and quarrels arose everywhere between the democratic leaders, who sought to bring in the Athenians, and the oligarchs, who wanted to bring in the Lacedaemonians.[1] Now in time of peace they could have had no pretext and would not have been so eager to call them in, but because it was war, and allies were to be had for either party to hurt their enemies and strengthen themselves at the same time, invitations to intervene came readily from those who wanted a new government. Civil war brought many hardships to the cities, such as happen and will always happen as long as human nature is the same, although they may be more or less violent or take different forms, depending on the circumstances in each case. In peace and prosperity, cities and private individuals alike are better minded because they are not plunged into the necessity of doing anything against their will; but war is a violent teacher: it gives most people impulses

---

1   I.e., the Spartans.

that are as bad as their situation when it takes away the easy supply of what they need for daily life.

Civil war ran through the cities; those it struck later heard what the first cities had done and far exceeded them in inventing artful means for attack and bizarre forms of revenge. And they reversed the usual way of using words to evaluate activities. Ill-considered boldness was counted as loyal manliness; prudent hesitation was held to be cowardice in disguise, and moderation merely the cloak of an unmanly nature. A mind that could grasp the good of the whole was considered wholly lazy. Sudden fury was accepted as part of manly valor, while plotting for one's own security was thought a reasonable excuse for delaying action. A man who started a quarrel was always to be trusted, while one who opposed him was under suspicion. A man who made a plot was intelligent if it happened to succeed, while one who could smell out a plot was deemed even more clever. Anyone who took precautions, however, so as not to need to do either one, had been frightened by the other side (they would say) into subverting his own political party. In brief, a man was praised if he could commit some evil action before anyone else did, or if he could cheer on another person who had never meant to do such a thing.

Family ties were not so close as those of the political parties, because their members would readily dare to do anything on the slightest pretext. These parties, you see, were not formed under existing laws for the good, but for avarice in violation of established law. And the oaths they swore to each other had their authority not so much by divine law, as by their being partners in breaking the law. And if their opponents gave a good speech, if they were the stronger party, they did not receive it in a generous spirit, but with an eye to prevent its taking effect.

To take revenge was of a higher value than never to have received injury. And as for oaths of reconciliation (when there were any!), these were offered for the moment when both sides were at an impasse, and were in force only while neither side had help from abroad; but on the first opportunity, when one person saw the other unguarded and dared to act, he found his revenge sweeter because he had broken trust than if he had acted openly: he had taken the safer course, and he gave himself the prize for intelligence if he had triumphed by fraud. Evildoers are called skillful sooner than the guileless are called honest, and people are ashamed to be called guileless but take pride in being thought skillful.

The cause of all this was the desire to rule out of avarice and ambition, and the zeal for winning that proceeds from those two. Those who led their parties in the cities promoted their policies under decent-sounding names: "equality for ordinary citizens" on one side, and "moderate aristocracy" on the other. And though they pretended to serve the public in their speeches, they actually treated it as the prize for their competition; and striving by whatever means to win, both sides ventured on most horrible outrages and exacted even greater revenge, without any regard for justice or the public good. Each party was limited only by its own appetite at the time, and stood ready to satisfy its ambition of the moment either by voting for an unjust verdict or seizing control by force.

So neither side thought much of piety, but they praised those who could pass a horrible measure under the cover of a fine speech. The citizens who remained in the middle were destroyed by both parties, partly because they would not side with them, and partly for envy that they might escape in this way.

83. Thus was every kind of wickedness afoot throughout all Greece by the occasion of civil wars. Guilelessness, which is the chief cause of a generous spirit, was laughed down and disappeared. Citizens were sharply divided into opposing camps, and, without trust, their thoughts were in battle array. No speech was so powerful, no oath so terrible, as to overcome this mutual hostility. The more they reckoned up their chances, the less hope they had for a firm peace, and so they were all looking to avoid harm from each other, and were unable to rely on trust. For the most part, those with the weakest minds had the greatest success, since a sense of their own inferiority and the subtlety of their opponents put them into great fear that they would be overcome in debate or by schemes due to their enemies' intelligence. They, therefore, went immediately to work against them in action, while their more intelligent opponents, scornful and confident that they could foresee any attack, thought they had no need to take by force what might be gotten by wit. They were, consequently, unprotected, and so more easily killed.

84.[1] Most of these atrocities, then, were committed first in Corcyra, including all the acts of revenge people take, when they have the opportunity, against rulers who have shown more arrogance than good sense, and all the actions some people choose unjustly to escape longstanding poverty. Most of these acted from a passionate desire for their neighbors' possessions, but there were also those who attacked the wealthy not for their own gain, but primarily out of zeal for equality, and they were the most carried away by their undisciplined anger to commit savage and pitiless attacks. Now that life had been thrown into confusion in the city, human nature—which is accustomed to violate justice and the laws—came to dominate law altogether, and showed itself with delight to be the slave of anger, the master of justice, and the enemy of anyone superior. Without the destructive force of envy, you see, people would not value revenge over piety, or profits over justice. When they want revenge on others, people are determined first to destroy without a trace the laws that commonly govern such matters, though it is only

---

1 Section 84 may well not be by Thucydides himself, but certainly continues his general line of thought.

because of these that anyone in trouble can hope to be saved, even though anyone might be in danger someday and stand in need of such laws.

FOR DISCUSSION:

Is human nature most clearly revealed in situations of civil strife such as Thucydides describes, or do such calamities distort it? What does your response imply about the rule of law?

(4) Bk.III, 37-38: CLEON ON THE DIFFICULTIES FOR A DEMOCRACY IN RUNNING AN EMPIRE[1]

The following is an excerpt from Thucydides' reconstruction of a speech given by the demagogue Cleon when, in 428 BCE, the Athenian assembly was reconsidering its earlier decision to punish the rebellious people of Mytilene, which had been an "ally" of Athens, by slaughtering all their males of military age. Cleon had been the most forceful of the speakers in favor of the punishment when it was first decided on. The reader should not assume that Cleon expresses opinions with which Thucydides himself would have sympathized, since generally Thucydides despised demagogues. But the speech does present thoughts held by many Greeks about the difficulties for democracy, and they are all the more remarkable for having come from the mouth of a man whose whole status in society depended on his oratorical ability to move the mass of the citizens. Fortunately for the Mytileneans the assembly overruled Cleon and rescinded their original decision.

37. For my part, I have often seen that a democracy is not capable of ruling an empire, and I see it most clearly now, in your change of heart concerning the Mytileneans. Because you are not afraid of conspiracies among yourselves in your daily life, you imagine you can be the same with your allies, and so it does not occur to you that when you let them persuade you to make a mistake, or you relent out of compassion, your softness puts you in danger and does not win the affection of your allies; and you do not see that your empire is a tyranny, and that you have unwilling subjects who are continually plotting against you. They obey you not because of any good turns you might do them to your own detriment, and not because of any good will they might have, but only because you exceed them in strength. But it will be the worst mischief of all if none of our decisions stand firm, and if we never realize that a city with inferior laws is better if they are never relaxed than a city with good laws that have no

---

1   From *History* iii, 37-38, translated by Woodruff, pp. 67-68.

force, that people are more use if they are sensible without education than if they are clever without self-control, and that the more common sort of people generally govern a city better than those who are more intelligent. For those intellectuals love to appear wiser than the laws and to win victory in every public debate—as if there were no more important ways for them to show their wisdom! And that sort of thing usually leads to disaster for their city. But the other sort of people, who mistrust their own wits, are content to admit they know less than the laws and that they cannot criticize a speech as powerfully as a fine orator can; and so, as impartial judges rather than as contestants, they govern a city for the most part very well. We should do the same, therefore, and not be carried away by cleverness and contests of wit, or give to you, the people, advice that runs against our own judgment.

38. As for me, I have the same opinion I had before, and I am amazed at these men who have brought this matter of the Mytileneans into question again, thus causing a delay that works more to the advantage of those who have committed injustice. After a delay, you see, the victim comes at the wrongdoer with his anger dulled; but the punishment he gives right after an injury is the biggest and most appropriate. I am also amazed that there is anyone to oppose me, anyone who will try to prove that the injustice the Mytileneans have committed is good for us and that what goes wrong for us is really damaging to our allies. Clearly, he must have great trust in his eloquence if he is trying to make you believe that you did not decree what you decreed. Either that, or he has been bribed to try to lead you astray with a fine-sounding and elaborate speech.

Now the city gives prizes to others in contests of eloquence like this one, but the risks she must carry herself. You are to blame for staging these rhetorical contests so badly. The habits you've formed: why you merely look on at discussions, and real action is only a story to you! You consider proposals for the future on the basis of fine speeches, as if what they proposed were actually possible; and as for action in the past, you think that what has been done in front of your own eyes is less certain than what you have heard in the speeches of clever fault-finders. You are excellent men—at least for being deceived by novelties of rhetoric and for never wanting to follow advice that is tried and proven. You bow down like slaves to anything unusual, but look with suspicion on anything ordinary. Each of you wishes chiefly to be an effective speaker, but, if not, then you enter into competition with those who are. You don't want to be thought slow in following their meaning, so you applaud a sharp point before it is even made; and you are as eager to anticipate what will be said, as you are slow to foresee its consequences. You seek to hear about almost anything outside the experience of our daily lives, and yet you do not adequately understand what is right before your eyes. To speak plainly, you are so overcome with the delight of the ear that you are more like an audience for the sophists than an assembly deliberating for the good of the city.

FOR DISCUSSION:

Are people well advised to leave their laws alone since there is likely more wisdom in the existing laws than in the clever designs of people who want to change them?

Do you think a democracy like Athens is any less capable of maintaining an empire than the other forms of government are, e.g., monarchy and oligarchy?

W.H. AUDEN, FROM "SEPTEMBER 1, 1939":[1]

Exiled Thucydides knew
All that a speech can say
About democracy,
And what dictators do,
The elderly rubbish they talk
To an apathetic grave;
Analyzed all in his book,
The enlightenment driven away,
The habit forming pain,
Mismanagement and grief:
We must suffer them all again.

---

1   This is the date of Germany's invasion of Poland, taken to be the start of World War II. Auden's poem was first published in *The New Republic*, 18 October 1939, and in book form in Auden's collection *Another Time* (New York: Random House: 1940). From *Collected Poems of W.H. Auden* by W.H. Auden, Random House, Inc.

B.3: ARISTOPHANES

B orn sometime around the mid-fifth century BCE, he became the greatest of the Athenian writers of comic drama, writing both during and after the war with Sparta, which Athens lost in 404. His last play, *Plutus*, was produced in 388 and it is assumed he died not long after. His plays often satirize Athenian political and social institutions and customs with biting sarcasm, reflecting, no doubt, a certain bitterness at the way the war was carried on, indeed that it was carried on at all. Plato knew him, competed unsuccessfully against him in one of the comedy competitions at the annual Dionysian Festival in Athens, and wrote him into his Socratic dialogue, *Symposium*.

Since Aristophanes was in Athens all during the disastrous war with Sparta his plays often reflect popular discontent with war and the conduct of government in Athens generally. One idea which he mines for its comic possibilities is turning over rule to women, who in fact had never had any direct say in political affairs, in Athens or in any other of the Greek city-states. This reversal of the universal patriarchal arrangements also gives him ample opportunities to scathingly satirize the way males handled government in Athenian democracy, where major decisions were made in an assembly to which all male citizens were encouraged to come and vote, indeed often even paid to come.

B.3.a: *LYSISTRATA*

Lines 480-613[1]

L *ysistrata* was produced early in 411, a little over a year after the disastrous collapse of Athens' attack on Syracuse. Many citizens were very
weary of the war with Sparta and its allies that had been going on
for more than a decade, and Aristophanes' play responds to this sentiment
and to a certain cynicism toward the leaders of the city, who seemed unable
to bring peace. Through the comic proposal that women take over the city
and its foreign policy Aristophanes both satirizes the male domination of
Greek society and lampoons the men currently in charge at Athens.

In the preceding sections of the play the main character, Lysistrata, abet-
ted by her friends Calonice and Myrrhine, has organized the women of
Athens into forcing an end to the war by refusing to have sex with their
husbands until the war is ended. They also seize the Acropolis where the
Athenian treasury is kept, so that they can keep the men from spending
more money on the war. A magistrate arrives to find the women inside the
gates to the Acropolis barring everyone else from entering.

MAGISTRATE (*to Lysistrata*):
> Well, the first thing I want to know is—what in Zeus' name do you
> mean by shutting and barring the gates of our own Acropolis against us?

LYSISTRATA:
> We want to keep the money safe and stop you from waging war.

MAGISTRATE:
> The war has nothing to do with money—

---

1 Translated by Sommerstein, pp. 199-205.

LYSISTRATA:

Hasn't it? Why are Peisander[1] and the other office-seekers always stirring things up? Isn't it so they can take a few more dips in the public purse? Well, as far as we're concerned they can do what they like; only they're not going to lay their hands on the money in there.

MAGISTRATE:

Why, what are you going to do?

LYSISTRATA:

Do? Why, we'll be in charge of it.

MAGISTRATE:

You in charge of *our* finances?

LYSISTRATA:

Well, what's so strange about that? We've been in charge of all your housekeeping finances for years.

MAGISTRATE:

But that's not the same thing.

LYSISTRATA:

Why not?

MAGISTRATE:

Because the money here is needed for the war!

LYSISTRATA:

Ah, but the war itself isn't necessary.

MAGISTRATE:

Not necessary! How is the city going to be saved then?

LYSISTRATA:

We'll save it for you.

MAGISTRATE:

You!!!

LYSISTRATA:

Us.

MAGISTRATE:

This is intolerable!

LYSISTRATA:

It may be, but it's what's going to happen.

MAGISTRATE:

By Demeter! I mean, it's against nature!

---

1   Peisander was a politician who leaned toward the oligarchic party in Athens. Soon after the production of this play he tried to set up a peace with Sparta.

LYSISTRATA (*very sweetly*):

    We've got to save you, after all, Sir.

MAGISTRATE:

    Even against my will?

LYSISTRATA:

    That only makes it all the more essential.

MAGISTRATE:

    Anyway, what business are war and peace of yours?

LYSISTRATA:

    I'll tell you.

MAGISTRATE (*restraining himself with difficulty*):

    You'd better or else.

LYSISTRATA:

    I will if you'll listen and keep those hands of yours under control.

MAGISTRATE:

    I can't—I'm too livid.

STRATYLLIS (*interrupting*):

    It'll be you that regrets it.

MAGISTRATE:

    I hope it's you, you superannuated crow! (*To Lysistrata*) Say what you have to say.

LYSISTRATA:

    In the last war[1] we were too modest to object to anything you men did—and in any case you wouldn't let us say a word. But don't think we approved! We knew everything that was going on. Many times we'd hear at home about some major blunder of yours, and then when you came home we'd be burning inside but we'd have to put on a smile and ask what it was you'd decided to inscribe on the pillar underneath the Peace Treaty.[2] And what did my husband always say? "Shut up and mind your own business!" And I did.

STRATYLLIS:

    I wouldn't have!

MAGISTRATE (*ignoring her—to Lysistrata*):

    He'd have given you one, if you hadn't!

---

1 The war that ended in 421 with the peace of Nicias.

2 Three years after the treaty was made, the Athenians inscribed on it 'The Spartans have not abided by their oaths.' This amounted to their denunciation of the whole thing.

LYSISTRATA:

>Exactly—so I kept quiet. But sure enough, next thing we knew you'd take an even sillier decision. And if I so much as said, "Darling, why are you carrying on with this silly policy?" he would glare at me and say, "Back to your weaving, woman, or you'll have a headache for a month. 'Go and attend to your work; let war be the care of the menfolk.'"[1]

MAGISTRATE:

>Quite right too, by Zeus.

LYSISTRATA:

>Right? That we should not be allowed to make the least little suggestion to you, no matter how much you mismanage the city's affairs? And now, look, every time two people meet in the street, what do they say? "Isn't there a man in this country?" And the answer comes, "Not one." That's why we women got together and decided we were going to save Greece. What was the point of waiting any longer, we asked ourselves. Well now, we'll make a deal. You listen to us—and we'll talk sense, not like you used to—listen to us and keep quiet, as we've had to do up to now, and we'll clear up the mess you've made.

MAGISTRATE:

>Insufferable effrontery! I will not stand for it!

LYSISTRATA (*magisterially*):

>Silence!

MAGISTRATE:

>You, confound you, a woman with your face veiled, dare to order me to be silent! Gods, let me die!

LYSISTRATA:

>Well, if that's what's bothering you—
>(*During the ensuing song the women put a veil on the magistrate's head, and give him a sewing basket and some uncarded wool.*)
>>With veiling bedeck
>>Your head and your neck,
>>And then, it may be, you'll be quiet.

MYRRHINE:

>This basket fill full—

CALONICE:

>By carding this wool—

---

1   Hector's parting words to his wife in the *Iliad*.

LYSISTRATA:

Munching beans—they're an excellent diet.

So hitch up your gown
And really get down
To the job—you could do with some slimmin'.
And keep this refrain
Fixed firm in your brain—

ALL:

That war is the care of the *women*!

(*During the song and dance of the women the magistrate has been sitting, a ludicrous figure, with not the least idea what to do with the wool. During the following chorus, fuming, he tears off the veil, flings away wool and basket, and stands up.*)

STRATYLLIS:

Come forward, ladies: time to lend a hand
Of succour to our heroine's brave stand!

CHORUS OF WOMEN:

I'll dance forever, never will I tire,
To aid our champions here.
For theirs is courage, wisdom, beauty, fire;
And Athens hold they dear.

STRATYLLIS (*to Lysistrata*):

Now, child of valiant ancestors of stinging-nettle stock,
To battle! Do not weaken, for the foe is seized with shock.

LYSISTRATA:

If Aphrodite of Cyprus and her sweet son Eros still breathe hot desire into our bosoms and our thighs, and if they still, as of old, afflict our men with that distressing ailment, club-prick—then I prophesy that before long we women will be known as the Peacemakers of Greece.

MAGISTRATE:

Why, what will you do?

LYSISTRATA:

Well, for one thing, there'll be no more people clomping round the Market Square in full armour, like lunatics.

CALONICE:

By Aphrodite, never a truer word!

LYSISTRATA:

You see them every day—going round the vegetable and pottery stalls armed to the teeth. You'd think they were Corybants![1]

MAGISTRATE:

Of course: that's what every true Athenian ought to do.

LYSISTRATA:

But a man carrying a shield with a ferocious Gorgon on it—and buying minnows at the fishmonger's! Isn't it ridiculous?

CALONICE:

Like that cavalry captain I saw, riding round the market with his lovely long hair, buying a pancake from an old stallholder and stowing it in his helmet! And there was a Thracian too—coming in brandishing his light-infantry equipment for all the world as if he were a king or something. The fruiteress fainted away with fright, and he annexed everything on her stall!

MAGISTRATE:

But the international situation at present is in a hopeless muddle. How do you propose to unravel it?

LYSISTRATA:

Oh, it's dead easy.

MAGISTRATE:

Would you explain?

LYSISTRATA:

Well, take a tangled skein of wool, for example. We take it so, put it to the spindle, unwind it this way, now that way (*miming with her fingers*). That's how we'll unravel this war, if you'll let us. Send ambassadors first to Sparta, this way, then to Thebes, that way—

MAGISTRATE:

Are you such idiots as to think that you can solve serious problems with spindles and bits of wool?

LYSISTRATA:

As a matter of fact, it might not be so idiotic as you think to run the whole city entirely on the model of the way we deal with wool.

MAGISTRATE:

How do you work that out?

LYSISTRATA:

The first thing you do with wool is wash the grease out of it; you can do

---

1   The Corybants were priests of the cult of Cybele and wore armour during their rituals.

the same with the city. Then you stretch out the citizen body on a bench and pick out the burrs—that is, the parasites. After that you prise apart the club-members who form themselves into knots and clots to get into power, and when you've separated them, pick them out one by one. Then you're ready for the carding: they can all go into the basket of Civic Goodwill—including the resident aliens and any foreigners who are your friends—yes, and even those who are in debt to the Treasury! Not only that. Athens has many colonies. At the moment these are lying around all over the place, like stray bits and pieces of fleece. You should pick them up and bring them here, put them all together, and then out of all this make an enormous great ball of wool—and from that you can make the people a coat.

MAGISTRATE:

Burrs, balls of wool, nonsense! What right have you to talk about these things? What have you done for the war effort?

LYSISTRATA:

Done, you puffed-up old idiot! We've contributed to it twice over and more. For one thing, we've given you sons, and then had to send them off to fight.

MAGISTRATE:

Enough, don't let's rub the wound.

LYSISTRATA:

For another, we're in the prime of our lives, and how can we enjoy it? Even if we've got husbands, we're war widows just the same. And never mind us—think of the unmarried ones, getting on in years and with never a hope—that's what really pains me.

MAGISTRATE:

But for heaven's sake, it's not only women that get older.

LYSISTRATA:

Yes, I know, but it's not the same thing, is it? A man comes home—he may be old and grey—but he can get himself a young wife in no time. But a woman's not in bloom for long, and if she doesn't succeed quickly, there's no one will marry her, and before long she's going round to the fortune-tellers to ask them if she's any chance.

MAGISTRATE:

That's right—any man who's still got a serviceable—

(*Whatever he's going to say, it is drowned by music. During the following*

song the women supply him with two half-obols, a filleted[1] head-dress and a
wreath, and dress him up as a corpse.)

LYSISTRATA:

> Shut up! It's high time that you died.
>
> You'll find a fine coffin outside.
>
> Myself I will bake
>
> Your Cerberus cake,[2]
>
> And here is the fare for the ride.[3]

CALONICE:

> Look, here are your fillets all red

MYRRHINE:

> And here is the wreath for your head—

LYSISTRATA:

> So why do you wait?
>
> You'll make Charon late!
>
> Push off! Don't you realize? You're dead!

MAGISTRATE (*spluttering with rage*):

> This is outrageous! I shall go at once and show my colleagues what these
> women have done to me.

LYSISTRATA:

> What's your complaint? You haven't been properly laid out? Don't worry;
> we'll be with you early the day after tomorrow to complete the funeral!
> (*The magistrate leaves. Lysistrata, Calconice and Myrrhine go back into the*
> *Acropolis.*)

FOR DISCUSSION:

What does Lysistrata's metaphor of the uncarded wool tell us about Aristophanes' likely diagnosis of Athens' ills?

---

1   A fillet is a thin strip of material, a ribbon.
2   A cake was traditionally placed in the hand of a corpse about to be buried, so that the dead
    person could use it to distract Cerberus, the frightful hound that guarded the gates to Hades.
3   To be rowed across the infernal lake to Hades the ferryman, Charon, had to be paid one
    obol.

B.3.b: *ASSEMBLYWOMEN*

T his is one of Aristophanes' last plays, having been produced probably in 390 or 391. As in *Lysistrata* Aristophanes plays with the idea that the bad governance by the men in Athens' democracy might be cured by turning power over to the women, a plan much more ludicrous in ancient society than in ours. But in *Assemblywomen* his main satirical target is the willingness of the Athenian citizens to consider experiments in non-traditional laws and ways of doing things. By having the leader of the women who have taken power espouse an extreme form of egalitarian communism Aristophanes takes this tendency to a ridiculous extreme and mines it for all its comic possibilities.

(1) LINES 169-240[1]

The play opens with the women, disguised as men, gathering in advance at the site of the assembly to practice what they will say to convince the other citizens who will come to the assembly to turn power over to the women. The leader of this female rebellion is Praxagora (the name itself means 'woman effective in public') and her speech recites the usual litany of bad behaviour engaged in by the male politicians. But then she defends her proposal for female rule by pointing to the bad habit of the male citizenry of constantly ignoring tradition and precedent in order to try some new, and usually bad, idea. Women, on the other hand, she says, always do what they have always done, and never look for change.

PRAXAGORA (taking the platform):

> Shoo, you go back to your seat over there too. (*To the seated women*) To judge
> from what I've seen of your abilities it seems best that I put on this garland

---

1 Translated by Henderson, pp. 267-73.

and make a speech myself. I beseech the gods to grant success to today's deliberations. My own stake in this country is equal to your own, and I am annoyed and depressed at all the city's affairs. For I see that she constantly employs scoundrels as her leaders. Even if one of them turns virtuous for one day, he'll turn out wicked for ten. You look to another one? He'll make even worse trouble. I realize how hard it is to talk sense to men as cantankerous as you, who fear those who want to befriend you and consistently court those who do not. There was a time when we convened no assemblies at all, but at least we knew Agyrrhius[1] for a scoundrel. Nowadays we do convene them, and the people who draw pay praise him to the skies, while those who draw none say that the people who attend for the pay deserve the death penalty.

FIRST WOMAN:

Well said, by Aphrodite!

PRAXAGORA:

Pitiful: you swore by Aphrodite. Wouldn't it be charming if you spoke that way in the Assembly?

FIRST WOMAN:

But I wouldn't have.

PRAXAGORA:

Well, don't get into the habit now. (*Resuming her speech*) And about this alliance: when we were examining the issue, the people insisted that the city would perish if we did not ratify it. But when it finally was ratified, the people were unhappy, and its staunchest supporter had to leave town in a hurry. We need to launch a fleet: the poor man votes yes, the wealthy and the farmers vote no. You get angry with the Corinthians, and they with you; now they're nice people, "so you be nice too." The Argives are morons, but Hieronymus is sage. And occasionally we get a fleeting glimpse of salvation, but Thrasybulus gets angry that you're not inviting him to take charge.[2]

FIRST WOMAN:

This man's smart!

PRAXAGORA:

Now that's the way to applaud! And you, the sovereign people, are responsible for this mess. For while drawing your civic pay from public funds, each of you angles for a personal profit. Meanwhile the public interest

---

1   Notorious embezzler of public money.
2   The reference is probably to the Athenian rejection of recently offered Spartan peace terms. The general Thrasybulus had been instrumental in persuading the city to take this course.

flounders like Aesimus.[1] But listen to my advice and you shall escape from your muddle. I propose we turn over governance of the city to the women; after all, we employ them as stewards and treasurers in our own households.

SECOND WOMAN:

Hear! Hear! Well said!

FIRST WOMAN:

Pray continue, sir!

PRAXAGORA:

And their character is superior to ours, as I will demonstrate. First, they dye their wool in hot water according to their ancient custom, each and every one of them; you'll never see them try anything new. But the Athenian State wouldn't hold on to that custom even if it worked just fine; no, they'd be fiddling around with some innovation. Meanwhile the women settle down to their cooking, as they always have. They carry burdens on their heads, as they always have. They celebrate the Thesmophoria,[2] as they always have. They bake cookies, as they always have. They drive their husbands nuts, as they always have. They hide their lovers in the house, as they always have. They buy themselves extra treats, as they always have. They like their wine neat, as they always have. They like a fucking, as they always have. And so, gentlemen, let us hand over governance of the city to the women, and let's not beat around the bush or ask what they plan to accomplish. Let's simply let them govern. Consider only these points: first, as mothers they'll want to protect our soldiers; and second, who would be quicker to send extra rations than the one who bore you? There's nobody more inventive at getting funds than a woman, and when in power she'll never get cheated, since women themselves are past masters at cheating. I'll pass over my other points. Adopt my resolution and you'll lead happy lives.

SECOND WOMAN:

Well said, Praxagora, my sweet! What skill! Where did you learn such fine talk, my dear?

PRAXAGORA:

During the displacements[3] I lived with my husband on the Pnyx,[4] and learned by listening to the orators.

---

1 Aesimus had commanded the democratic forces in a civil war in 403, but his career had gone into eclipse since then.
2 A festival in honour of Demeter, goddess of fertility, which was presided over by women.
3 During the Peloponnesian wars there had been times when the people of the countryside had to move into the city for the protection of its walls.
4 The area where the Assembly was held.

(2) LINES 569-710

Praxagora, along with the chorus of women, confronts her rather dissipated husband, Blepyrus, and a neighbour of his. She proceeds to explain what changes the women have introduced in the way the city is to be run. It is immediately apparent that instead of returning to traditional ways, as, according to her speech to the assembly, was supposed to be what women would do if given power, they have instituted the most radical reforms imaginable with the end of establishing complete political, economic and sexual equality among all the citizens, male and female alike. Blepyrus and his neighbour are sceptical at first and think of all sorts of difficulties that might attend the scheme, but Praxagora cleverly answers all these, and then secures the final acquiescence of the two men by setting before them the prospect of a life of unending banquets and sexual favours. Clearly Aristophanes is not here presenting us with a serious utopian scheme but with a parody of the sort of crackpot ideas that he had seen voiced by clever thinkers around the city as citizens searched for reforms that might save them from their own corrupt ways. Nevertheless, Praxagora's egalitarian, communistic society bears some comparison with the serious utopia that Plato was to put forth in the *Republic* , particularly its arrangements for the so-called guardians. (See selection **B.5.e (1)** below.) One can imagine the sarcasm with which Aristophanes would have greeted Plato's innovative proposals had he lived to know of them.

PRAXAGORA:

> Let me explain it; you'll have to side with me, and even my mister here
> will have no rebuttal to *me*.

CHORUS:

> Now you must summon up
> a shrewd intelligence
> and a philosophic mind
> that knows how to fight for your comrades.
> For it's to the prosperity of all alike
> that from your lips comes a bright idea
> to gladden the lives of the city's people
> with countless benefits;
> now's the time to reveal its potential.
> Yes, our city needs
> some kind of sage scheme;
> describe it in full, making sure only

that none of it's ever been
said or done before:
they hate to watch the same old stuff
over and over again!

CHORUS LEADER:

No more delay! Here and now you must put your idea in play: what spectators most appreciate is speed.

PRAXAGORA:

Well, I'm sure my proposals are worthwhile, but I'm awfully worried about the spectators: are they ready to quarry a new vein and not stick with what's hoary and conventional?

NEIGHBOUR:

Don't worry about quarrying new veins; for us, indifference to precedent takes precedence over any other principle of government.

PRAXAGORA:

Then let no one object or interrupt until you've heard the speaker out and understand the plan. Very well: I propose that everyone should own everything in common, and draw an equal living. No more rich man here, poor man there, or a man with a big farm and a man without land enough for his own grave, or a man with many slaves and a man without even an attendant. No, I will establish one and the same standard of living for everyone.

BLEPYRUS:

How will it be the same for everyone?

PRAXAGORA:

If we were eating dung, you'd want the first bite!

BLEPYRUS:

We'll be sharing the dung too?

PRAXAGORA:

God no. I mean you cut me off by interrupting; I was just about to explain that point. My first act will be to communize all the land, money, and other property that's now individually owned. We women will manage this common fund with thrift and good judgment, and take good care of you.

NEIGHBOUR:

And what about the man who owns no land but has invisible wealth, like silver coin and gold darics?[1]

---

1   The daric was a Persian coin worth about 20 drachmas.

PRAXAGORA:

> He'll contribute it to the common fund.

BLEPYRUS:

> And if he doesn't, he'll perjure himself; after all, that's how he got it in the first place!

PRAXAGORA:

> But see, it won't be of any use to him anyway.

BLEPYRUS:

> What do you mean?

PRAXAGORA:

> No one will be doing *anything* as a result of poverty, because everyone will have all the necessities: bread, salt fish, barley cakes, cloaks, wine, garlands, chickpeas. So where's his profit in not contributing? If you can find it, do tell me.

BLEPYRUS:

> But even now, aren't the people who have all this the bigger thieves?

NEIGHBOUR:

> That was before, my friend, when we lived under the previous system. But now that everyone will be living from a common fund, where's his profit in not contributing?

BLEPYRUS:

> If he spots a girl and fancies her and wants a poke, he'll be able to take her price from this common fund and have all that's commonly wanted, when he's slept with her.

PRAXAGORA:

> No, he'll be able to sleep with her free of charge. I'm making these girls common property too, for the men to sleep with and make babies with as they please.

BLEPYRUS:

> Then won't everyone head for the prettiest girl and try to bang her?

PRAXAGORA:

> The homely and bob-nosed women will sit right beside the classy ones, and if a man wants the latter he'll have to ball the ugly one first.

BLEPYRUS:

> But what about the older men? If we go with the ugly ones first, our cocks won't have anything left when we get where you said.

PRAXAGORA:

> They won't fight about you, don't worry. Never fear, they won't fight.

BLEPYRUS:

Fight about what?

PRAXAGORA:

About not getting to sleep with you! Anyway, you've got that problem as it is.

BLEPYRUS:

Your side of the equation makes a certain sense; you've planned it that no woman's hole will go unplugged. But what do you mean to do for the men's side? Because the women will shun the ugly men and go for the handsome ones.

PRAXAGORA:

Well, the homely men will tail the handsomer ones as they leave their dinner parties, and keep an eye on them in the public places, for it won't be lawful for handsome and tall men to sleep with any women who haven't first accommodated the uglies and the runts.

BLEPYRUS:

So now Lysicrates'[1] nose will be up there with the beautiful people's!

NEIGHBOUR:

Absolutely. What's more, it's an idea that favours ordinary people, and it'll be a great joke on the big shots with signet rings when a guy wearing clogs speaks up and says, "Step aside and wait till I'm finished; then I'll give you seconds!"

BLEPYRUS:

Well, if we live this way, how will any man be able to recognize his own children?

PRAXAGORA:

Why should he? They'll regard all older men of a certain age to be their fathers.

BLEPYRUS:

Then from now on won't sons methodically strangle each and every older man? Because even now they strangle their acknowledged father; what will happen when he's unacknowledged? Won't they shit on him as well?

PRAXAGORA:

No the bystanders won't allow it. They didn't used to care who was beating other people's fathers, but now if they hear a man getting beaten they'll worry that the victim is their own dad, and fight the attackers.

---

1 Presumably some homely man around town, but otherwise unknown.

BLEPYRUS:

There's nothing wrong with your analysis, but if Epicurus or Leucolophus[1] start hanging around and calling me "daddy", it's going to be frightful to listen to.

NEIGHBOUR:

Well, I can think of something a lot more frightful.

BLEPYRUS:

Such as?

NEIGHBOUR:

If Aristyllus[2] claims you're his father and kisses you!

BLEPYRUS:

If he does he'll sorely regret it!

NEIGHBOUR:

And you'd smell of *eau d'ordure*!

PRAXAGORA:

But he was born before our decree, so there's no need to worry that he'll kiss *you*.

BLEPYRUS:

He'd still have been sorry if he did. But who will there be to farm the land?

PRAXAGORA:

The slaves. Your only concern will be to get slicked up and head for dinner when the shadow stick's[3] at ten feet.

BLEPYRUS:

Then about overcoats, who will supply them? It's a reasonable question.

PRAXAGORA:

Your current supply will do for now; later we'll weave you new ones.

BLEPYRUS:

One more question: what happens if someone loses a lawsuit to somebody before the archons?[4] How will he pay the judgement? It wouldn't be fair to take that from the common pool.

PRAXAGORA:

But there won't be any lawsuits in the first place.

BLEPYRUS:

That statement will be your undoing.

---

1 Evidently two well known malefactors.
2 Apparently a known coprophiliac, i.e., someone who is sexually excited by feces.
3 Ancient method of telling time.
4 Chief magistrates.

NEIGHBOUR:

> That's my verdict too.

PRAXAGORA:

> But what, poor dear, will they sue over?

BLEPYRUS:

> My god, lots of things. Foremost, of course, is when a debtor refused to pay.

PRAXAGORA:

> But where did the creditor get the money to lend, all funds being in common? He's obviously a thief—of course!

NEIGHBOUR:

> By golly, that's right.

BLEPYRUS:

> But let her answer me this; when people act rowdy after a dinner party and get into fights, how will they pay their fines for assault? That one, I think, will stump you.

PRAXAGORA:

> He'll pay out of his own bread ration. A decrease there will hit him right in the belly, so he'll think twice before he gets rowdy again.

BLEPYRUS:

> And will no one be a thief?

PRAXAGORA:

> Of course not: how can anyone steal what he's got a share in?

BLEPYRUS:

> So no more muggers at night?

NEIGHBOUR:

> Not if you sleep at home!

PRAXAGORA:

> Not even when you go out as you used to, for all will be content with their condition. If someone tries to steal a cloak, the victim will let him have it. Why should he put up a fight? He can go to the common store and get a better one.

BLEPYRUS:

> And people won't gamble at dice?

PRAXAGORA:

> What would they use for stakes?

BLEPYRUS:

> And what standard of living will you establish?

PRAXAGORA:

> The same for all. I mean to convert the city into one household by breaking down all partitions to make one dwelling, so that everyone can walk into everyone else's space.

BLEPYRUS:

> And where will you serve dinner?

PRAXAGORA:

> I'll turn all the courthouses and porticoes into dining rooms.

BLEPYRUS:

> What will you do with the speakers' platform?

PRAXAGORA:

> I'll use it to store mixing bowls and water jugs, and the children can use it to recite poetry about brave men in battle, or about anyone who was cowardly, so they'll be ashamed to share the meal.

BLEPYRUS:

> An absolutely charming idea! And what will you do with the ballot boxes?

PRAXAGORA:

> I'll have them set up in the marketplace by Harmodius' statue and have everyone draw lots, till each one has got his letter and gone off happily to whatever dining hall it assigns. Thus the Herald will instruct everyone with the letter R to proceed to dinner at the Royal Stoa; the Thetas will go to the one next to it; and the G's to the Grain Market.

BLEPYRUS:

> G as in guzzle?

PRAXAGORA:

> No, as in gourmandise.

BLEPYRUS:

> But people who draw no letter for dinner, will everyone push them away from the table?

PRAXAGORA:

> That won't happen with us; we'll provide everything for everyone unstintingly. Every single man will leave drunk, garland still on and torch in hand, and along the streets as they come from dinner the ladies will accost them like this: "Come over here to our place; there's a lovely girl in here." "And over here," another one will cry from a second storey window, "is a very fine and exquisitely pale girl. Of course, you'll have to sleep with me before her." And the inferior men will chase after the

handsome lads, saying "Hey you, where do you think you're off to? You're going to get nothing anyway: the law says that the pug-nosed and the ugly get first fuck, while you grab the petals of your double-hung fig branch and jerk off in the doorway!" So tell me does my plan meet with your approval?

BLEPYRUS *and* NEIGHBOUR:

Very much so!

PRAXAGORA:

Then I'll be going off to the marketplace to receive the goods as they come in, after I pick up a girl with a strong voice to be my herald. These are my duties as the woman elected to office. I must also organize the communal dinners, so you can have your first banquet this very day.

BLEPYRUS:

The banquets are to start right away?

PRAXAGORA:

That's what I'm telling you. Then I want to put all the prostitutes out of business.

BLEPYRUS:

Why?

NEIGHBOUR:

(*indicating Praxagora and the chorus*) That's obvious: so that these women can have their pick of the young men!

PRAXAGORA:

What's more, slave girls will no longer be allowed to wear makeup and steal away the fond hearts of the free boys. They'll be allowed to sleep only with slaves, with their pussies trimmed like a woollen barn jacket.

BLEPYRUS:

Say, I'd like to tag along at your side, and share the spotlight, with people saying, "Look, that's none other than the Lady Commander's husband!"

B.4: SOCRATES

There is no doubt that Socrates was an actual historical figure and not just a creation of later writers such as Plato. He was born around 470 BCE, lived all his life in Athens, and was executed by the civic authorities in 399. There is also agreement that he was a loyal and courageous soldier on at least two military campaigns. But his chief claim to fame was as a teacher at Athens both during and after the war with Sparta, and it was this activity which brought him into conflict with the authorities. Beyond that little is certain about the historical Socrates. Many scholars think that the dialogues taken to be written early in Plato's career portray the spirit of Socrates as a teacher, although everyone agrees that the conversations are works of fiction, not renderings of actual events. A quite different picture of Socrates emerges in Xenophon's *Memorabilia*, and still a third portrayal, very satirical, in Aristophanes' play *Frogs*. However, it is Plato's Socrates that came to be accepted in the ancient world as the true picture, and established Socrates as a kind of moral hero for later philosophers. In this volume the editors have placed under the heading of 'Socrates' selections from two of Plato's "early" dialogues and then treated dialogues scholars think were written later, like *Republic* and *Laws*, as reflecting Plato's own views even though Socrates is still portrayed in the *Republic* as leading the discussion.

B.4.a: PLATO, *CRITO*

48b-54e[1]

O nly in the *Crito* does Plato give us a view of what was likely his teacher's own beliefs about the authority of the law and of the state. At least
nothing quite like it appears elsewhere in the Platonic dialogues.

The scene of this dialogue finds Socrates in prison awaiting execution
where he is visited early one morning by his friend Crito, come to try to persuade him to save himself by escaping from Athens. The following picks up
the conversation between them just after Socrates has argued that we ought
not to be swayed by the opinion of the many but listen to those who genuinely
understand the matter we are concerned with. Socrates proceeds to defend
his decision to remain in Athens and allow himself to be put to death.

At first Socrates secures Crito's agreement to the archetypical Socratic
positions that the good life is the life lived justly and honourably, that doing
injustice is always wrong, even when it is in return for an injustice done
to oneself. In fact, doing something bad is never justifiable, even if one is
treating someone badly because they have so treated you. Socrates notes
that few people agree to this, but he expects Crito to agree since he has been
part of the discussions within Socrates' circle of friends in which the topic
was fully explored.

> *Socrates*: ... Now see whether we agree on another proposition: that not living
> but living well is chiefly to be valued.
> *Crito*: Yes, we definitely hold to that.
> *Soc.*: And living well is equivalent to living honourably and justly; do we hold to that?

---

1 Translated by Jowett, vol.1, pp. 432-38, with modifications.

Cr.: Yes we do.

Soc.: From these premises we must argue the question whether it is just or not for me to try and escape without the consent of the Athenians; and if it appears just, then I will make the attempt; if not, I'll give that up. The other considerations which you mention, of money and loss of reputation and the duty to educate one's children, are, I fear, merely the opinions of the many, of those who would be as ready to restore people to life, if they were able, as they are to put them to death, and with as little reason.

But now, given the way the argument so far constrains us, the only question which remains to be considered is whether we would behave justly by paying these men who are to aid in our escape and thanking them as well as by escaping ourselves, or whether in fact this would not be just. If the latter, then death or any other calamity which might result from my staying put must not be allowed to figure in our reasoning.

Cr.: I think you are right, Socrates, but how should we proceed?

Soc.: Let's investigate the matter together, and you refute me if you can, and I will be convinced, or, otherwise, stop, my dear friend, from repeating over and over that I ought to escape despite the wishes of the Athenians. For I am anxious to act on this with your approval and not contrary to what you want. Please, then, see if you agree with my starting premise, and see how you can best answer me.

Cr.: I will try.

Soc.: Are we to say that we are never willingly to act unjustly, or are we to act unjustly in some circumstances but not in others? Or is acting unjustly never good or fine, as I was just now saying, and as we have often already agreed? Are all our former conclusions to be thrown away in a few days? Have we, at our age, been seriously conversing with each other all our life long only to discover that we are no better than children? Or, in spite of the opinion of the many, and in spite of the consequences, whether for the better or for the worse, shall we insist on the truth of what we said back then, that injustice is always bad and disgraceful to him who acts unjustly? Shall we say that or not?

Cr.: Yes.

Soc.: Then we should not act unjustly at all.

Cr.: Certainly not.

Soc.: Nor should we return injustice by doing injustice, as the many think; for in fact we must not act unjustly at all?

Cr.: Clearly not.

Soc.: Again, Crito, should we do bad things or not?

Cr.: Surely not, Socrates.

Soc.: And what of doing something bad in return for suffering something bad, which is what the many think, is that just or not?

Cr.: Not just.

Soc.: For doing something bad to a person is no different from acting unjustly?

Cr.: Very true.

Soc.: Then we ought not to retaliate or return what is bad for what is bad to anyone, whatever bad thing we may have suffered from him. But please consider, Crito, whether you really mean what you are saying; for this opinion has never been held, and never will be held, by any but a few people, and those who agree to this and those who do not, have no common ground and can only despise one another when they see how far apart they are. Tell me, then, whether you agree with and assent to this first principle, that it is never correct to do injustice nor to retaliate or ward off what is bad by doing what is bad. Shall that be the starting point for our argument, or do you decline and dissent from this? For this is what I have always thought and continue to think; but, if you are of another opinion, let me hear what you have to say. On the other hand, if you are still of the same mind as formerly, I will get on to the next step.

Cr.: You may proceed; I haven't changed my mind.

FOR DISCUSSION:

Given Socrates' position against retaliation, can punishment of wrongdoers possibly be justified?

To show that illegally escaping the city and the judgement of the court would be unjust and thus not something it could be correct to do, Socrates gives the laws of Athens a voice of their own in which they can argue how they would be wronged by such an action. The first step is the claim that the proposed escape would in fact amount to an attempt to destroy the laws and the state, while the second step is to secure assent to the extremely high respect which is to be paid both to the laws and to the state, a respect exceeding even that which one should pay to one's parents.

Soc.: Now the next point may be put in the form of a question: Ought a person to do what he has agreed is just, or may he cheat?

Cr.: He ought to do it.

Soc.: Then consider this. If I leave here without the consent of the state, is there anyone I treat badly, in fact the very ones I least ought to, or not? And are we abiding by what we agreed was just, or not?

Cr.: I cannot tell, Socrates, for I don't understand.

Soc.: Then consider it this way. Suppose I were on the point of skedaddling off (or whatever you'd like to call it), and the laws, i.e. the common bond of the city, were to come and question me: "Tell us, Socrates, what are you about to do? Are you not going by an act of yours to overturn us, the laws and the whole state, as far as in you lies? Do you imagine that a state can continue existing and not be overthrown in which the decisions of the courts have no power but are set aside and trampled on by private individuals?" What will be our answer, Crito, to this and similar questions? Anyone, and especially a rhetorician, will have lots to say on behalf of the law which says sentences of a court must be carried out. He will argue that this law should not be set aside. And are we going to reply: "Yes, but the state has treated us unjustly and given an unjust sentence." Shall we say that, or what?

Cr.: Yes, Socrates, by Zeus, let's say that.

Soc.: "And was that the agreement you made with us?" the laws would answer; "Or were you to abide by whatever judgments the state pronounced?" And, if I were astonished at their words, the laws would probably add: "Answer, Socrates, and don't look surprised; you are used to asking and answering questions. Tell us, what complaint have you to make against us which justifies you in attempting to destroy us and the state? In the first place, did we not bring you into existence? Your father married your mother by our aid and sired you. Now tell us whether you have any objection to raise against those of us who regulate marriage." None, would be my reply. "Or against those of us who after birth regulate the nurture and education of children, which you, like others, received? Weren't the laws which are in charge of education right to command your father to train you in music and gymnastic?" Right, I would reply. "Well, then, since you were brought into the world and nurtured and educated by us, can you deny first of all that you are our child and slave, as your ancestors were before you. And if this is true, you are not on equal terms with us, nor can you think it just to do to us what we are doing to you. Would you have any right to strike or revile or do any other bad thing to your father or your master, if you had one, just because you had been struck or reviled by him, or received something bad at his hands? And because we think it just to destroy you, do you think that it is just to destroy us in return, and your country, so far as you are able—you who are so concerned about true excellence? Or are you so wise that you fail to see that your country is more to be valued and higher and holier far than mother or father or any ancestor, and more highly regarded by gods and men of understanding? And that she is to be reverenced, obeyed, and approached in humility when she is angry, even more than a father, and either to be persuaded, of if not persuaded, to be obeyed? And when she orders you punished, whether with imprisonment or flogging, you must endure it in silence? And if she sends you to war where you are wounded or killed, there you must go, as that is just? And that no one may yield or retreat or leave his post, but whether in battle or in a court of law, or anywhere else, he must do what his city and country order him to do; or he must change her view of what is just? And, if he may do no violence to his father or mother, much less may he do violence to his country?" What answer shall we make to this, Crito? Do the laws speak the truth, or not?

Cr.: I think they do.

FOR DISCUSSION:

From the fact that the state through its laws has made one's existence, nurture and education possible, does it follow that one should give the same regard to the laws and the state as to one's parents, or regard oneself as a "slave" of the state? Does anything at all follow about what respect one should have for the laws and the state?

The argument now shifts to emphasizing a sort of tacit agreement Socrates has supposedly made with the state to respect its laws, including the decisions of its courts, just by continuing to live in the state when the option to leave is open, and when the possibility exists of convincing the state that some of its commands are unjust and should be rescinded.

Soc.: Then perhaps the laws will say this: "Notice, Socrates, that, if we are speaking the truth, then in your present attempt you are going to do us an injustice. For, having brought you into the world, and nurtured and educated you, and given you and every other citizen a share in every good which we had to give, we further proclaim to any Athenian by the liberty which we allow him that, if he does not like us when he has come of age and has seen the ways of the city and familiarized himself with us, he may go where he pleases and take his goods with him. None of us laws will forbid him or interfere with him. Anyone who does not like us and the city, and who wants to emigrate to a colony or to any other city, may go where he likes while retaining his property. But he who has experience of the way we administer justice and govern the state and still remains, has entered into an implied contract that he will do as we command him. He who disobeys us, however, is, we maintain, acting unjustly in three ways: first, because in disobeying us he is disobeying his parents; because he disobeys us who nurtured him; and because he has made an agreement with us that he will obey our commands, but he neither obeys nor convinces us that out commands are unjust. We do not impose these sternly, but give him the alternative of obeying or convincing us. That is what we offer, and he does neither.

"These are the charges to which, as we were saying, you, Socrates, will be open to if you carry out your intentions, and you more than other Athenians." Suppose now I ask why I more than anyone else? They will reply justly that I more than others have acknowledged the agreement. "There is clear proof," they will say, "Socrates, that you liked us and the city. Of all Athenians you have been the most constant resident, and, since you never leave the city, you may be supposed to love it. You never went outside the city either to see the festivals or to any other place unless when you were on military service; nor did you travel in the way other people do. Nor did you have any curiosity to know other states and their laws; you were quite contented with us and our state; we were your special favourites and you agreed to be governed by us. It is here in this city that you sired your children, which proves your satisfaction with us. Moreover, in the course of your trial you might, if you had liked, to fix the penalty at banishment; the state, which refuses to let you go now, would have let you go then. Instead, you pretended that you preferred death to exile, and that you were quite willing to die. Now you have forgotten these fine sentiments and pay no respect to us the laws, whom you are about to destroy. You are doing what only a wretched slave would do, running away and turning your back on the compacts and agreements which you made as a citizen. Are we right in saying that you agreed to be governed by us in deed and not just in word? Is that true or not?" How shall we answer, Crito? Don't we have to agree?

Cr.: We cannot help but agree, Socrates.

FOR DISCUSSION:

Is the position the laws put forward here claiming that as long as you continue to live within a state you may protest the laws but you may not disobey them?

Is the argument here independent of the earlier claim about the laws and the state deserving the highest respect, or would it lack force without that earlier assumption?

The laws continue by showing how Socrates would be violating his own teachings and throwing them into contempt if he were to escape Athens in order to avoid his own death. It is clear by the end that Socrates finds these arguments totally conclusive.

Soc.: Then, won't they say: "You, Socrates, are breaking the covenants and agreements which you made with us at your leisure, not in haste or under any compulsion or deception, but after you have had seventy years to think of them, during which time you were free to leave the city if you did not like us or if our covenants appeared to you to be unfair. You had your choice and could have gone either to Lacedaemon or Crete, both of which you often praised for their good government, or to some other Greek or foreign state. But, in fact, you, more than all other Athenians, seemed to be so fond of this state, or, in other words, of us her laws (and who would care about a state which had no laws?) that you never stirred out of her; the halt, the blind, the maimed stayed put in her no less than you did. Now you skedaddle off and forsake your agreements. Don't do it, Socrates, if you will take our advice; do not make yourself a laughing-stock by escaping from the city.

"For just consider, if you transgress and err in this sort of way, what good will you do either for yourself or for your friends? That your friends will be driven into exile and deprived of citizenship, or will lose their property is close to certain; and you yourself, if you flee to one of the neighbouring cities, Thebes or Megara, for example, both of which are well governed, will come to them as an enemy, Socrates, and their government will be against you and all patriotic citizens will look askance at you as a subverter of the laws, and you will confirm in the minds of the jurors the justice of their own condemnation of you. For someone who destroys the laws is more than likely to be a corrupter of the young and foolish portion of mankind. Are you going to flee, then, from well-ordered cities and from civilized men? Is existence worth having on these terms? Or will you go to them without shame and talk to them, Socrates? And what will you say to them? Will you talk about what you talk about here, about excellence and justice and institutions and laws being the best things in the world of humans? Would that be a decent thing to do? Surely not. But if you go away from well-governed states to Crito's friends in Thessaly, where there is found utter disorder and licence, they will be charmed to hear the tale of your escape from prison, told with hilarious particulars of how you were wrapped in a goatskin or some other disguise, your appearance altered as is the practice of runaways. But will there be no one to remind you that in your old age you were not ashamed to break the most sacred laws just out of a miserable desire for a little more life? Perhaps not, if you keep them in a good mood. But if they are in a bad mood, you will hear a lot of disparaging remarks. You will live, but how? As the flatterer of everybody, and everybody's servant? And doing what? Eating and drinking in Thessaly, as though you had gone there to get a dinner? And where will be your fine sentiments about justice and excellence? Suppose you say that you want to live for the sake of your children; you want to bring them up and educate them. Will you take them along to Thessaly and deprive them of Athenian citizenship? Is this the benefit you will confer on them? Or are you under the impression that they will be better cared for and educated here if you are still alive, even though absent, for your friends will take care of them? Do you imagine that if you reside in Thessaly they will take care of them, but if you reside in the other world they will not? Surely not; if they who call themselves friends are good for anything, they will—to be sure they will.

"So listen, Socrates, to us who brought you up. Don't put life and children first and justice afterwards, but rather justice first so that you will be justified before the rulers of the world below.[1] For neither you, nor any that belong to you, will be happier or more pious or more just in this life, or happier in another, if you do as Crito bids. Now you depart a victim, not a doer, of injustice, the injustice not of the laws but of men. But if you go out there returning something bad for something bad, injustice for injustice, breaking the covenants and agreements you have made with us and treating unjustly those whom you ought least of all to treat that way, that is to say yourself, your friends, your country, and us, we shall be angry with you while you live, and our brothers, the laws in the world below, will receive you as an enemy, for they will know that you have done your best to destroy us. Listen, then, to us, and not to Crito."

---

1   The "underworld", below the surface of the earth, where the souls of the departed live.

This, dear Crito, is the voice which I seem to hear whispering in my ear, like the sound of the flute in the ears of the initiates to the cult of Cybele;[1] that voice, I say, is humming in my ear and prevents me from hearing any other. I know that anything more you may say will be futile. But speak, if you have anything to say.

Cr.: I have nothing to say, Socrates.

Soc.: Let it be, then, Crito; and let us act that way, since that's the way the god is leading us.

FOR DISCUSSION:

Supposing the laws themselves to be just under which Socrates was convicted, could the conviction itself be unjust? And could it then possibly be just to evade that conviction illegally?

DIOGENES LAERTIUS, FROM *LIVES*: ABOUT SOCRATES:[2]

He used to express his astonishment that the sculptors of marble statues should take pains to make the block of marble into a perfect likeness of a man, and should take no pains about themselves lest they should turn out mere blocks, not men.

---

1 This mystery cult was imported into Greece from Asia Minor, with Cybele often identified with Aphrodite.
2 Translated by Hicks, vol.1, pp. 163-65.

B.4.b: PLATO, *GORGIAS*

466a-495b[1]

Although Plato's *Gorgias* is mainly a defense of the personal ethic which has been associated with Socrates by most later writers, it also deals with important issues in political philosophy. There is, for a start, the question of how power within a community should be defined if it is to be considered something worth having. Then there is also the place of justice, i.e., morality, in public life, as well as the role of the philosopher in politics. When the cynical Callicles enters the conversation, he introduces the distinction between the justice established by nature and that based on human conventions and uses it to defend the manipulation of political life to serve the self-interest of a few. The confrontation between him and Socrates is one of the most dramatic moments in all of ancient philosophical literature.

Beyond the ideas Socrates espouses is the picture the *Gorgias* paints of his character and personality. Warnings of how his refusal to compromise his principles will lead to his destruction and perhaps death only seem to deepen his resolve to stay on the path of moral purity, which he takes to be what is of most benefit not only to himself but to anyone. It is not difficult to see how this figure could become not just a guide to the good life but also a hero and inspiration to generations of later readers with a philosophical bent. This impression is reinforced by the realization that Plato has here created a fictional encounter which is supposed to have occurred not long before Socrates was to face his own execution with complete equanimity, as is told in Plato's *Phaedo*.

---

1 Translated by Jowett, vol.1, pp. 524-55, with modifications.

The dialogue's beginning, not given here, portrays a meeting between the celebrated teacher of rhetoric, Gorgias, and Socrates, who has doubts about the extravagant claims the former has been making as to the efficacy of the skill he teaches. But Gorgias' role in the discussion is taken over by his brashly over-confident acolyte, Polus, and the portion of the dialogue given below begins with Socrates engaged with him about whether rhetoricians have any real power. It is here that the question of how to define political power comes to the fore. Once Socrates has secured Polus' agreement that power is always something good to its possessor, he is willing to allow that someone who is able to do whatever he wants to do has power, but, to Polus' amazement (and in all likelihood the modern reader's), Socrates denies that rhetoricians and tyrants ever in fact do what they want to. His point rests on drawing a distinction between doing what one thinks is best and what one wants to do. Of course, it is possible to do what one thinks is best but be mistaken, and in this case it can be said that one does not do what one wants to do. But the mistake can arise in two ways: (1) what one thinks best to do is something one wants to do only because it leads to some desirable goal, but in fact it does not lead to that goal; (2) doing what one thinks is best leads to what one expected, but that turns out to be something which is not in fact beneficial for the agent. It is the latter sort of mistake that Socrates has in mind, for the tyrant or other foolish person takes himself to be doing what he thinks best because he thinks the end result will be beneficial to him. If you say that still such a person wants to do what he is doing as long as he *thinks* its end result will be beneficial, then Socrates can reply that power to do what one wants to in that sense is not necessarily something good, since in the case of foolish people, who don't know what is genuinely beneficial and what is not, it merely magnifies their ability to ruin themselves; thus Polus would have to go back on the initial assumption about power being good.

Pol.: What are you saying, then? Do you think rhetoric is flattery?

Soc.: No, I said a part of flattery. If at your age, Polus, you can't remember, what will you do by-and-by when you are older?

Pol.: And are good rhetoricians counted as worthless in cities, under the idea that they are flatterers?

Soc.: Is that a question or the beginning of a speech?

Pol.: I am asking a question.

Soc.: Then my answer is that they don't count for anything at all.

Pol.: How are they not counted for something? Don't they have very great power in cities?

Soc.: Not if you mean to say that power is a good to the possessor.

Pol.: That is what I do mean to say.

Soc.: Then, if so, I think that they have the least power of all the citizens.

Pol.: What! Aren't they like tyrants? They kill and expropriate and exile anyone whom they please?

Soc.: By the dog, Polus, I cannot make out every time you speak whether you are giving your own opinion or asking a question of me.

Pol.: I am asking a question of you.

Soc.: All right, my friend, but you ask two questions at once.

Pol.: How two questions?

Soc.: Why, did you not say just now that rhetoricians are like tyrants, and that they kill and expropriate and exile anyone whom they please?

Pol.: I did.

Soc.: Well, then, I say to you that here are two questions in one, and I will answer both of them. I tell you, Polus, that rhetoricians and tyrants have the least possible power in states, as I was just now saying; for they do literally nothing which they want to, but only what they think best.

Pol.: And is not that a great power?

Soc.: No—at least Polus does not agree.

Pol.: What do you mean I do not agree? Of course I agree.

Soc.: Now I swear by... You don't, for you say that power is a good to him who has the power.

Pol.: Yes, I still do.

Soc.: And would you maintain that if a person with no intelligence does what he thinks is best, this is a good, and would you call that great power?

Pol.: No, I would not.

Soc.: Then you must show that the rhetorician has intelligence, and that rhetoric is an art and not just a form of flattery; then you will have refuted me. But, if you leave me unrefuted, the rhetoricians who do what they think best in cities, and the tyrants, will have gained no benefit, if as you say power be indeed a good while admitting at the same time that what is done without intelligence is bad.

Pol.: Yes, I admit that.

Soc.: How then can the rhetoricians or the tyrants have great power in cities, unless Polus can refute Socrates and prove to him that they do what they want?

Pol.: This fellow...

Soc.: I say that they do not do what they want. Now refute me.

Pol.: But didn't you already say that they do what they think best?

Soc.: Yes, and I still say so.

Pol.: Then surely they do what they want.

Soc.: I deny that.

Pol.: But they do what they think best?

Soc.: Right.

Pol.: That, Socrates, is monstrous and absurd.

Soc.: Don't scold me, most polished of Poluses, if I may speak in your own way. Rather, if you have any questions to ask me, either prove I am in error or take on the role of answering yourself.

Pol.: All right, I'm willing to answer so that I can find out what you mean.

Soc.: Do people appear to you to want what they do or to want the thing for the sake of which they do what they do? When they take medicine, for example, on a physician's orders, do they want the drinking of the medicine which is painful, or the health for the sake of which they drink it?

Pol.: Clearly the health.

Soc.: And when people go on a voyage or engage in business, they don't want what they are doing at the time, for who would desire to take the risk of a voyage or all the trouble of business? Rather, they want to have the wealth for the sake of which they go on a voyage.

Pol.: Certainly.

Soc.: And is this not universally true? If a person does something for the sake of something else, he wants not what he is doing, but rather that for the sake of which he does it?

Pol.: Yes.

Soc.: Now isn't everything either good, or bad, or intermediate between these and so neither good nor bad?

Pol.: To be sure, Socrates.

Soc.: Wisdom and health and wealth and things like those you would call goods, and their opposites bad things?

Pol.: I would.

Soc.: And the things which are neither good nor bad, and which sometimes share in the good and at other times in the bad, or neither, are such as sitting, walking, running, sailing; or, again, wood, stones, and the like; these are the things which you call neither good nor bad?

Pol.: Exactly.

Soc.: Are these intermediate things done for the sake of the good, or is the good done for the sake of the intermediate?

Pol.: Clearly, the intermediate are done for the sake of the good.

Soc.: When we walk, then, we walk for the sake of what's good, thinking it is better to walk, and when we stand we stand equally for the sake of what's good?

Pol.: Yes.

Soc.: And when we kill a person we kill him or exile him or expropriate his goods, because, we think, it will conduce to our good?

Pol.: Yes.

Soc.: People who do any of these things do them for the sake of the good?

Pol.: I agree.

Soc.: Now, didn't we admit that when we do something for the sake of something else, we do not want what we are doing but that other thing for the sake of which we do what we're doing?

Pol.: Very true.

Soc.: Then, we don't want simply to kill a person or exile him or expropriate his goods; rather we want to do these things only if they are beneficial, and not if they are harmful; for we want, as you say, what is good, while what is neither good nor bad, or simply bad, we do not want. Why are you silent, Polus? Aren't I right?

Pol.: You are right.

Soc.: From that we may infer that if anyone, whether a tyrant or a rhetorician, kills another, or exiles another, or deprives him of his property, under the idea that the act is better for him when in fact it is worse, he can be said to do what seems best to him?

Pol.: Yes.

Soc.: But does he do what he wants if he does what is bad? Why do you not answer?

Pol.: Well, I suppose not.

Soc.: Then if great power is a good as you allow, will such a person have great power in a city?

Pol.: He won't.

Soc.: Then I was right in saying that a person may do what seems good to him in a city, yet not have great power nor do what he wants?

FOR DISCUSSION:

Can a person consciously decide to do something they do not want to do? In what circumstances would you say this happens?

Is this reasoning any good: X does not want to do things bad for him; action
A is bad for him; therefore X does not want to do A.

The discussion with Polus now shifts to whether doing injustice can
ever be more beneficial to a person than doing justice. (Here it is important to know that 'just' and 'unjust' translate too narrowly the Greek
words, which might well be rendered by 'moral' and 'immoral'.) Socrates goes so far as to claim that a person who does injustice is worse
off than the person who suffers it, and that unjust people, like flagrant
tyrants, can never be happy, but are more wretched than the people they
unjustly torment. All of which leads Polus to relate the gruesome career of Archelaus, who made himself the tyrannical ruler of Macedon.

> *Pol.*: And as though you, Socrates, would not like to have the power of doing
>   what seemed good to you in the city rather than not; or would not be
>   jealous when you saw anyone killing or expropriating or imprisoning
>   whomever he pleased. Oh, no!
>
> *Soc.*: Justly or unjustly, do you mean?
>
> *Pol.*: Is he not equally to be envied in either case?
>
> *Soc.*: Please, Polus, quiet down!
>
> *Pol.*: Why "quiet down"?
>
> *Soc.*: Because you ought not envy wretches who are unenviable, but rather just
>   pity them.
>
> *Pol.*: The people I was speaking of are wretches?
>
> *Soc.*: Yes, certainly they are.
>
> *Pol.*: So you think that he who slays anyone whom he pleases, and slays him
>   justly, is pitiable and wretched?
>
> *Soc.*: No, I don't say that of him; but neither do I think that he is to be envied.
>
> *Pol.*: Didn't you just say that he is wretched?
>
> *Soc.*: Yes, my friend, if he killed another *unjustly*, and in that case he is also to
>   be pitied; but he is not to be envied if he killed him justly.
>
> *Pol.*: At any rate you will allow that he who is unjustly put to death is wretched,
>   and to be pitied?
>
> *Soc.*: Not as much, Polus, as the person who kills him, and not so much as he
>   who is justly put to death.
>
> *Pol.*: How can that be, Socrates?
>
> *Soc.*: This way: because doing injustice is the worst of bad things.
>
> *Pol.*: But is it the worst? Is not suffering injustice even worse?

Soc.: Certainly not.

Pol.: Then would you prefer to suffer rather than do injustice?

Soc.: I wouldn't like to do either, but if I had to choose between them, I would prefer suffering to doing injustice.

Pol.: Then you have no wish to be a tyrant?

Soc.: Not if you mean by tyranny what I mean.

Pol.: I mean, as I said before, the power of doing whatever seems good to you in a city, killing, banishing, doing in everything just as you like.

Soc.: Well then, my splendid man, let me talk a bit, and then bring up your objections. Suppose that I go into a crowded market square with a dagger under my arm. Polus, I say to you, I have just acquired a rare power and become a tyrant, for if I think that any of these people you see ought to be put to death, the person whom I have a mind to kill is as good as dead; and if I think his head should be broken or his garment torn, he will have his head broken and his garment torn in an instant. This is how great my power is in this city. Now, if you do not believe me, and I show you the dagger, you would probably reply: Socrates, in that way anyone may have great power; he can burn any house he pleases, as well as the docks and triremes of the Athenians, and all their other ships, whether public or private; but can you believe that this mere doing as you think best is great power?

Pol.: Certainly, it is not.

Soc.: But can you tell me why you disapprove of that sort of power?

Pol.: I can.

Soc.: Why, then?

Pol.: Because the person who acted in that way would be certain to be punished.

Soc.: And punishment is bad?

Pol.: Certainly.

Soc.: Now you would admit once more, my good friend, that great power is a good to a person if his actions are beneficial when he does what seems best to him; otherwise, it is something bad and not power. But let us look at the matter another way. Don't we acknowledge that the things we were mentioning—infliction of death, exile, and expropriation of property—are sometimes good and sometimes not a good?

Pol.: Certainly.

Soc.: About that you and I may be supposed to agree?

Pol.: Yes.

Soc.: Tell me, then, when do you say they are good and when they are bad; how do you draw the line?

Pol.: Socrates, I'd rather you answer as well as ask that question.

Soc.: Very well, Polus, since you would rather have the answer from me, I say they are good when they are just, and bad when they are unjust.

Pol.: You are hard to refute, Socrates, but couldn't a child refute that and show it isn't true?

Soc.: Then I shall be very grateful to the child, and equally grateful to you, if you will refute me and deliver me from my foolishness. I even hope you will refute me and not get tired of benefitting a friend.

Pol.: Well, Socrates, I need not go far afield or appeal to ancient history; events which happened just a few days ago are enough to refute you, and to prove that many men who do injustice are happy.

Soc.: What events?

Pol.: You see, I presume, that Archelaus the son of Perdiccas is now the ruler of Macedonia?

Soc.: If I don't, I hear tell he is.

Pol.: And do you think that he is happy or wretched?

Soc.: I cannot say, Polus, for I've never met the man.

Pol.: What! You could tell if he was happy if you met the man, but otherwise you can't tell right off that he is happy?

Soc.: Certainly not.

Pol.: Then clearly, Socrates, you would say that you did not know even whether the Great King[1] was a happy man?

Soc.: And I would be saying the truth, for I do not know how he is off for education and justice.

Pol.: What! Is that all happiness amounts to?

Soc.: Yes, that's right, Polus, that is what I teach: the men and women who are fine and good are also happy, as I maintain, and those who are unjust and depraved are wretched.

Pol.: Then according to what you teach the said Archelaus is wretched?

Soc.: Yes, my friend, if he is unjust.

Pol.: How could he not be unjust! He had no title at all to the throne which he now occupies, seeing that he was the only son of a woman who was the slave of Alcetas, Perdiccas's brother; so in strict right he himself was

---

1   The king of Persia, generally recognized at the time as the most powerful and wealthy ruler in the known world.

Alcetas's slave; and if he had wanted to act justly he would have stayed his slave, and, then, according to what you teach, he would have been happy. But as things are, he has turned out incredibly wretched, for he has been guilty of the gravest crimes. First of all, he invited his uncle and master, Alcetas, to visit him, under the pretense that he would restore to him the throne which Perdiccas had usurped, and after entertaining him and his son, Alexander, his own cousin and nearly the same age as he, he got them drunk, threw them into a wagon and carried them off into the night, murdered them, and got rid of them.

After he had committed all these crimes, he never noticed that he was the most wretched of men and had no inclination to repent. He had a younger brother, a child seven years old, who was Perdiccas's legitimate son and to whom the kingdom rightly belonged. Archelaus, however, had no intention of bringing him up as he ought and restoring the kingdom to him; that was not his notion of happiness; rather, not long afterwards he threw him into a well and drowned him, telling his mother Cleopatra that he had fallen in while chasing a goose and had been killed. So now, as he is the greatest criminal among all the Macedonians, he may be supposed to be the most wretched and not the happiest of them, and I dare say there are many Athenians, and you at the head of them, who would rather be any Macedonian other than Archelaus!

Polus' tale of depravity and tyranny does not have the desired effect on Socrates, who proceeds to explain that Polus is trying to refute him by bringing up things which will persuade the multitude, whereas Socrates believes that the effort should be to bring the very person whom one is conversing with around to seeing that his view is wrong. Here Socrates is implying that he has a method of persuasion different from that of rhetoric, the method of dialectic.

Socrates begins by increasing the contrast between his own view and Polus' by asserting that not only is the doer of injustice worse off than the sufferer, but a person who does injustice and escapes punishment is worse off than the person who does it but gets punished. Nothing could seem more absurd to Polus at this point. To argue the first thesis Socrates first secures Polus' agreement that doing injustice is more shameful than suffering it. But then Polus will not agree that what is more shameful is worse. Then comes an argument which runs, in outline, as follows:

1. What is fine is so either by giving pleasure or being useful.

2. Therefore, what is shameful is so either by giving pain or being bad.

3. Doing injustice is certainly not more painful than suffering it.

4. Therefore, since doing injustice is more shameful, it must be worse.

The argument depends on treating badness as the opposite of utility and also shamefulness as the opposite of being fine, and here Socrates may well be guilty of playing on hidden ambiguities in Greek words that lack a precise meaning. He even goes so far as to draw a further conclusion:

5. No one would prefer doing what is more shameful and worse to what is not shameful and not as bad.

But, of course, they might very well if they thought the shameful option was a lot less painful, or not painful at all, in comparison to the option that was not shameful. Socrates has not shown that no one prefers what they know to be detrimental but not painful to what they know to be beneficial or neutral but very painful. And this is just what we have in the case of doing injustice as opposed to suffering it. Still Polus might well be ashamed to admit that he personally would prefer something more detrimental, i.e., worse, just because it wasn't painful like the alternative. A real Greek male would not be so lacking in courage.

> *Soc.*: I praised you at first, Polus, for being good at rhetoric, though I thought then, as now, that you had neglected dialectic. So this, I am to suppose, is the sort of argument with which you fancy that a child might refute me, and by which I stand refuted when I say that the unjust person is not happy. But, my good friend, where is the refutation? I do not concede any of the things which you have been saying.
>
> *Pol.*: That's just because you don't want to. In fact you must think as I do.
>
> *Soc.*: Not so, my gifted friend; it's rather because you try to refute me in the way that rhetoricians refute people in courts of law. There the one party thinks they refute the other once they bring forward a number of respectable witnesses who back their allegations, while their adversary has only a single one, or none at all. But this kind of proof is of no value where truth is the aim; a person may often be beaten down by a crowd of false witnesses who have a great air of respectability. So, now, in our argument nearly everyone, Athenians and strangers alike, would be on your side, if you want to bring witnesses to disprove what I say. You may, if you want, summon Nicias the son Niceratus, and let his brothers, who donated the row of tripods that stand in the precinct of Dionysus, come with him; or you may summon Aristocrates, the son of Scellius, who made that famous

donation which is at Delphi; summon, if you want, the whole house of Pericles, or any other great Athenian family whom you choose; they will all agree with you. I alone don't agree, for you do not convince me, even though you produce many false witnesses against me in the hope of depriving me of my property, which is the truth.

I, on the other hand, consider that nothing worth speaking of will have been accomplished by me unless I make you the sole witness backing what I say; nor has anything been accomplished by you, unless you make me the sole witness for what you say; the rest of the world does not matter. For there are two ways of refuting, one which is yours and of the world in general, and then there is mine, which is of another sort. Let's compare them and see in what they differ. For the matters on which we differ are not trivial but concern things which are the finest to know and most shameful not to know; they amount to knowing or not knowing who is happy and who is not.

Therefore, I'll begin by asking you whether you do not think that a man who is unjust and doing unjust things can be happy, seeing that you think Archelaus unjust and yet happy? May I assume this to be your opinion?

Pol.: Certainly.

Soc.: But I say that this is impossible; here is one point at issue between us— very good. Now do you mean to say also that, if he meets with retribution and punishment, he will still be happy?

Pol.: Certainly not; in that case he will be totally wretched.

Soc.: On the other hand, if the unjust person is not punished, then, according to you, he will be happy?

Pol.: Yes.

Soc.: But in my opinion, Polus, the unjust doer of unjust actions is wretched in any case; more wretched, however, if he is not punished and does not meet with retribution, and less wretched if he is punished and meets with retribution at the hands of gods and humans.

Pol.: That's an absurd doctrine you're maintaining, Socrates.

Soc.: I will try to get you to agree with me, my friend, for I do regard you as a friend. So these are the points at issue between us, are they not? I was saying that to do injustice is worse than suffering it?

Pol.: Exactly.

Soc.: And you said the opposite?

Pol.: Yes.

Soc.: I also said that those who do injustice are wretched, and you refuted me?

Pol.: By Zeus, I did.

Soc.: In your own opinion, Polus.

Pol.: Yes, and I think I was in the right.

Soc.: You further said that the wrongdoer is happy if he goes unpunished?

Pol.: Certainly.

Soc.: And I affirm that he is most wretched, and that those who are punished are less wretched. Are you going to refute this claim as well?

Pol.: That's something even harder to refute than the other, Socrates.

Soc.: Say rather, Polus, impossible, for who can refute the truth?

Pol.: What do you mean? If someone is caught in an unjust attempt to make himself a tyrant, and then is put on the rack, mutilated, his eyes burnt out, and after having been tortured in all sorts of ways, and having seen his wife and children suffer the same, is finally crucified or tarred and burned alive, will he be happier than if he escapes and becomes a tyrant, and then continues all through life doing what he wants and holding the reins of power, the envy and admiration both of citizens and foreigners? Is this what you say cannot be refuted?

Soc.: Oh, Polus, you're just trying to scare me with hobgoblins instead of refuting me; what you did just now is call witnesses against me. Nevertheless, please refresh my memory a little. Did you say: "in an unjust attempt to make himself a tyrant"?

Pol.: Yes, I did.

Soc.: Then I say that neither of them will be happier than the other, neither he who unjustly acquires tyranny, nor he who suffers in the attempt, for of two wretched people one cannot be happier; but I do say that he who escapes and becomes a tyrant is the more wretched of the two. Polus, why are you laughing? Is this some new kind of refutation: whenever anyone says anything, instead of refuting him just laugh at him?

Pol.: But don't you think, Socrates, that you have been refuted enough when you say what no human being will allow? Ask the company.

Soc.: Polus, I am not a politician, and only last year when I was serving on the Council and my tribe held the presidency, and it became my duty as president to take the votes, people laughed at me because I didn't know how to put the question. So don't tell me now to put the question to the company; rather, if, as I was saying, you have no better argument than these, let me have a turn, and you face the sort of refutation I think should be used. For I will produce just one witness for the truth of my words, the very person with whom I am arguing; his vote I know how to take, but with the crowd I have nothing to do, and do not even hold a dialogue with them. May I ask, then, whether you will answer questions in turn and have what you say subjected to possible refutation? For I certainly think that I and you and everyone really do believe that to do injustice is worse than to suffer it, and not to be punished worse than to be punished.

Pol.: And I, on the other hand, say that neither I nor anyone believes this.

Would you yourself, for example, prefer to suffer rather than do injustice?

Soc.: Yes, and you too. I or anyone would.

Pol.: It's quite the reverse. Neither you, nor I, nor anyone.

Soc.: But will you answer questions?

Pol.: To be sure. I am really curious to hear what you can have to say.

Soc.: Tell me, then, so you will know, as though we were starting at the beginning: Which of the two, Polus, in your opinion is worse, to do injustice or to suffer it?

Pol.: I say that suffering it is worse.

Soc.: And which is more shameful, to do or to suffer injustice?

Pol.: To do it.

Soc.: And what is more shameful is worse?

Pol.: Certainly not.

Soc.: I see. If I am not mistaken, you are saying that fine and good are not the same, nor are bad and shameful?

Pol.: They certainly are not.

Soc.: Let me ask you a question: When you speak of fine things, such as bodies, colours, shapes, sounds, practices, do you not call them fine by reference to some criteria? Bodies, for example are fine either to the extent that they are useful or to the extent that the sight of them gives pleasure to whoever looks at them. Can you give any other account of what makes a body fine?

Pol.: I cannot.

Soc.: And would you say of shapes and colours generally that they were fine either by reason of the pleasure which they give or by reason of their utility, or both?

Pol.: Yes, I would.

Soc.: And would you call sounds and music fine for the same reason?

Pol.: I would.

Soc.: Conventions and practices also have no fineness in them except in so far as they are useful or pleasant or both?

Pol.: I agree.

Soc.: And shouldn't the same be said of fineness in branches of knowledge?

Pol.: You're absolutely right, Socrates, and I very much approve of your judging fineness by the criteria of pleasure and utility.

Soc.: And the shameful must be judged by the opposites, pain and badness?

Pol.: Certainly.

Soc.: Then when of two fine things one is finer, it is finer by exceeding in respect of one or both of these, i.e. of pleasure or utility?

Pol.: Very true.

Soc.: And further of two shameful things, when one is more shameful than the other, it must exceed the other either in respect of pain or of badness— isn't that right?

Pol.: Yes.

Soc.: Now, what were you just now saying about doing and suffering injustice? Didn't you say that suffering injustice was worse and doing injustice more shameful?

Pol.: I did.

Soc.: Then, if doing injustice is more shameful than suffering it, isn't it either more painful and thus more shameful by exceeding in pain, or by exceeding in badness, or in both?

Pol.: Of course.

Soc.: First, then, let us consider whether the doing of injustice exceeds the suffering of it in pain. Do the doers of injustice suffer more pain than do the sufferers of injustice?

Pol.: No, Socrates, that's certainly not the case.

Soc.: Then it does not exceed in pain?

Pol.: No.

Soc.: And if not in pain, then not in both?

Pol.: Certainly not.

Soc.: Then all that's left is the other?

Pol.: Yes.

Soc.: That is to say, in badness?

Pol.: It seems so.

Soc.: Then doing injustice will exceed in respect of badness, and will thus be worse than suffering injustice?

Pol.: Clearly.

Soc.: But haven't you and the mass of mankind already agreed that doing injustice is more shameful than suffering it?

Pol.: Yes.

Soc.: But that has now turned out to be worse?

Pol.: It seems so.

Soc.: Now would you prefer something worse and more shameful to what is
 less bad and shameful? Answer, Polus, and don't be afraid. No harm will
 come to you if you nobly present yourself to the argument as to a physician
 without shrinking and say either 'Yes' or 'No' to me.

Pol.: Well no, Socrates, I would not prefer it.

Soc.: Would anyone else prefer what is worse to what is less bad?

Pol.: No, not according to this argument, at least.

Soc.: Then I was right, Polus. Neither you, nor I, nor anyone would prefer to do
 injustice rather than suffer it, for of the two doing injustice is worse.

Pol.: Apparently.

Soc.: You see, Polus, how unlike this sort of refutation is to that other.
 Everybody, myself excepted, thinks as you do, but your one assent and
 witness are enough for me, I have no need of any other; I take your vote
 and disregard everybody else.

FOR DISCUSSION:

Suppose we substitute for 'fine and good' 'desirable'. Is it true that only
 what is either pleasant or useful is what is desirable?

Does being detrimental to the doer tend to make an action "shameful"?
 What would you say makes an action shameful?

How much of Socrates' argumentation depends on finding Polus willing to
 accept things we would not?

Now for the even more astounding thesis that getting punished for injustice
is better than going unpunished afterwards. Socrates' argumentation here reveals his basic view of injustice as a kind of disease of the soul and punishment
as a kind of painful treatment for that disease. (By 'soul' Socrates means the
"self" which exercises intentional control over what the person does.) But since
the soul is far more important to a person than his body, treating and curing
a disease in the former is of far more benefit than doing so in the latter. One
ought to welcome punishment, then, even more than one welcomes painful
medical cures. Of course, it is better for the soul never to fall into injustice in the
first place; if it remains just, it remains in good health, so to speak.

Enough of this; let's go on to the next question: whether what is worse is to be
 guilty of injustice and suffer the punishment, as you supposed, or whether avoiding the punishment is worse, as I supposed. Consider. You would say that to suffer
 punishment is another name for being justly corrected when you do injustice?

Pol.: I would.

Soc.: And wouldn't you allow that all just things are fine insofar as they are just? Please think about it before you answer.

Pol.: Yes, Socrates, I think they are.

Soc.: Consider again. Where someone does something, must there not also be something affected by the doer?

Pol.: I would say so.

Soc.: And won't the thing affected be affected by what the doer does? And won't the being affected have whatever quality the doing of the doer has? I mean, for example, that if someone strikes there must be something which is struck?

Pol.: Necessarily.

Soc.: And if the striker strikes violently or quickly, the thing struck will be struck violently or quickly?

Pol.: True.

Soc.: So whatever is done to the thing struck is of the same sort as the doing of him who strikes?

Pol.: Yes.

Soc.: And if someone sets on fire, there is something set on fire?

Pol.: Certainly.

Soc.: And if he sets on fire excessively or painfully, the thing set on fire will be set on fire in the same way?

Pol.: Right.

Soc.: And if he cuts, the same principle holds; there will be something cut?

Pol.: Yes.

Soc.: And if the cutting be large or deep or painful, the being cut will be of the same sort?

Pol.: That seems right.

Soc.: Then would you agree generally to what I was saying about everything: that the thing affected is affected in just the way the doer does what he does?

Pol.: I agree.

Soc.: Given we agree about that, let me ask whether being punished is a being affected or a doing?

Pol.: A being affected, Socrates; there can be no doubt about that.

Soc.: And being affected implies there is a doer?

Pol.: Certainly, Socrates; he is the punisher.

Soc.: And he who punishes in the right way does so justly?

Pol.: Yes.

Soc.: So, therefore, he does something just?

Pol.: Something just.

Soc.: So, then, isn't the person who is punished and pays just retribution being affected by something just?

Pol.: That is evident.

Soc.: So what is just has been admitted to be fine?

Pol.: Certainly.

Soc.: Then the punisher does something fine, and the punished is affected by something fine?

Pol.: True.

Soc.: And if by something fine, then by something good, for the fine is either pleasant or useful?

Pol.: Certainly.

Soc.: Then he who is punished is affected by something good?

Pol.: So it seems.

Soc.: Then he is benefitted?

Pol.: Yes.

Soc.: Now do you mean by 'benefitted' what I mean? I mean that if he is justly punished his soul is improved.

Pol.: Yes, that's likely.

Soc.: Then he who is punished is delivered from something bad in his soul?

Pol.: Yes.

Soc.: And is he not delivered from the worst sort of thing? Look at it this way: So far as a person's possessions go, do you see any bad state besides poverty?

Pol.: There is nothing worse.

Soc.: And as regards a person's bodily condition, would you say its bad state is weakness, disease, ugliness, and the like?

Pol.: I would.

Soc.: And wouldn't you imagine that the soul likewise has some depraved state of its own?

Pol.: Of course.

Soc.: And would you call this injustice and stupidity and cowardice, and the like?

Pol.: Certainly.

Soc.: So, then, in soul, body and possessions, which are three, you have noted three corresponding depravities: injustice, disease, poverty?

Pol.: True.

Soc.: And which of these depravities is the most shameful? Is not the most shameful of them injustice, and in general depravity of the soul?

Pol.: By far the most.

Soc.: And if it is the most shameful, isn't it the worst?

Pol.: What do you mean, Socrates?

Soc.: I mean to say, that what is most shameful has already been admitted to be most painful or most harmful or both.

Pol.: Certainly.

Soc.: And now injustice and all bad states of the soul have been admitted by us to be most shameful?

Pol.: That was admitted.

Soc.: And most shameful either because most painful and exceeding in pain, or most harmful, or both?

Pol.: Certainly.

Soc.: Therefore, to be unjust and immoderate and cowardly and stupid is more painful than to be poor and sick?

Pol.: No, Socrates. That doesn't seem to follow from what we've said.

Soc.: Then if, as you would argue, it is not more painful, and the bad state of the soul is of all bad things the most shameful, the extra shamefulness must be due to some exceedingly great or serious harmfulness of the bad state?

Pol.: Clearly.

Soc.: So what has such a high degree of harmfulness turns out to be the worst of all bad things?

Pol.: Yes.

Soc.: Then injustice, immoderation, and in general depravity of the soul, are the worst of bad things.

Pol.: That is evident.

Soc.: Now, what art is there which delivers us from poverty? Isn't it the art of money-making?

Pol.: Yes.

Soc.: And what art frees us from disease? Isn't it the art of medicine?

Pol.: Very true.

Soc.: And which art delivers us from depravity and injustice? If you are not able to answer at once, ask yourself where we go with the sick and to whom we take them.

Pol.: To the physicians, Socrates.

Soc.: And to whom do we go with the unjust and immoderate?

Pol.: To the judges, do you mean?

Soc.: And there they go to pay just retribution?

Pol.: Yes.

Soc.: Then don't those who punish rightly punish them in accord with some kind of justice?

Pol.: Clearly.

Soc.: Then the art of money-making frees a person from poverty; medicine from disease; and justice from immoderation and injustice?

Pol.: Apparently.

Soc.: Which, then, is the finest of these three?

Pol.: Which three?

Soc.: Money-making, medicine, and justice?

Pol.: Justice, Socrates, is far and away superior.

Soc.: And justice, if the finest, gives the greatest pleasure or benefit or both?

Pol.: Yes.

Soc.: But is medical treatment a pleasant thing? Do the patients enjoy it?

Pol.: I don't think so.

Soc.: Something beneficial, then?

Pol.: Yes.

Soc.: Yes, because the patient is delivered from something very bad, and this is the benefit of enduring the pain: you get well?

Pol.: Certainly.

Soc.: Now who would be happier: the person who was healed by medical treatment of his body or the person who was never sick to begin with?

Pol.: Clearly he who was never sick to begin with.

Soc.: Yes; for happiness surely does not consist in being delivered from bad things, but in never having had them.

Pol.: True.

Soc.: Now take the case of two people who have something bad in their bodies and where one of them is healed and delivered from that bad thing while the other is not healed but retains the bad thing. Which of them is the more wretched?

Pol.: Clearly the one who was not healed.

Soc.: And was not punishment said by us to be a deliverance from the worst of bad things, namely depravity?

Pol.: True.

Soc.: And justice moderates us and makes us more just, and is the medicine for our depravity?

Pol.: True.

Soc.: So the person who has first place on the scale of happiness is the one who never had depravity in their soul, for this has been shown to be the worst of bad things.

Pol.: Clearly.

Soc.: In second place is the person who gets delivered from depravity?

Pol.: So it seems.

Soc.: And this is the person who is corrected, reprimanded and who pays just retribution?

Pol.: Yes.

Soc.: The person who, having been unjust, has no deliverance from injustice, is the one who lives worst?

Pol.: Certainly.

Soc.: Which is to say that he lives worst who commits the greatest crimes and who, while being the most unjust of men, succeeds in escaping correction and punishment and paying just retribution. This is what you say has been accomplished by Archelaus and other tyrants and rhetoricians and men in high places?

Pol.: So it seems.

Soc.: Is not their way of living, my friend, comparable to that of a person who is afflicted with the worst of diseases and yet contrives not to pay the penalty to the physician for the faults of his body, and doesn't go to be cured, because, like a child, he is afraid of the pain of being burned or cut? Isn't that a fair comparison?

Pol.: Yes, it truly is.

Soc.: It seems that he does not know what health and excellence of body are like. Now, if we are right, Polus, in our previous conclusions, the people who try to evade justice are similar; they see justice to be painful, but are blind to the benefit which comes from it, not realizing how far more wretched a companion a diseased soul is than a diseased body, i.e. a soul which is corrupt, unjust and impious. Hence they do all they can to avoid punishment and to avoid being released from the worst of bad things. They provide themselves with money and friends, and cultivate to the utmost their powers of persuasion. But if we, Polus, are right, do you see what follows, or shall we work it all out?

Pol.: If you think we should.

Soc.: Is it not a fact that injustice, and the doing of injustice is the worst of bad things?

Pol.: That is clear.

Soc.: And further, suffering punishment is the way to be released from this bad thing?

Pol.: True.

Soc.: And not to suffer punishment is to perpetuate this bad thing?

Pol.: Yes.

Soc.: So doing injustice is only second in the scale of bad things; but to do injustice and not to be punished is first and greatest of all?

Pol.: So it seems.

Soc.: Well, was this not the point in dispute, my friend? You judged Archelaus happy because he was a very great criminal and unpunished. I, on the other hand, maintained that he or any other like him who has done injustice and has not been punished, is, and ought to be, the most wretched of all men; and that the doer of injustice is more wretched than the one who suffers it; and he who escapes punishment more wretched than he who suffers it. Wasn't that what I said?

Pol.: Yes.

Soc.: And it has been proved true?

Pol.: Apparently.

Soc.: Well, Polus, if this is true, what is the great use of rhetoric? From what we just said it follows that every person ought in every way to watch himself and keep from doing injustice, for if he does it he will suffer something very bad. Isn't that right?

Pol.: True.

Soc.: And if he, or anyone he cares about, does do injustice, he ought of his own accord go where he will be immediately punished, to the judge, just as he would to a physician, in order to prevent the disease of injustice from becoming chronic and so become an incurable growth. Isn't this what we must say, Polus, follows from the points we agreed to earlier? Is any other inference consistent with them?

Pol.: What else can we possibly say, Socrates?

Soc.: Then rhetoric is of no use to us, Polus, in helping someone excuse his own injustice, or that of his parents, friends, or children or his native country. It might be of use to anyone who holds that instead of excusing he ought to accuse—himself above all, and in the next place his family or any of his friends who may be doing injustice; he should bring to light the wrongdoing and not conceal it so that the wrongdoer may pay just retribution and be made healthy. And he should even force himself and others not to shrink back, but with closed eyes like brave men to let the physician operate with knife or searing iron, not regarding the pain, in the hope of attaining what is good and fine. Let him who has done things worthy of flogging, offer himself up to be flogged; if worthy of prison, to be imprisoned; if of a fine, to be fined; if of exile, to be exiled; if of death, to die; himself being the first to accuse himself and his own relations, and use rhetoric in order to make manifest his and their unjust actions so that they themselves may be delivered from injustice, which is the worst of bad things. Then, Polus, rhetoric would indeed be useful. Do you say 'yes' or 'no' to that?

Pol.: It seems very absurd to me, Socrates, although it probably agrees with what was said earlier.

Soc.: Is this not the conclusion, if the things agreed to earlier are not disproven?

Pol.: Yes, it certainly is.

Soc.: Looking at it in the opposite way, if we really should harm someone else, whether an enemy or not, we should first of all take special care that we ourselves do not suffer any injustice; but if an enemy treats someone else unjustly, then in every sort of way, by word as well as deed, we should try to prevent his being punished, or appearing before a judge; and if he does appear, we should arrange for him to escape and not pay just retribution: if he has stolen a sum of money, let him keep it and spend it on himself and his relatives, paying no attention to justice or the gods; and if he has done things deserving of death, we must keep him from dying and let him be immortal in his depravity; or, if this is not possible, we should ensure he lives as long as he can. For purposes like that, Polus, rhetoric may be useful, but it is of little use to anyone who is not intending to commit injustice; at least, no such use was discovered by us in the previous discussion.

FOR DISCUSSION:

Does the analogy of a judge with a physician seem very plausible?

Is the purpose of punishment of wrongdoers just to reform them? Would the infliction of pain be likely to have a reformative effect?

The dialogue now takes another turn with the intervention of Callicles, who turns out to be a much more sophisticated opponent than Polus, and also a far more cynical one. After Socrates assures Callicles that he is perfectly serious in the position he has taken with Polus (while not omitting to get in the barb about Callicles' desire to please one of his loves, the Athenian *dem-os*, i.e., masses), Callicles launches into an explanation of how what is just, or unjust, by nature (*phusis*) differs from what is so by convention (*nomos*). Nature declares that it is just and fine for the stronger to rule and take the lion's share of the goods available; convention dictates that it is unjust and shameful for people to take an unequal share and that the stronger must take account of the interests of the weaker. This is because it is the masses who create the conventions, and they do so to frighten the stronger into refraining from taking advantage of the weaker. (From these remarks it is clear that Callicles' supposed love for the *demos* masks a cynical contempt for them.) Callicles holds that the stronger should break free from these conventions and take what is theirs by nature. He also tells Socrates that, although as a youth it is good to have some interest in philosophy, once one is fully a man, occupying oneself with philosophy is ridiculous and renders one unfit for public life. At the end of his great speech he advises Socrates to turn to rhetoric and the skills needed for public life instead, so that he can properly defend himself in court and elsewhere and not be utterly helpless in his own cause as well as his friends'. There is also the charge that Socrates is ruining the lives of the group of young men who gather round him for guidance, one of the accusations that was levelled at him in the trial that preceded his execution. Plato is clearly trying to pin the blame for Socrates' death at least in part on the kind of cynical thinking which Callicles is not ashamed to express openly.

Callicles: Tell me, Chaerephon, is Socrates serious or is he just joking?

Chaerephon: I'd say, Callicles, that he is deadly serious, but there's nothing like asking him.

Cal.: By the gods, I will do just that. Tell me, Socrates, are you serious or just joking? If you are serious, and what you say is true, isn't the whole of human life turned upside-down; and are we not doing, as would appear, in everything the opposite of what we ought to be doing?

Soc.: O Callicles, if human beings did not have some feelings in common, however much they may vary from person to person, I mean to say if everyone's feelings were peculiar to himself and not shared by the rest of mankind, it would not be easy to communicate one's feelings to someone else. I say this because I notice that you and I have a common feeling, for both of us are lovers and both of us each have two loves. I am the lover of Alcibiades, the son of Cleinias, and of philosophy; and you the lover of

the Demos [people] of Athens and of Demos the son of Pyrilampes. Now
I observe that you with all your cleverness do not dare to contradict your
beloved in any word or opinion of his; rather as he changes so you change,
backwards and forwards. When the Athenian Demos denies anything you
are saying in the assembly, you change and go over to his opinion; and you
do the same with Demos, the good-looking young son of Pyrilampes. For
you are incapable of resisting the words and opinions of your beloveds; and
if a person were to express surprise at the absurdity of what you say from
time to time when under their influence, you would probably reply, if you
were honest, that unless someone stopped them from saying these things,
you cannot help saying them too, and that you can only be silent when
they are. Now you must realize that you'll hear the same sort of thing from
me. Don't be surprised at what I say, but if you want to silence me, silence
my beloved, philosophy, for she is always telling me what I am now telling
you, my friend. Nor is she capricious like my other beloved, for the son
of Cleinias says one thing today and another tomorrow, while philosophy
always says the same thing. She is the one whose words surprised you,
and you heard her yourself. It is she you must refute and show, as I was
saying, that to do injustice and to escape punishment is not the worst of all
bad things; or, if you leave her unrefuted, by the Dog, the god of Egypt,
I declare, O Callicles, that Callicles himself will not agree with you, but
will be in discord with you for all of your life. And yet, my friend, I would
rather have my lyre out of tune and in discord, or some chorus which I
have provided, yes, even that the whole world should be at odds with me,
than that I should be at odds with myself and contradict myself.

Cal.: Socrates, you seem to be going completely wild in your speeches, just like
some mob-orator. And now you're going on this way because Polus has
fallen into the same error himself which he accused Gorgias of. He said
that when Gorgias was asked by you whether, if someone came to him
who wanted to learn rhetoric and did not know justice, he would teach
him justice; Gorgias, out of shame, replied that he would, thus going
along with the usual ways of mankind, who would be indignant if he
said he wouldn't. It was in consequence of this admission that Gorgias
was compelled to contradict himself, that being just the sort of thing
in which you delight. At that point, Polus laughed at you, deservedly, I
think; but now he has himself fallen into the same trap. But I really can't
approve of his performance when he conceded to you that to do injustice
is more shameful than to suffer it, for that was the admission which led to

his being entangled by you, and because he was ashamed to say what he thought, he had his mouth stopped.

For, Socrates, you who pretend to be pursuing truth are appealing now to the popular and common notions of what is fine, but these are not fine by nature, only by convention. Convention and nature are generally at odds with one another, and so, if a person is ashamed to say what he thinks, he is compelled to contradict himself. You, cleverly perceiving how to take advantage of this, slyly ask him who is arguing conventionally a question which is to be determined by nature; or, if he is arguing as to nature, you slip over to convention, as, for instance, you did in this very discussion about doing and suffering injustice. When Polus was speaking of what is conventionally shameful, you attacked him from the point of view of nature; for by nature suffering injustice is more shameful because it is worse, but conventionally doing injustice is more shameful. Suffering injustice is not what happens to a man, but to a slave, who would be better off dead than alive, since when he is wronged and trampled on, he is unable to help himself or anyone else about whom he cares. The reason for this, as I see it, is that those who make the conventions are the mass of people, who are weak, and they make conventions and distribute praise and censure with themselves in mind and their own advantage. They terrify the stronger sort of people and those who can get the better of them, and in order that they may not get the better of them, they say that this is shameful and unjust, meaning by the word 'injustice' the desire to have more than one's neighbours; for knowing how inferior they are, I suspect they are only too glad to gain equality. This is why trying to have more than the mass of people is conventionally said to be shameful and unjust, and is called injustice, whereas nature herself indicates that it is just for the better to have more than the worse, and the more powerful than the weaker. In many ways she shows among humans as well as animals, and indeed among whole cities and races, that justice consists in the superior ruling over and having more than the inferior. For what sort of justice did Xerxes rely on when he invaded Greece, or his father the Scythians? There are numberless other examples. These are the men who I think act according to what is just by nature, and, yes, by Zeus, according to the convention of nature; not, no doubt, according to that convention people lay down, which we invent and impose on the best and the strongest from their youth on and so tame them like young lions, charming them with incantations until they are enslaved, and telling them to be content with equality and that equality is fine and just.

But if there were a man who had enough strength, he would shake off and break out of and escape from all this; he would trample under foot all our formulas and spells and charms, and all our conventions which are against nature. This slave of ours would rise in rebellion and be our master, and then nature's justice would shine forth. This is what I take to be Pindar's meaning when he says in his poem that

> Convention is the lord of all,
>
> Of mortals as well as immortals.

And it, he continues,

> Justifies the utmost violence
>
> With overpowering hand. My witness is
>
> The deeds of Heracles, for without making payment...

I do not remember the exact words, but the meaning is that without paying for them and without their being given to him, he drove off the cattle belonging to Geryon, as though this were his right by nature, that the cattle and other property of weaker and inferior beings properly belonged to the stronger and superior.[1]

This is what the truth is. You can be convinced of it yourself, if you will just leave philosophy and go on to more important things. For philosophy, Socrates, if pursued in moderation and at the proper age, has a certain charm, but too much philosophy is the ruin of people. Even if a man is well endowed by nature, still, if he carries on philosophy into later life, he is bound to be ignorant of all those things which it is necessary for a gentleman and highly respected person to know; he is inexperienced in the conventions of the state, and in the language which ought to be used in dealings between man and man, whether public or private, and utterly ignorant of the pleasures and desires of mankind and of human character in general. So people of this sort, when they go off to the realms of politics or business are as ridiculous as I imagine politicians are when they get involved in your conversations and debates. For as Euripides says,

> Every man shines in that and pursues that and devotes the greatest
>
> portion of the day to that in which he most excels.

But anything in which he is inferior, he avoids and denigrates, while praising the opposite out of regard for himself, because he thinks he will in

---

1   The reference is to one of the "ten labours" of Heracles ("Hercules" to the Romans) done in expiation for having killed his own children; the tenth labour involved shooting and stealing the cattle of the monster Geryon.

this way praise himself.

But I think the best thing is to have a share in both. Philosophy, as a part of education, is an excellent thing, and there is no disgrace to a man while he is young in pursuing such a study; but when he is older, it becomes ridiculous, and I feel towards philosophers as I do towards those who lisp and mumble like a child. For I love to see a little child, who is not old enough to speak plainly, lisping and mumbling playfully; I find this charming in how free it is and suitable to the child's age. But when I hear a child speaking clearly, I find it unpleasant; the sound is annoying and more suited to a slave. So, when I hear a man lisping, or see him mumbling like a child, his behaviour strikes me as ridiculous, unmanly, and deserving of a blow.

Well, I have the same feeling about students of philosophy. When I see a youth engaged in it, it strikes me as suitable and becoming a free man; him who neglects philosophy I regard as an inferior person, who will never aspire to anything fine or noble. But when I see him continuing in philosophy later in life, and not leaving off, I'd like to give him a beating, Socrates; for, as I was saying, such a person, even though he is well-endowed by nature, becomes unmanly. He shuns the city centre and the market place, in which, as the poet says, "men win distinction". He creeps into a corner for the rest of his life, and talks in a whisper with three of four admiring youths, but never speaks out like a free man in a great and powerful way.

Now, Socrates, I have very friendly feelings toward you, and my feeling may be compared with that of Zethus towards Amphion in the play by Euripides which I just mentioned. I feel like saying to you much what Zethus said to his brother, that you, Socrates, are careless about the things you ought to be careful of, and that you

Who have a soul so noble are twisting it into a childish shape;
Neither in a court of justice could you state a case, or give any reason or proof,
Or offer bold counsel on another's behalf.

And you must not be offended, dear Socrates, for I am speaking out of good will towards you. Aren't you ashamed of being the way I say you are, which is the condition not just of you but of all those who go deeper and deeper into the abysses of philosophy? For suppose that someone were to take you, or anyone of your sort off to prison, declaring you had done wrong when you had done no wrong, you have to grant that you would not know what to do. There you would stand, dizzy and gaping, and not having a word to say. And when you went up before the court, even if your accuser were some inferior type and not good for much, you would end up executed if he sought the death penalty for you.

And yet, Socrates, how can this be wise, "this art which converts a good man and makes him worse," a man who is helpless and has no power to save either himself or others, this art which lets him live with all his property expropriated by his enemies and simply deprived of his rights as a citizen—a man who, to put it bluntly, can be punched out with impunity. So, my friend, take my advice and engage no more in refutations, "practice the sweet art of practical affairs and what will earn you a reputation for wisdom, but leave to others the subtleties", whether we should call them nonsense or absurdities: "they will only put you in a house where no one visits." Stop emulating, then, these worthless word splitters, and emulate only the man with a life, a reputation, and every other good.

FOR DISCUSSION:

Do you think that our notions of what is just and unjust (moral and im-moral) are rooted in conventions humans have created for their own purposes? Would such a view necessarily imply that if doing injustice was profitable for a person and he could get away with it, he should?

Supposing human conventions were entirely removed, and we lived in what we might call a "state of nature", would the stronger feel no constraint on their taking advantage of the weaker?

Is there such a thing as too much regard for truth and for taking positions which make sense? Can it, when carried to an extreme, make a person impotent and defenceless?

FRIEDRICH NIETZSCHE, FROM *ON THE GENEALOGY OF MORALS:*[1]

The reason the subject (or, as we more colloquially say, *the soul*) has been, until now, the best doctrine on earth, is perhaps because it facilitated that sublime self-deception whereby the majority of the dying, the weak, and the oppressed of every kind could construe weakness itself as freedom, and their particular mode of existence as an accomplishment.

---

1   Initially published in German as *Zur Geneologie der Moral* (Leipzig: Nauman, 1887). This translation is by Carol Diethe, *On the Genealogy of Morality*, Keith Ansell-Pearson, ed. (Cambridge: Cambridge UP, 1994).

Socrates begins his response to Callicles' speech by congratulating Callicles on being just the sort of respondent he needs: someone who is educated, a friend, but above all perfectly candid about what he thinks, never letting himself be ashamed to express the views he holds. Just how much Socrates' tongue is in his cheek when he says these things is hard to judge, but doubtless some of his famous irony is at work. There is no doubt, however, that Socrates is perfectly serious when he says that the inquiry in which he is now engaged, into how people should run their lives, is the most important anyone can undertake.

> *Soc.*: If my soul, Callicles, were made of gold, don't you think I would be delighted to discover one of those stones with which they test gold, and the very best one possible, to which I might bring my soul, so that if I brought my soul to it and it agreed that my soul was well cared for, then I would know that I was in a satisfactory condition and that no other test was needed?
>
> *Cal.*: What is your point in asking, Socrates?
>
> *Soc.*: I will tell you: in you I think I have had the luck to find just such a stone.
>
> *Cal.*: Why?
>
> *Soc.*: Because I am sure that if you agree with me in any of the opinions which my soul forms, I have at last found the truth. For I think that if a person is to make a completely adequate test of the life his soul is living, of its correctness or the opposite, he should have three qualities: knowledge, good-will, and candor, all of which are possessed by you. Many people I meet are unable to test me, because they are not wise as you are; others are wise, but they will not tell me the truth because they don't have my interests at heart in the way you do; and these two foreigners, Gorgias and Polus, are doubtless wise men and my very good friends, but they do not have sufficient candor and are too prone to shame. Why, their proneness to shame is so great that they are driven to contradict themselves, first one and then the other, in front of a large company and on matters of the greatest importance. But you have all the qualities in which these others are deficient. You received an excellent education, as many Athenians can testify. Also you are well-disposed to me. Shall I tell you why I think so? I know that you, Callicles, and Tisander of Aphidnae, and Andron the son of Androtion, and Nausicydes of the deme of Chorlarges, studied together. There were four of you, and I once heard you advising each other as to the extent to which the pursuit of philosophy should be carried, and, as

I know, you came to the conclusion that the study should not be pushed into minute precision. You were cautioning each other not to become over-wise, and afraid that too much wisdom might without your being aware of it ruin you. So now, when I hear you giving the same advice to me which you then gave to your closest friends, that's enough evidence to convince me of your real good will toward me. As for your being the sort to speak candidly without shame, you've said as much yourself and that assurance is confirmed by the speech you gave just now.

So, then, in the present situation this is the way things stand: If you agree with me in an argument about any point, that point will have been adequately tested by us and will need no further testing. For you would not have agreed with me either from lack of knowledge, or from excess of shame, or from a desire to deceive me, for you are my friend, as you tell me yourself. And, therefore, when you and I agree on something, the result will be the attainment of final truth.

Now, there is no finer inquiry, Callicles, than the one you censure me for making: What ought the character of a man to be, what his pursuits, and how far should he pursue them both when he is older and in his youth? For be assured that if I go wrong in my own conduct, I do not do so intentionally but from ignorance. So don't cease reproving me, now that you have begun, until I have learned exactly what it is I should be pursuing and how I can acquire it. And if you catch me agreeing with what you say and then later not doing what I agreed with, just call me a dolt and consider me unworthy of receiving further censures.

The first round of questioning opens up an apparent inconsistency in Callicles' speech. The many, though individually weaker than any of the strong men Callicles speaks of, are collectively stronger, and hence by Callicles' own reasoning they are collectively better and should by nature rule. Hence their conventions are in accord with nature, not against it. However, Socrates does not make it clear that there is this ambiguity between what is true of each individual in a group and what is true of the group as a whole.

Once more, then, tell me what you and Pindar mean by 'just by nature': Didn't you say that the superior should take the property of the inferior person by force, that the better should rule the worse, the noble have more than the ordinary? Or am I not recollecting correctly?

Cal.: Yes, that is what I was saying, and I still say it.

Soc.: And do you mean by the better the same as the superior? For at the time
I could not make up my mind what you were saying: whether you meant
by the superior the stronger, and that the weaker must obey the stronger,
as you seemed to imply when you said that great states attack small ones
according to what is just by nature, because they are superior and stronger,
as though the superior and the stronger and the better were the same;
or whether the better may also be inferior and weaker, and the superior
the more wretched, or whether better is to be defined in the same way as
the superior. This is the point which I want to have cleared up: Are the
superior and the better and the stronger the same or different?

Cal.: I say unequivocally that they are the same.

Soc.: Then aren't the many by nature superior to the single individual, against
whom, as you were saying they make the conventions?

Cal.: Certainly.

Soc.: Then the conventions of the many are the conventions of the superior?

Cal.: Very true.

Soc.: Then aren't the conventions of the many the conventions of the better,
since on your account the superior are better?

Cal.: Yes.

Soc.: And since they are superior, the conventions made by them are fine by
nature?

Cal.: Yes.

Soc.: And are not the many of the opinion, as you were just saying, that equality
is just and that to do injustice is more shameful than to suffer it? Is that
not so, or not? Answer Callicles, and don't let any shame get in the way.
Do the many think, or do they not think that? Please do answer so that if
you agree with me, I can take myself to be confirmed by the agreement of
someone so competent on these matters.

Cal.: Yes, the opinion of the many is what you say.

Soc.: Then it is not mere convention but nature which affirms that to do
injustice is more shameful than to suffer injustice, and it seems you were
wrong when you accused me and said that nature and convention are
opposed, and that I, knowing this, was dishonestly playing between them,
appealing to convention when the argument is about nature, and to nature
when the argument is about convention.

Callicles feels compelled to backtrack and admit that a group of decidedly
inferior people is not simply by their joint strength superior to one genu-

inely good person. But this means he has to come up with a new criterion for what makes someone better.

Cal.: This man will never cease talking nonsense. At your age, Socrates, aren't you ashamed to be playing with words and thinking it great to pounce on someone when they make a verbal slip? Don't you see, haven't I told you already, that by superior I mean better? Do you really imagine me to say that if a rabble of slaves and ne'er-do-wells, who are of no use except perhaps for their physical strength, get together and make pronouncements that those are the laws?

Soc.: So, wisest Callicles, is that what you say?

Cal.: Certainly.

Soc.: I was thinking, Callicles, that something like that had to be in your mind, and that is why I repeated the question: What is the superior? I wanted to know clearly what you meant; for surely you do not think that two men are better than one, or that your slaves are better than you because they are stronger? So please begin again, and tell me who the better are, if they are not the stronger; and I will ask you, gifted friend, to be a little gentler in your censures, or I shall have to run away from you.

Cal.: You're speaking ironically, Socrates.

Soc.: No, by Zethus, Callicles, on whose aid you called when you directed a lot of irony towards me, I am not. Just tell me who you say are the better men.

Cal.: I mean the more worthy.

Soc.: Don't you see that you are yourself using words which have no meaning and that you explain nothing? Will you tell me whether you mean by the better and superior the wiser, or if not, whom?

Cal.: Most definitely, I do mean the wiser.

Soc.: Then according to you, one wise man may often be superior to ten thousand fools, and he ought to rule them, and they ought to be his subjects, and he ought to have more than they. This is what I believe you mean—and you must not suppose I am just playing with words—if you allow that the one individual is superior to the ten thousand?

Cal.: Yes, that is what I mean, and that is what I take to be the just by nature: that the better and wiser should rule and have more than the inferior.

Soc.: Stop there, and let me ask you what you would say in this case. Let us suppose that we are all together as we are now; there are several of us, and we have a large common store of meats and drinks, and there are all sorts of persons in our company having various degrees of strength and weakness, and one of us, being a physician, is wiser in the matter of food than all the rest, and he is probably stronger than some and not so strong as others of us. Will not this person, since he is wiser, be also better than the rest of us and superior to us in the matter of food?

Cal.: Certainly.

Soc.: Is he, then, to have a larger share of the meats and drinks because he is better, or should he be in charge of distribution since he is ruling, but not then lavish a larger portion of them on his own body lest he damage himself. His share will exceed that of some and be less than that of others, and, if he is the feeblest of all, the share assigned to this best man will be the smallest, Callicles. Am I not right, my friend?

Cal.: You talk about meats and drinks and physicians and other nonsense. I'm not speaking about them.

Soc.: Well, but don't you admit that the wiser is the superior? Answer 'yes' or 'no'.

Cal.: Yes.

Soc.: And shouldn't the superior person have a larger share?

Cal.: Not of meats and drinks.

Soc.: I see. Then, perhaps, of coats; the most artful weaver should have the largest coat, and the greatest number of them, and go about dressed up in the best and most good-looking ones?

Cal.: Really, coats?

Soc.: Then the most artful and best in making shoes ought to have more shoes; the shoemaker, clearly, should walk about in the largest shoes and have the greatest number of them?

Cal.: Really, shoes? What nonsense!

Soc.: Well, if that's not what you mean, perhaps you would say that a farmer who in cultivating the soil is wise and fine and good should actually have a larger share of seeds, and have as much seed as possible for his own land?

Cal.: How you go on, always talking in the same way, Socrates!

Soc.: Yes, Callicles, and about the same things too.

Cal.: Yes, by the gods, you are literally always talking about cobblers, fullers, cooks and physicians, as if these had anything to do with our argument!

Soc.: But why won't you tell me in what a man must be wiser and superior in order to claim a larger share? Since you won't accept my suggestions, won't you propose one yourself?

Cal.: I've already told you. In the first place, I mean by superiors not cobblers or cooks but wise politicians who understand the administration of a state,

and who are not only wise but brave as well and able to carry out their
designs, and not the sort who give up from weakness of spirit.[1]

Soc.: Just see now, excellent Callicles, how different my accusation against
you is from the one you bring against me, for you charge me with always
saying the same, while I charge you with never saying the same about
the same things, for at one time you were defining the better and the
superior as the stronger, then later as the wiser, and now you bring forward
something else: the better and the superior are now declared by you to be
the more courageous. Please do tell me, my good friend, once and for all,
whom you affirm to be the better and superior, what it is they are better
and superior in.

Cal.: I just told you that I mean those who are wise and courageous in the
administration of the state. They ought to be the rulers of their states, and
justice consists in their having more than their subjects.

Socrates now shifts the discussion to ruling over oneself so as to exhibit the
virtue of moderation. But to Callicles this is no virtue at all, and the best
way to live is to leave one's cravings unrestrained so that one can have more
of the pleasure that comes in satisfying them. The wise person will strive
to be in a position of power where he can satisfy his cravings and then give
free rein to them, ignoring all the conventions which the many inferior
people have established to check just this sort of behaviour.

Soc.: What? More than themselves, my friend? In what are they rulers or ruled?

Cal.: What are you talking about?

Soc.: I mean that everyone is his own ruler. But, perhaps, you think there is no
necessity for him to rule himself; he is only required to rule others?

Cal.: What do you mean by 'ruling over himself'?

Soc.: Something simple enough. What is commonly said: that a person should
be moderate and master of himself, and ruler over his own pleasures and
cravings.

Cal.: How simple-minded! You mean to call those fools the moderate?

Soc.: What? Anyone would realize that that's not what I'm saying.

Cal.: But it certainly is, Socrates. How can someone be happy who is the slave
of anything? I plainly then assert the opposite, and I shall freely tell you
what the fine and just are by nature: the person who is to live rightly

---

1   Literally, softness of soul.

should let his cravings grow as much as possible and not repress them; and when they have grown to their maximum he should have the courage and wisdom to serve them and satisfy all his longings. The many, however, are not capable of this, and they blame the powerful because they are ashamed of their own weakness, and out of a desire to conceal it they say that immoderation is shameful. As I have already said, they enslave the nobler natures and, being unable to satisfy their own desire for pleasure, they praise moderation and justice because of their own cowardice. For if a man had originally been the son of a king, or had a nature capable of acquiring an empire or a tyranny or absolute power, what could be more truly depraved or bad than moderation—to a man like him, I say, who could freely enjoy every good, with no one to stand in his way, and yet has allowed convention and speech and the opinions of other people to be masters over him? Must he not be wretched whom the reputation for justice and moderation hinders from giving more to his friends than to his enemies, even though he be a ruler in the state? No, Socrates, the truth, for you claim to be devoted to truth, is this: that luxury, immoderation, and freedom, if they are supplied with the means, are virtue and happiness. All the rest is mere bauble, agreements of men contrary to nature, foolish talk, worth nothing.

FOR DISCUSSION:

Are we living as fully as possible just when we are satisfying strong desires and enjoying that?

Socrates likens the life advocated by Callicles to that of a person who is constantly filling leaky jars, and Callicles unashamedly accepts that a person who has satisfied his desires is no longer enjoying himself and hence no longer happy. He must keep his cravings going so that he can keep experiencing pleasure, for it is pleasure that Callicles identifies with what makes life good. Socrates tries, without success, to get Callicles to admit that some pleasures are not good but just disgusting, for that would of course contradict the radical hedonism that Callicles accepts.

Soc.: There is nobility in the freedom, Callicles, with which you carry on speaking, for what you say is what the rest of the world think but do not want to say. Please do keep this up, so that the true way we should live will become clear. You say, do you not, that in the man who lives as he ought the cravings should not be repressed, but that they should be allowed to grow as great as possible and then somehow or other be satisfied, and that this is virtue.

Cal.: Yes, I do.

Soc.: Then those who are in need of nothing are not rightly said to be happy?

Cal.: Certainly not, for then stones and corpses would be happiest of all.

Soc.: But surely life according to your view is an awful thing. Indeed, I think Euripides may have been right in saying:

Who knows if life be not death and death life?

And we are very likely dead. Once I heard a wise man say that right now we are actually dead, and that the body is our tomb, and that the part of the soul which is the seat of the cravings is liable to be persuaded and shifts back and forth. Some ingenious person, probably a Sicilian or an Italian, played with the word in a tale in which he called the soul, because it is persuadable [*pithanon*] and impressionable, a jar [*pithon*], and called the foolish [*anoētous*] the uninitiated [*amuētous*]. In the uninitiated the part of soul in which the cravings exist, being the immoderate and insatiable part, he compared to a leaky jar, because it can never be filled. He was not of your way of thinking, Callicles, for he declares that of all the souls in Hades, meaning the invisible ones, those uninitiated or leaky persons are the most wretched, and that they pour water into a leaky jar with a sieve similarly full of holes. The sieve is the soul, my informer told me, and he compares the soul of the foolish to a sieve because it was leaky and so unable to retain anything because of its bad memory and unreliability.

This is all, to be sure, very strange, but it shows what I would like to prove to you: that you should change your mind and, instead of the immoderate and unrestrained life, choose one that is orderly and adequately supplied and satisfied with what it has. Am I making any impression on you, and are you coming over to the view that the orderly are happier than the immoderate? Or will I fail to persuade you, and no matter how many tales I relate to you you still won't change your mind?

Cal.: The latter, Socrates, is closer to the truth.

Soc.: Well, I will give you another simile, from the same source as the earlier one. See how far you would accept the following simile as an account of the lives of the moderate person and the immoderate. There are two men, each of whom has a number of jars; the one man has sound and full jars, one full of wine, another with honey, and a third with milk, as well as others filled with other things, and the sources for these things are scarce and he can only obtain them with a great deal of toil and trouble. But once his jars are filled, he has no need to refill them anymore and doesn't worry about them or pay any attention to them. The other man, in a similar way, can obtain sources though not without trouble; but his jars are leaky and unsound, and night and day he is forced to keep filling them, and, if he pauses for a moment, he is in an agony of pain. Such are their respective lives. Now would you say that the life of the immoderate person is happier than that of the moderate? Don't I convince you that the opposite is true?

Cal.: You don't convince me, Socrates. For the person who has filled up no longer has any pleasure left, and this is, as I was just saying, the life of a stone. He has neither joy nor sorrow once he is filled. No, pleasure depends on having as much as possible flowing in.

Soc.: So, then, if the intake is great so must also the outflow be great, and the holes must be large for that to happen.

Cal.: Certainly.

Soc.: The life you are now depicting is not that of a corpse or of a stone, but more that of a cormorant.[1] Do you mean that he is to be hungry and eating?

Cal.: Yes.

Soc.: And he is to be thirsty and drinking?

Cal.: Yes, that is what I mean. He is to have all his cravings and with the power to satisfy them enjoy life and be happy.

Soc.: That's splendid, my excellent man. Go on as you have begun and have no shame. I, too, must get rid of shame. First, will you tell me whether you include itching and scratching; provided you have enough itches and pass your life scratching you're living happily?

Cal.: What an absurd being you are, Socrates; really just a mob-orator.

Soc.: That was the reason, Callicles, why I scared Polus and Gorgias until they were too ashamed to say what they really thought. But you will not be too ashamed and not scared away, for you are a brave man. So now, answer my question.

Cal.: All right, I'll say that even the scratcher would live pleasantly.

Soc.: And if pleasantly, also happily?

Cal.: To be sure.

Soc.: But what if the itching were not confined to the head? Shall I carry on here? Callicles, consider how you would reply if you were forced to confront the full implications of this, especially if at the end you were

---

1   It is uncertain exactly what species of bird is referred to, but it must be one which was known for spending most of its time eating and excreting.

asked whether the life of a catamite[1] is not absurd and shameful and wretched. Are you really going to say that they too are happy as long as they get enough of what they want?

Cal.: Aren't you ashamed, Socrates, to introduce such topics into the discussion?

Soc.: Well, my fine friend, am I really the one who introduces these topics, or is it he who says without any qualification that all who feel pleasure in whatever manner are happy, and who admits no distinction between good and bad pleasures? And I still ask: Do you say that pleasure and good are the same, or that some pleasures are not good?

Cal.: Well, all right, for the sake of being consistent in what I say I will say that they are the same.

Soc.: You are breaking the original agreement, Callicles, and it will no longer be possible to continue with you the search for truth, if you say what is contrary to your real opinion.

Cal.: But that's just what you do too, Socrates.

Soc.: If I do, then we are both in the wrong. Still, my dear friend, I ask you to consider whether pleasure, no matter where it comes from, is good; for, if this is true, then all the shameful things just hinted at must follow, and many others.

Cal.: That, Socrates, is only your opinion.

Soc.: And do you, Callicles, seriously maintain what you are saying?

Cal.: Indeed I do.

Soc.: Then, shall we proceed with the argument on the assumption that you are serious?

Cal.: By all means.

FOR DISCUSSION:

Can it be reasonable to claim that some pleasures are *of themselves* bad? Or are pleasures bad only when they arise from some action which is bad?

Could it be reasonable to define the welfare of the citizenry as simply the maximizing of its pleasures and the minimizing of its pains?

---

1   A boy kept by an older man for sexual purposes.

B.5: PLATO

orn in Athens in 428 BCE to an aristocratic family, he took a great
interest in both politics and the theatre as a young man. At some
point he came under the influence of Socrates, whose death by execution in 399 seems to have moved him to take up the study of philosophy,
the vocation which dominated the rest of his life. His abilities as a dramatist
were put to good use in the writing of numerous dialogues (such as the
Crito and *Gorgias*, excerpts from which are found in the previous two readings) in which he pictures Socrates as cross-examining men he meets on
questions of ethics and in the course of the conversation puncturing their
pretensions to genuine knowledge.

When Plato was 40 years old he visited Italy and Sicily where he was a
guest at the court of Dionysus I, the tyrant of Syracuse. He seems to have
fallen out of favour there and returned to Athens in 387, where he founded
a school called the Academy. Perhaps it was while in the western parts of
the Greek world that Plato encountered Pythagoreans and learned about
the developing science of mathematics, for certainly this was a formative
influence on his thought.

Plato undertook two more trips to Syracuse, in 367 and 361, with hopes
of educating the new ruler, Dionysus II, in philosophy and thereby bringing
about some form of government resembling that which is argued for in
the *Republic*. These efforts failed and Plato spent his remaining days at the
Academy, dying in 348.

The selections in this section are drawn almost entirely from Plato's
Republic, a work which starts off in the style of the early Socratic dialogues
but shifts somewhat abruptly at the beginning of book II into something
much more speculative and constructive. Although the overarching aim
of the dialogue is to show that the just life is its own reward, so to speak,

Socrates asks his young audience to first investigate what justice is by look-ing for it in a maximally well governed political state, the assumption being that there will be an analogy between justice in the best sort of state and justice in an individual. That gives Socrates the opportunity to construct a utopian political arrangement and say how it might be possible to bring it into reality. He also allows himself to say exactly what he finds wrong with the forms of government commonly found in Greece and why these forms turn out to be unstable, falling eventually into tyranny.

Plato's utopia will strike the reader as hopelessly unrealistic and probably not at all the sort of community in which they would be comfortable living. It has fairly rigid class divisions; the vast majority of the population has no role in governance; and there is a need for total deference to the expertise of a specially educated elite. Democracy, Greek-style, is lampooned merci-lessly; freedom and equality are treated as qualities which a society can eas-ily have too much of. One might well wonder why Plato was led to put this whole fantasy forward in the first place. The answer lies partly, to be sure, in the ills to which the Greek city states, Athens in particular, were so obvi-ously susceptible. Plato had seen first-hand how the Athenian democracy had led to disaster, and he would also have known how civil strife followed on the division of citizens into the rich and the poor. Ghastly tyrants were also a frequent affliction of the Greek world. Couple this with his belief that he had a method which would lead especially intelligent people who had received a proper education as youths to a secure knowledge of what was good and to be aimed at in life, and you can see that he may well have thought that radical reform on the basis of that knowledge was both needed and possible.

It is easy to find fault with many of the particulars in Socrates' argument, but the basic premises of it are still live options today and it is a challenge to say why they are wrong, if they are. There is the premise that there is something like a science of the goal which human society should aim at and an expertise which can be learned in how to achieve it. Further, this science and expertise can only be acquired by a specially educated few, but the rest of the population can be brought by their own less demanding education to accept leadership from that highly educated class. Finally the science that the members of that class acquire reinforces in them a moral character that is not easily corrupted by self-interest. Given these three assumptions it is difficult not to reach the conclusion that it would be good to institute the educational program that would allow for society to produce the elite class as well as the docile majority needed to give it the best leadership possible and thus the greatest chance of achieving what society ought to achieve. Socrates always makes clear that his proposals are tentative and that he welcomes opposition, although he gets only a little from his acolytes in the dialogue. Readers should feel themselves invited to formulate just where the premises go wrong, while, of course, enjoying the panache with which Socrates carries out his enterprise.

B.5.a: *REPUBLIC* I

336b-344c[1]

The first book of Plato's *Republic* is in style very like Plato's early Socratic dialogues where there is a highly dramatic encounter between Socrates and some noted sophist. In this case the drama is engendered by Thrasymachus who impatiently interjects into a rather sedate discussion of how to define justice his own quite cynical take on the subject. The challenge of his position, however, sets the topic for the whole rest of the book, viz. how to show that the life lived justly will always be happier and more satisfying than a life of injustice. ('Justice' here has a broader meaning than we normally give the word; it covers most matters of morality in our dealings with others. To be just is to be moral in our dealings with others.) For Thrasymachus, justice is merely the restraints placed on the conduct of most people by the stronger people who rule and rule in their own interest. If a person can get away with it, it is in his interest to act unjustly, i.e., for his own benefit rather than that of the rulers. Such perversions of government were as common in Plato's day as they are in our own, and just as much cause for cynicism then as they are now.

This selection begins just after Socrates and his companions admit they have not yet been able to find a satisfactory definition of what justice really is.

Several times during the course of the discussion Thrasymachus had tried to break into the argument but had been put down by the rest of the company, who wanted to hear the end. But when Polemarchus and I had finished speaking and there was a pause, he could no longer hold his peace. Gathering

---

1 Translated by Jowett, with modifications.

himself up he came at us like a wild beast seeking to devour us. We were panic-stricken at the sight of him.

He roared out to the whole company: What idiocy, Socrates, has taken possession of you all? And why, you simpletons, do you keep on politely deferring to each other. I say that if you really want to know what justice is you should not only pose questions but answer them, and you should not seek to score points just by refuting an opponent, but have an answer of your own. For there are many who can ask a question but cannot answer one. Now I am not going to put up with your saying that justice is duty or advantage or profit or gain or interest; I don't stand for that sort of nonsense. I demand clearness and accuracy.

I was panic-stricken at his words, and could not look at him without trembling. Indeed I believe that if I had not fixed my eye on him, I would have been struck dumb. But when I saw his fury, I looked at him first, and so was able to frame a reply.[1]

Thrasymachus, I said, with a quiver, don't be hard on us. Polemarchus and I may have been guilty of a little mistake in the argument, but I can assure you that the error was not intentional. If we had been seeking for a piece of gold, you would not imagine that we were deferring to one another and so losing our chance of finding it. So why, when we are seeking justice, a thing more precious than many pieces of gold, do you say that we are meekly yielding to one another and not doing our best to get at the truth? No, my good friend, we are genuinely anxious to do so, but in fact we lack the ability. If so, you people with superior insight should pity us and not be angry with us.

Isn't that just like you, Socrates, he replied, with a sarcastic laugh. An example of your ironic style! Didn't I see this coming? Didn't I tell you that whatever he was asked he would refuse to answer, and turn to irony or some other evasion in order to avoid giving an answer?

You are wise, Thrasymachus, I replied, and know full well that if you ask a person what numbers make up twelve, while carefully ruling out any answer like 'twice six' or 'three times four', or 'six times two', or 'four times three' as the sort of nonsense you don't stand for, then obviously, if you put the question that way, no one can answer you. But suppose he were to reply: "Thrasymachus, what do you mean? If one of these numbers which you prohibit is the right answer, am I supposed to say some other one which is not right? Is that your point?" How would you answer him?

---

1   It was a saying that if you kept your eye on a wolf it would not attack you.

As though those two cases were alike, he said.

Why aren't they? I replied. Even if they aren't but just appear to be so to the person who asked, shouldn't he say what he thinks regardless of whether you or I forbid him?

So then, I can suppose that you are going to give one of the prohibited answers?

I may very well do that, despite the danger, if after due reflection I approve of any.

But what if I give you an answer about justice different and better than any of these? What penalty do you think you deserve?

Penalty! Whatever is appropriate for the ignorant: I must learn from the wise. That's what I deserve to suffer.

What nerve! In addition to learning you have to pay me a fee.

I'll pay when I have the money, I replied.

But you do have it, Socrates, said Glaucon. And you, Thrasymachus, need not worry about the money; we'll all contribute to a fund for Socrates.

Yes, he replied, and then Socrates will do what he always does: refuse to answer himself but take and pull to pieces whatever answer someone else gives.

But, my good friend, I said, how can someone who does not know, and says he doesn't, answer, especially if, supposing he does have some vague ideas, he is told by some respected authority that he is not to utter them? The reasonable course is for someone like yourself who claims to know and can say what he knows to do the speaking. Will you, then, be kind enough to give us your answer, so that I and the rest of the company can benefit from it?

Glaucon and the rest joined in my request, and Thrasymachus, as anyone could see, was in reality eager to speak, for he thought he had an excellent answer that would do him credit. But at first he pretended to insist on my answering and only after a while consented to begin.

Behold, he said, the wisdom of Socrates: he refuses to teach himself and goes about learning from others, to whom he never even says "Thank you."

It's certainly true, I replied, that I learn from others, but I totally deny that I am ungrateful. Money I have none, and so I pay with praise, because that's all I have. How ready I am to praise anyone who seems to me to speak well you will soon find out once you've answered, for I expect you will answer well.

Listen, then, he said; I proclaim that justice is nothing else than the interest of the stronger. All right, why aren't you praising me? But of course you won't.

First I have to understand you, I replied. Justice, you say, is the interest of the stronger. What, Thrasymachus, does that mean? You cannot mean to say that because Polydamus, the pancratiast,[1] is stronger than we are and finds eating beef conducive to his physical strength, that eating beef is therefore equally good for us weaker persons and right and just for us?

How outrageous of you, Socrates; you take the words in the sense most damaging to the argument.

Not at all, my good sir, I said; I'm just trying to understand them. Please be a little clearer.

Well, he said, have you never heard that forms of government differ: there are tyrannies, and democracies, and aristocracies?

Yes, I know.

And the government is the ruling power in each state?

Certainly.

And these different forms of government make democratic laws, or aristocratic laws, or tyrannical ones, to suit their different interests. These laws, designed to suit the ruling class and made in their own interests, constitute the justice which they deliver to their subjects. Anyone who violates them they punish as a law-breaker and someone unjust. That is what I mean when I say that in all states there is the same principle of justice, namely the interest of the government. And since the government must be supposed to have power, it is only reasonable to conclude that everywhere the interest of the stronger is the single basis for justice.

Thrasymachus' definition of justice founders because it is really two definitions: (1) justice is obeying the laws, (2) justice is what is for the interests of the stronger, i.e., the ruling class. But, of course, when the ruling class makes a mistake and frames laws which are not in its own interest, the two definitions lead to contradictory results, and in what follows Socrates quickly pounces on this difficulty.

Now I understand you, I said; and whether you are right or not I'll try to discover. But first note that in defining justice you yourself used the word 'interest', which you forbade me to use. However, it's true that you did add the words 'of the stronger'.

A minor addition, no doubt!

Minor or major, never mind about that. We must first inquire whether what you are saying is true. Now we are both agreed that justice is an interest of some

---

1   The Greek equivalent of mixed martial arts.

sort, but you go on to say 'of the stronger', and that's what I'm not so sure
about. Let's consider that.

Proceed.

I will. First tell me: Do you admit that it is just for subjects to obey their
rulers?

I do.

But are the rulers always right, or do they sometimes make mistakes?

To be sure, they sometimes make mistakes.

So in making the laws they may sometimes make them correctly, and
sometimes not?

True.

When they make them correctly, they make them conform to their own
interests; when they make a mistake, contrary to their interests? Do you admit
that?

Yes.

And the laws that they make must be obeyed by their subjects; that's what
you call justice?

No doubt.

Then, according to your thesis, it is just not only to serve the interest of the
stronger but also the opposite?

What are you saying?

I'm just repeating what you said, I think. But let's look at it more closely.
Have we not admitted that the rulers may be mistaken about their own interest
in what they command, and also that justice is obeying the rulers. Didn't we
admit that?

Yes.

Then you must also acknowledge that doing what's just is not in the interest
of the stronger when the rulers unintentionally command things to be done
which injure them. Given, as you say, justice is the obedience the subject
renders to the rulers' commands, in that case, most wise Thrasymachus, how
can we avoid the conclusion that the weaker are commanded to do, not what is
in the interest of the stronger, but what injures them.

Nothing could be clearer, Socrates, said Polemarchus.

Yes, said Cleitophon, interrupting, given Polemarchus is allowed to be a
witness.

But there is no need for witnesses, said Polemarchus; for Thrasymachus
himself grants that rulers may sometimes command what is not in their own
interest and that it is just for subjects to obey them.

Yes, Polemarchus, Thrasymachus did say that for subjects to do what their rulers commanded was just.

Yes, Cleitophon, but he also said that what is just is in the interest of the stronger, and, while admitting both these, he further granted that the stronger may command the weaker, who are his subjects, to do what is not in his own interest. From that it follows that what injures the ruler is just as just as what is in the ruler's interest.

FOR DISCUSSION:

Do we have any standards by which to judge laws themselves to be unjust? Are any of these standards ones that people in different societies would agree on for the most part?

The obvious move for Thrasymachus to make at this point is to say that justice is what the rulers *think* is in their interest, even if in fact it is not. But Plato has him take a different line, where he distinguishes a ruler in the ordinary sense of the term from a ruler insofar as he is a ruler, and he then claims that the latter cannot make a mistake, just as a physician, insofar as he is a physician, cannot prescribe the wrong treatment. The analogy with an expert in an art like medicine will prove crucial to the rest of the argument, and Socrates is careful to get Thrasymachus to grant that it is the interest of the ruler in the second sense that is involved in his definition. In other words it is the interest of the ruler *qua* ruler that we are talking about.

But, said Cleitophon, he meant by the interest of the stronger what the stronger thought to be in his interest. This is what the weaker was supposed to do, and that is what he affirmed to be just.

That's not what he said, replied Polemarchus.

Never mind, I replied, if he now says that this is what he meant, let's accept that. Tell me, Thrasymachus, I said, did you mean by justice what the stronger thought to be in his interest, whether it really was or not?

Certainly not, he said. Do you suppose that I would call a person who is mistaken the stronger at the very time when he is mistaken?

Yes, I said, my impression was that you said that when you admitted that the ruler was not always correct but could sometimes be mistaken.

You argue like a quibbling lawyer, Socrates. Do you mean, for example, that someone who makes a mistake about a sick person is a physician in respect of what he is mistaken about, or that someone who makes a mistake in arithmetic or grammar is an arithmetician or a grammarian at the very time he is making the mistake and in respect of the mistake? True, we say that the physician or arithmetician or grammarian has made a mistake, but this is just a way of speaking. The fact is that neither the grammarian nor any other person with an expert skill ever makes a mistake insofar as he is what the name of that skill implies, though none of them make a mistake unless their skill fails them, and then they cease to be expert in that skill. No artisan or wise person or ruler makes a mistake at the time when he is what that name implies; though he is commonly said to make a mistake, and I adopted the ordinary way of speaking. But to be perfectly precise, since you love precision so much, we should say that the ruler, insofar as he is a ruler, never makes a mistake, and consequently he always commands what is in his own interest, and the subject is required to execute his commands. Therefore, just as I said at the start and I now repeat, justice is what is in the interest of the stronger.

Really, Thrasymachus, do I seem to you to argue like a quibbling lawyer?

You certainly do, he replied.

Do you think I ask these questions with the purpose of injuring you through the argument?

'Think' is not the word; I *know* it. But your tactics won't work; nor will you win by the sheer force of your argument.

My dear man, I'd never attempt such a thing. But to avoid any misunderstanding occurring in the future, let me ask in what sense do you speak of a ruler or stronger person. Do you mean that the ruler in the ordinary sense, or the ruler in the strict sense you just mentioned, is the person in whose interest, as being superior, it is just for the inferior person to do things?

The ruler in the strictest of all senses, he said. So now bring on your tricks and play the quibbling lawyer, if you can. I ask for no quarter from you. You'll not be able to snare me.

Do you imagine, I said, that I am mad enough to try and trick Thrasymachus?! I might as well try to shave a lion's mane.

But, he said, you just tried to a minute ago, and you failed.

FOR DISCUSSION:

If Thrasymachus had taken up Cleitophon's suggestion and said justice is what the ruler *thinks* is in this interest, how might Socrates have attacked that?

In confining the interest in question to those of the ruler insofar as he is a ruler, what sort of interests of the person who is ruling do Socrates and Thrasymachus rule out?

Socrates proceeds to equate what is in the interest of any expert in an art, *qua* expert in that art, with what is the good the art aims at, and in the case of arts dealing with people and animals this seems to be what is in the interest of those people and animals insofar as they are subject to that art. Then, if the ruler is an expert in an art—and Thrasymachus has suggested already that he is—that art aims at the interest of those it rules over and hence so does the ruler insofar as he is a ruler. His own interests are irrelevant. Thus the laws he frames will not necessarily be in his own interest but rather in the interests of the weaker people, the subjects. So once again justice as obeying the laws distinguishes itself from acting in the interest of the rulers.

Enough of this exchange of compliments, I said. Let me ask you this: Is the physician, taken in that strict sense you mentioned, a healer of the sick or a maker of money? And remember I am now speaking of the true physician.

A healer of the sick.

And the ship's captain, the true one, that is, is he a commander of sailors or a mere sailor?

A commander.

That he sails in the ship is irrelevant; neither is he to be called a sailor. The name 'captain' that distinguishes him has nothing to do with sailing, but rather signifies his skill and his authority over the sailors.

Very true.

Each of these arts, then, has an interest it attends to?

Certainly.

And the art has to consider that interest and provide for it?

Yes, that is the aim of an art.

And the interest of any art is its perfection, this and nothing else?

What do you mean?

Let me illustrate by the example of the body. Suppose you asked me whether the body is self-sufficient or has need of something else. I would reply: Certainly the body has needs, for it may be sick and need to be cured; therefore, it has interests to which the art of medicine caters, and this is the origin and purpose of medicine. Don't you think that's right?

Quite right.

But now is the art of medicine, or any other art, faulty or deficient in some quality in the way that the eye may be deficient in sight or the ear in its ability to hear so that it requires an art to provide for its interests in seeing or hearing?

Has art itself, I say, an analogous liability to fault or defect, so that every art requires another additional art to provide for its interests, and then that art still another and so on without end? Or is each art such that it has no faults or defects, hence no need to correct them either through itself or through some other art? It has only to consider the interest of what it is dealing with, and as long as it is true to that it will stay perfect and unimpaired. Taking the words in your precise sense, tell me whether I am not right.

Yes, clearly.

So medicine does not consider the interest of medicine, but the interest of the body?

True.

Nor does the art of horse training consider the interests of the art of horse training, but rather the interests of the horse. Nor do any other arts care for themselves, for they have no needs; they care just for what they are dealing with?

True.

But, Thrasymachus, surely the arts are superior to and rulers of the things they deal with?

To this he assented with a good deal of reluctance.

So, I said, no expert knowledge or art attends to the interests of the stronger but only to the interests of the weaker that it deals with?

After trying to contest this he eventually acquiesced.

Then, I continued, no physician, insofar as he is a physician, considers his own good, but just the good of his patient. For the true physician is also a ruler with the human body as his subject, and is not just a money-maker. You admitted that?

Yes.

And the captain, too, in the strict sense of the term, is a ruler over sailors and not a mere sailor?

That we admitted.

And such a captain and ruler will provide and prescribe for the interests of the sailors who are under him, and not for his own, i.e. the ruler's, interest?

He gave a reluctant 'Yes'.

Then, I said, Thrasymachus, one who governs, insofar as he is a ruler, does not consider and command what is for his own interests, but rather always what is in the interest of his subjects and is demanded by his art. This is what he aims at, and this alone is what he considers in everything that he says and does.

FOR DISCUSSION:

Could Thrasymachus evade Socrates' line of argument by denying that ruling is an art? What other difficulties might attend that defence?

In exasperation over Socrates' reasoning Thrasymachus reveals the full dimensions of his cynical view. Injustice when carried out on a grand scale always secures more benefits for its practitioners than does justice for those who act justly. The just person will always end up being taken advantage of by the unjust, and people praise justice only because they are seeking some defence against people with no scruples, not because they have some positive liking for just behaviour in itself.

At this point in the argument everyone saw that the definition of justice had been completely overturned. Instead of replying to me, Thrasymachus said: Tell me, Socrates, do you have a nurse?

Why do you ask such a question, I said, when you should be answering questions?

Because she leaves you snivelling and never wipes your nose. She has not even taught you how to distinguish the shepherd from the sheep.

What makes you say that?

Because you imagine that the shepherd or cowherd fattens and tends the sheep or oxen with a view to their own good and not to the good of himself or his master. And you further imagine that the rulers of states, if they are true rulers, never think of their subjects as sheep and are not studying their own advantage day and night. Oh, no; and you are so totally off in your ideas about the just and the unjust as not even to know that justice and the just are in reality someone else's good, that is to say, the interest of the ruler and stronger party, and detrimental to the subject. Injustice is just the opposite, for the unjust lords it over truly simple and just people; he is the stronger, and his subjects do what is in his interest, and attend to his happiness, which is far from being their own.

Notice too, my naïve Socrates, that the just person always loses out in comparison with the unjust. First of all, in private contracts: Wherever the unjust partners with the just and then the partnership is dissolved, the unjust man, you will find, always ends up with more and the just person with less. Secondly, in dealings with the state: when taxes come due, the just person will pay more and the unjust less on the same amount of property; and when it comes to getting something back, the one gains nothing and the other much. Notice too what happens when they fill an office; there is the just man neglecting his own affairs and maybe suffering other losses, while getting nothing out of the public, because he is just; moreover he ends up hated by his friends and associates for refusing to unlawfully help them out. But this is all reversed in the case of the unjust man.

I am speaking, as before, about injustice of a grand sort where the advantage of the unjust person is more evident; and my meaning will be most clear if we turn to that highest form of injustice where the criminal is the happiest of men, and his victims or those who refuse to do injustice are the most wretched, i.e. tyranny, which by fraud and force confiscates the property of others, not just little by little but wholesale. He makes no distinctions between the sacred and the profane, private and public. If he were found perpetrating any of these wrongs singly, he would be punished and disgraced; the people who do such wrong in individual cases are called robbers of temples, kidnappers, burglars, swindlers and thieves. But once a man besides taking away the money of the citizens has also made slaves of them, then, instead of being called by those pejorative terms, he gets called happy and blessed, and not just by the citizens but by everyone who hears of the way in which he has achieved the ultimate in injustice. People generally censure injustice because they fear becoming its victim, not because they shrink from committing it. Thus, Socrates, as I have shown, injustice, when it is sufficiently grand, has more strength and freedom and mastery than justice. So, just as I said at first, justice is what is in the interest of the stronger, while injustice is what is to a person's own benefit and interest.

FOR DISCUSSION:

How does Thrasymachus' position here compare with that of Callicles in the *Gorgias* (see preceding selection)?

Is speculating about what a genuinely good government would be like a waste of time, since in reality all politics is just a struggle for power in order to use the community for one's own personal interests?

B.5.b: *REPUBLIC* II

368c-376c[1]

The following passage begins just after Glaucon and Adeimantus have each implored Socrates to give a defence of the just life which does not rely on the supposed external rewards which might attend it, neither on the honours bestowed by fellow citizens nor on the favours of the gods. After warning that the inquiry is going to be difficult, Socrates proposes that instead of proceeding directly to justice in the individual person they look at what it is in a community (i.e., city or state), and then see if there isn't something analogous in the individual. This approach allows Plato, through the character of Socrates, to discuss how a state is properly constructed and so to build up a picture of the ideal city and how it is governed.

First Socrates puts forward a theory of the origins of community. Why do people group together in the first place? In his view it is to facilitate the provision of the necessities of life, for these needs can be met far more efficiently if people are allowed to specialize in different occupations and then exchange the resulting goods and services. From this beginning Socrates plausibly suggests how trades proliferate, foreign trade begins, and the classes of merchants, retailers, and hired labourers are established in addition to the farmers and artisans that we began with.

[*Socrates:*] Glaucon and the rest entreated me by all means not to let the question drop, but to proceed in the investigation. They wanted to arrive at the truth, first, about the nature of justice and injustice, and secondly, about their

---

1 Translated by Jowett, with modifications.

149

relative advantages. I told them, what I really thought, that the inquiry would be into something very obscure and would require very keen sight. Seeing then, I said, that we are not all that clever, I think we had better adopt a method which I may illustrate as follows: suppose that a short-sighted person had been asked by someone to read small letters from a distance, and it occurred to someone else that they might be found in another, larger place where the letters were writ larger. If they were the same and he could read the larger letters first, and then proceed to the smaller, wouldn't he think that he had been lucky indeed?

Very true, said Adeimantus; but how does the illustration apply to our inquiry?

I will tell you, I replied; justice, which is what we are inquiring about, is, as you know, sometimes treated as something belonging to an individual person and sometimes as belonging to a whole city.

True, he replied.

And is not the city larger than an individual?

It is.

Then in the larger thing there is likely to be more of justice and it is likely to be more easily discerned. I propose, then, that we inquire into the nature of justice and injustice first as they appear in the city, and secondly in the individual, proceeding from the larger to the smaller and comparing them.

That sounds like an excellent proposal.

And if we imagine the state[1] in process of coming into existence, we shall see the justice and injustice of the state also in process of coming into being.

I dare say.

Once that is done, what we are looking for will be more easily found.

Yes, far more easily.

Shall we try to do this? I said; for to do so, it would seem to me, will be no light undertaking. Think about that, then.

I have thought about it, said Adeimantus, and am eager to see you get on with it.

A state, I said, arises, as I think of it, out of the needs of mankind; no one is self-sufficing, but all of us have many needs. Can any other origin of the state be imagined?

There can be no other.

So, as we have many needs, and many persons are needed to supply them,

---

1   'State' and 'city' translate the same Greek word, 'polis'.

one calls in one helper for one purpose and another for another; and when these partners and helpers are gathered together in one habitation the group of inhabitants is termed a state.

True, he said.

And they exchange with one another; one gives and another receives, each being under the idea that this will be for his own good.

Very true.

Then, I said, let's start and create a state in our minds, although the real creator is our own needs.

Of course, he replied.

Now the first and greatest of necessities is food, which is the condition of life and existence.

Certainly.

The second is a dwelling, and the third clothing and the like.

True.

And now let us see how our city will be able to supply this great demand: We may suppose that one person will be a farmer, another a builder, and someone else a weaver. Shall we add to them a shoemaker, or perhaps some others to cater to our personal needs?

By all means.

The minimal sort of state, then, must include four or five people.

Clearly.

And how will they proceed? Will each contribute the result of his work to a common stock—the individual farmer, for example, producing for four and working four times as long and as much as he would need to for himself to provide food, or will he have nothing to do with the others and not go to the trouble to produce for them, but rather provide for himself alone a fourth of the food in a fourth of the time, and in the remaining three fourths of his time be employed in making a house or a coat or a pair of shoes, not partnering with the others but just supplying by himself all his own wants?

Adeimantus thought that he should aim at producing food only and not at producing everything.

Probably, I replied, that would work better; and when I hear you say this, it occurs to me that we are not all alike; we come with different innate capacities which suit us for different occupations.

Very true.

And is the work done better when the workman has many occupations, or when he has only one?

When he has just one.

Further, there can be no doubt that a job is spoiled when it is not done at the right time?

No doubt.

For a job does not wait until the doer of it is at leisure; rather the doer must get on with his job and make it his first priority.

He must.

Given that, we must infer that all things are produced more plentifully and easily and of better quality when one person does one single thing which they are naturally suited for, does it at the right time, and does not attend to other jobs.

Undoubtedly.

Then more than four citizens will be required; for the farmer will not make his own plough or hoe, or other agricultural implements, if they are to be good for anything. Neither will the builder make his tools, and he too needs lots of them. Likewise for the weaver and the shoemaker.

True.

So carpenters, smiths, and many other artisans will be part of our little state, which is already beginning to grow?

True.

Yet even if we add cowherds, shepherds, and other herdsmen, so that our farmers can have oxen for ploughing, and builders as well as farmers can have draught-animals, and shoemakers and weavers can have fleeces and hides, still our state will not be very large.

True, but neither will it be a very small state if it contains all these.

Then, again, there is the city's location; finding a place where nothing needs to be imported is well-nigh impossible.

Impossible.

This means there must be another class of citizens who import goods from other cities?

There must.

But if these traders go abroad having nothing that those other cities require, they will return empty-handed.

For sure.

And therefore what is produced at home must not just be enough for home consumption but also enough to trade to those others from whom supplies are required.

Very true.

So more farmers and more artisans will be required?

Yes.

Not to mention those in the business of importing and exporting, who are called merchants?

Yes.

So we are going to need merchants?

We shall.

And if merchandise is to be carried over the seas, skilful sailors will also be needed, and quite a few of them?

Yes, quite a few.

Then, again, inside the city how are producers to exchange their products? Our principal aim, you will recall, in forming a community and establishing a state was to facilitate such an exchange.

Clearly they will buy and sell.

Then they will need a market-place and some currency as a medium for exchange.

Certainly.

Suppose now that a farmer or an artisan brings their product to market, and they come at a time when there is no one to trade with, is he to forget his work and sit idle in the market-place?

Not at all. They will find people there who seeing the need undertake to sell things. In properly run states they are usually those who are physically the weakest and so of little use for any other purpose. Their job is to be in the market, give money in exchange for goods from those who want to sell and take money from those who want to buy.

This need, then, creates a class of retail traders in our state. Is not 'retailer' the term applied to those who sit in the market-place engaged in buying and selling, while those who travel from one city to another are called 'merchants'?

Yes, he said.

And there is another class, whose minds are such that they are hardly worth including in our society, but still they have lots of physical strength for hard work, and so they sell themselves out and are called, if I am not mistaken, hired labourers, because they sell the use of their strength for wages.

True.

Then hired labourers will help make up our population?

Yes.

So now, Adeimantus, has our state reached its full growth; is it complete?

Where, then, is justice, and where injustice, and in what part of the state did they spring up?

Probably in the dealings of these citizens with one another. I can't imagine
that they would be found anywhere else.

You might well be right in that suggestion, I said. We had better think this
whole matter through and not hold back from the inquiry.

FOR DISCUSSION:

Is the need to provide the necessities of life the only thing which impels
people to live together? What other motivations might there be?

Do you think the state as so far described would require much in the way of
government? What would the government have to do?

The life of the citizens of the community so far described will be, according to Socrates, simple but happy. However, he characterizes it in such a
way that it obviously lacks many of the conveniences and pleasures any
Athenian would expect to be provided, and, consequently, Glaucon thinks
it is fit only for pigs. Socrates acknowledges that many people will not be
satisfied with this way of life and want all sorts of luxuries in diet, accou-
trements, and sophisticated entertainments. Such a life style is doubtless
less healthy than the earlier one, and it also puts greater demands on the
economy so that the city needs more land. That in turn leads to war with
neighbouring and similarly oriented states. There is no reason to doubt that
Plato was serious in thinking that in the end more is lost than gained by the
transition to the luxurious state, but he has Socrates treat it as more or less
inevitable. As for justice and injustice, Socrates suggests that they might
show up even more clearly in this less than ideal order of society.

Let us then consider, first of all, what will be their way of life, now that we
established them in this sort of community. Won't they produce grain, and wine,
and clothes, and shoes, and build houses for themselves? And once housed, they
will work in summer for the most part without clothes or shoes, but in winter
they will make use of both. They will feed on barley-meal and wheat flour, baking
and kneading them, making beautiful cakes and loaves; these they will serve up
on mats of reeds or on clean leaves, while they themselves lie back on beds strewn
with yew or myrtle. And so they and their children will feast, drinking the wine
which they have made, wearing garlands on their heads, and singing songs of
praise to the gods, and happily talking away with each other. But they will be
careful not to have too many children, so that their families do not become too
large, and then run the risk of poverty or war.

But, said Glaucon interrupting, you have not given them any relish for their feast.

True, I replied, I forgot that. Of course, they must have a relish: salt, and olives, and cheese, and they will boil roots and herbs such as country folk prepare; for a dessert we shall give them figs, peas, and beans; and they will roast myrtle-berries and acorns over the fire, while they sip their wine. Living this way they can be expected to live in peace and health to a ripe old age, and bequeath a similar life to their children.

Yes, Socrates, he said, that is just the sort of fare you would provide for a city of pigs.

But what would you have, Glaucon? I replied.

Why, he said, you should give them the usual conveniences of life. Let them be comfortable and lie on couches, dine off tables, and have sauces and sweets such as those we have nowadays.

Oh, I said, now I get it. The question which you would have me consider is not just how a state but how a *luxurious* state comes into existence. Well, maybe there is no harm in this, for in that sort of state we might be more likely to see how justice and injustice come to be. In my opinion, it is the sort of state I just described that is the ideal and healthy one, but if you want to see a state suffering from inflammation, I have no objection. I suspect that many people will not be satisfied with the simpler way of life. They will want to add couches, tables and other furniture, and also delicacies, perfumes, incense, and courtesans, and cakes, not just one sort but many types. We will have to go beyond the necessities of which I spoke earlier, such as houses, clothes, and shoes; the arts of the painter and the embroiderer will have to be set going, and gold and ivory and various other materials procured.

True, he said.

So, we'll have to enlarge our city further, for the original, healthy state is no longer sufficient. Now the city will have to fill up and swell with all sorts of other occupations which are not required by any natural need: such as the whole gang of hunters, and the imitators, of whom one large class deal with shapes and colours, another with making music, poets and their associates the rhapsodists, actors, dancers, and impresarios, as well as the makers of different kinds of goods such as women's dresses. Also we shall need more servants. Won't tutors too be in demand, and nurses, both wet and dry, barbers and beauticians, as well as confectioners and cooks? And won't we need swineherds, too, who were not required for the earlier form of our state? We shouldn't forget them; and there will be many sorts of new animals, if people are going to live on meat.

Certainly.

This life style will mean we have much greater need of physicians than before?

Much greater.

Now the country, which was enough to support the original inhabitants, will be too small and not enough?

Quite true.

Then we will want a slice of our neighbour's land for ploughing and pasture, and they will want a slice of ours, if, like ourselves, they go beyond what is necessary and dedicate themselves to the unlimited accumulation of wealth?

That, Socrates, will be inevitable.

And so we shall go to war, Glaucon. Won't we?

Most certainly, he replied.

Then, leaving aside the question of whether war does good or harm, we can affirm this much: we have discovered war to be derived from causes which are also the causes of almost all the evils afflicting states, both private and well as public.

Undoubtedly.

FOR DISCUSSION:

Why do you think people want more than just the simple life of the earlier society Socrates describes?

Do you think the early, non-luxurious society could possibly put limits on its population so as to curtail its need for land?

War requires a specially trained class of soldiers, whom Socrates calls guardians. Like any other job for which there is an art, the practitioners of war must specialize in it and be well-trained. They also need to be suited for it by nature, but what sort of nature? Socrates suggests it is the spirited nature of the guard-dog. And then, in a somewhat far-fetched comparison, he says that the dog's ability to distinguish friend from stranger argues a philosophic disposition, and this too must be something innate in those suited to be guardians. Why philosophy is important here becomes a lot clearer later on in the dialogue.

So our state will have to be added to once more, and this time the addition will be nothing short of a whole army that will have to go out and fight off invaders defending the citizens and all the possessions they have as earlier described.

Why is that? he said. Are they not capable of defending themselves?

No, I said; not if we were right about that principle we all agreed to when we were framing our state: the principle, as you will recall, was that one single person cannot practise more than one art with success.

True enough, he said.

But is not war an art?

Certainly.

And an art requiring just as much attention as shoemaking?

Quite true.

And we did not allow the shoemaker to also be a farmer, or a weaver, or a builder, because we wanted our shoes to be well made. Rather, to this person and to every other worker we assigned just one job for which that person was innately suited, and he was to continue working at that job his whole life long and at no other; he was never to be off doing something else at the time when his job needed to be done, and then he would become a good workman. Now nothing can be more important than that the work of a soldier should be well done. But is war an art so easily acquired that a man may be a warrior who is also a farmer, or a shoemaker, or some other artisan, even though no one in the world would be a good player of dice or draughts who merely took up the game as a recreation and had not from their earliest years devoted themselves to this and nothing else? No tools will make a person a skilled workman or athlete, nor be of any use to one who has not learned how to handle them and has never bestowed any attention on them. How then will someone who takes up a shield or other weapon of war become a good fighter all in a day, whether we talk of the heavily armed troops or any other kind.

Yes, he said, tools that would teach people how to use them would be priceless.

Now these guardians, I said, given the importance of their duties, will need most of all to be free from other jobs so they can have the time to apply themselves and acquire the requisite skill and practice.

No doubt, he said.

Will they not also require a natural aptitude for their calling?

Then it will be our responsibility to select, if we can, natures which are fitted for the task of guarding the city?

It will.

This selection will be no easy matter, I said; but we must do the best we are capable of.

We must.

In respect of keeping guard, do you think there is any difference between the nature of a well-bred dog and a well-born young man?

What do you mean?

I mean that both of them ought to be quick to spy things, swift to overtake the enemy when they have spied them, and strong too, in case once they have caught the enemy they have to fight them.

They'll certainly need all those qualities, he replied.

And your guardians must be brave too, if they are to fight well?

Certainly.

And is that likely to be brave which has no spirit, whether a horse, dog, or other animal? Have you ever noticed how invincible and unconquerable is spirit and how the presence of it makes the soul of any creature absolutely fearless and indomitable?

I have.

So now we have a clear idea of the physical qualities which the guardian will require.

True.

And the mental ones, too; his soul is to be full of spirit?

Yes.

But aren't these spirited natures apt to be savage with one another, and everyone else?

A problem not easily overcome, he replied.

What, in fact, they ought to be is dangerous to their enemies and gentle to their friends; if not, they will destroy themselves without waiting for their enemies to destroy them.

True.

What is to be done, then? I said. How shall we find a gentle nature which has also a great spirit, for the one conflicts with the other?

True.

People will not be good guardians who lack either of these two qualities, and yet the combination of them appears to be impossible; hence we have to infer that it is impossible to be a good guardian.

I'm afraid what you say is right, he replied.

At this point I felt perplexed, and I began to review what we had said earlier. My friend, I said, no wonder we're so perplexed; we've lost sight of the comparison we had made.

What do you mean? he said.

I mean that in fact there do exist natures gifted with those opposing qualities.

Where?

Lots of animals are good examples; our friend the dog is a very good one. You know that well-bred dogs are perfectly gentle to those they know and are accustomed to, but the reverse to strangers.

Yes, I know.

Then there is nothing impossible or contrary to nature in our finding a guardian with a similar combination of qualities?

Evidently.

Wouldn't the person suited to be a guardian have to have, in addition to a spirited nature, the qualities of a philosopher?

I don't see what you mean.

The trait I mean, I replied, is also seen in dogs, and is really quite a remarkable one in them.

What trait?

Why, a dog, whenever it sees a stranger, gets fierce; when it sees someone it knows, it becomes friendly, even though the former has never done it any harm nor the latter any good. Did this never strike you as curious?

That never occurred to me before, but you're quite right about it.

And surely this trait in the dog is very admirable; indeed, it makes the dog a real philosopher.

Why?

Why, because it distinguishes the face of a friend from that of an enemy only by the criterion of knowing and not knowing. Must not an animal be a lover of learning if it determines what it likes and dislikes by the test of knowledge and ignorance?

Definitely.

And is not the love of learning the love of wisdom, which in turn is philosophy?

They are the same, he replied.

And can't we say confidently of people too, that they who are likely to be gentle to their friends and people they know must by nature love wisdom and knowledge.

We can safely affirm that.

So those who are to be really good and fine guardians of the state must unite in themselves philosophy, spirit, swiftness, and strength?

Undoubtedly.

FOR DISCUSSION:

Would a real lover of knowledge be hostile to unfamiliar things?

B.5.c: *REPUBLIC* III-IV

412b-421c[1]

Socrates has just finished saying how music, poetry and gymnastics are to be used in the upbringing of future guardians. Now he turns to the question of how from among the guardian class those that are rulers are to be selected. (It is noteworthy that Plato seems, at this point, at any rate, to assume that it is from the guardians, rather than from among those skilled in arts other than war, that the rulers are to come.) The chief criterion, in his mind, is the person's firmness of resolve to give first priority always to the welfare of the state as a whole. Obviously Socrates is very anxious to avoid among the rulers any form of corruption in which the commonweal is sacrificed to the interests of the rulers themselves, or of some narrow group to which the rulers belong. Once this selection is made, the term 'guardian' receives a narrower and fuller sense in which only the rulers are called guardians, while the rest of the military class are called 'auxiliaries' in virtue of their function of enforcing the commands of those who are guardians in the strict sense.

> [*Socrates*:] Very good, I said; then what is the next question. Must we not ask who are to be rulers and who subjects?
> [*Glaucon*:] Certainly.
> There can be no doubt that the elder must rule the younger.
> Clearly.
> And that the best of these must rule.
> That is also clear.

---

1 Translated by Jowett, with modifications.

Now, aren't the best farmers those who are most skilled at farming?

Yes.

So if we want the best guardians, we must have those who are most skilled in guarding the city?

Yes.

Then they must be, to begin with, wise and intelligent in civic affairs, and have a concern for the interests of the city?

True.

A person will be most likely to care about that which they love?

To be sure.

And they will be most likely to love what they regard as having the same interests as they do, and whose fortunes for better or worse will be the same as their own?

Very true, he replied.

It follows that we must select from all the guardians those who in their whole life show the greatest zeal to do what is for the good of their country, and the greatest aversion to doing what is against the country's interests.

Those would be the right ones.

They will have to be watched at every age, so that we can see whether they stay firm in their resolution and never, under any influences of force or beguilement, forget or cast off their sense of duty to the state.

How would they cast it off? he said.

Let me explain. A resolution may go out of a person's mind either with their will or against their will; with their will when they get rid of a falsehood and learn better, against their will whenever they are deprived of truth.

I understand, he said, how one can willingly lose a resolution, but I don't see yet how it happens against their will.

Why, do you not see that people are unwillingly deprived of good, but willingly of what's bad? Isn't it bad to lose the truth, while possessing the truth is good? And wouldn't you agree that to possess the truth is to think of things as they in fact are?

Yes, he replied, I agree with you in thinking that people are deprived of true belief against their will.

When that happens to them, then, it is by theft, force, or beguilement?

Still, I don't understand.

I'm afraid I must have been talking darkly, like the tragic poets. I only mean that some people are changed by persuasion and others forget; arguments steal away their beliefs in the one case, time in the other. This is what I call theft. Now do you understand?

Yes.

Those again who are forced are those whom the violence of some pain or grief compels to change their opinion.

I understand, he said, and you are quite right.

And you would also acknowledge that the beguiled are those who change their minds either under the softer influence of pleasure or the sterner influence of fear?

Yes, he said, everything that deceives may be said to beguile.

Therefore, as I was just now saying, we have to find out who are the best guardians of their own conviction that they must always serve what they take to be the best interest of the state. We must watch them from youth on, and make them engage in activities where they are most likely to forget or be deceived, and those who remember and are not deceived are to be selected, while those who fail the trial are to be rejected. Won't that be the way?

Yes.

And we should also put them through ordeals of toil and pain and conflict, where they will be made to give further proof of the same qualities.

Very right, he replied.

And then, I said, we must subject them to beguilement, that will be a third sort of test, and see how they behave. Like those who take colts out in noise and tumult to see if they are timid, so we must take our youth out into terrors of some kind, and then into situations of pleasures, and test them more thoroughly than gold is tested in the furnace, so that we can discover whether they are resistant against beguilement and always bear themselves well, true guardians of themselves and of the music which they have learned, retaining under all circumstances a rhythmical and harmonious nature, the sort that will be most of service both to the persons themselves and to the state. Those who at every age, as a child and youth and in mature life, have emerged from the trial victorious and pure shall be appointed a ruler and guardian of the state; they shall be honoured in life, and in death shall receive funeral rites and memorials of honour, the greatest we have to give. But those who fail, we must reject. I am inclined to think, Glaucon, that this is the way in which our rulers and guardians should be chosen and appointed. I am just giving an outline here and do not pretend to exactness.

My thinking is much the same as yours, he said.

So perhaps the word 'guardian', taken in the fullest sense, ought to be reserved for just this higher class who will defend us against foreign enemies from without and friends at home, so that the former will not have the power and the latter will not have the wish to do us harm. The young people whom we before called guardians can be more properly designated auxiliaries, and they will aid the rulers in enforcing their decisions.

I agree with you, he said.

FOR DISCUSSION:

What would make Plato suppose that the best rulers will be found among the class of soldiers? Do you think he is right about this?

Socrates now engages in a little myth-building. Plato thought myths could be of use for inculcating certain values and customs in the mass of people and is keen to compose his own, given his low opinion of most myths traditional in Greek culture. The one composed here is supposed to get the citizens to care for each other and accept the class division between guardians, auxiliaries, and the economic class of farmers and artisans. He does not, however, claim that children born of parents in one of these classes must themselves be in that class. Although generally parents pass on their own traits, there are always exceptions, and the rulers must be alert to spot these and put the child in the class that he or she is innately suited for. Note that one cannot just by one's own effort lift oneself out of a lower class into a higher; one is suited to a class by the character one is born with.

Now, some time ago we spoke of useful lies. Could we now contrive some single, high-minded lie[1] that the rulers themselves might be persuaded of, or at least the rest of the city?

What sort of lie? he said.

Nothing new, I replied; only an old Phoenician tale of what has often occurred before now in other places (as the poets say, and have made the world believe), though not in our time, and it would be hard to persuade anybody that it could ever happen again.

You seem hesitant to put this into words.

You will not wonder at my hesitation once you have heard it.

Out with it! Don't be afraid.

Well then, I will say it, although I hardly know how to look you in the face or what words to utter. I propose to persuade first the rulers, then the soldiers,

---

1   Often misleadingly translated as "noble lie". The point is that the person telling the lie has the best of purposes in doing so.

and finally the people. They are to be told that their youth was a dream, and the education and training which they received from us all just something that appeared in a dream. In reality during all that time they were being formed and fed in the womb of the earth, where they themselves and their arms and equipment were being fashioned. When they were finished, the earth, their mother, sent them up to the surface; their land being then their mother and also their nurse, they are bound to care for her and to defend her against all attacks, and her citizens they are to regard as children of the earth and their own siblings.

It's no wonder that you were hesitant to come out with that piece of fiction!

True, I replied, but there is still more; I have only told you half. Citizens, we shall say to them in our tale, you are brothers, yet the god has formed you in different ways: in those of you who are fit to rule he mixed in gold, hence they are most to be prized; others he has made of silver and they are to be auxiliaries; others again who are to be farmers and craftsmen he has composed of brass and iron. Although usually the offspring will preserve the quality of their parents, sometimes, as we all are of the same original stock, a golden parent will have a silver child, or a silver parent a golden child. Now the god proclaims as a chief duty of a ruler, that there is nothing which they should more anxiously watch, if they are to be good guardians, than the mixture of metals in the souls of the children; for if the child of a golden or silver parent has a mixture of brass and iron, then they must without any pity assign him a station appropriate to his nature and place him among the farmers and craftsmen. On the other hand, if there is among the offspring of artisans some who are composed of gold or silver, they are to be raised, in accord with their value to become guardians or auxiliaries. For there is an oracle which says that when a person of brass or iron guards the state, it will be destroyed. Such is the tale. Is there any chance of making our citizens believe it?

Not in the first generation, but maybe their children, or their children's children, and their posterity after that.

Well, said I, even that will have the good effect of making them care more for the city and for one another, but I see the problem. We'll leave it all to the care of popular lore.

FOR DISCUSSION:

Do you agree that fictions people are expected to believe in can play a positive role in promoting social cohesion? Can you think of any modern ones?

Socrates now turns to the life-style of the guardians and auxiliaries. He is very conscious of the possibility that this armed military class will oppress the rest of the citizens, and he expresses some doubt that the sort of education previously described will be sufficient to prevent this. (Plato foreshadows here the more elaborate education system that he will describe later.) Certainly it is also necessary to rid the members of this class of any desire for a luxurious private life, so Socrates institutes a thoroughgoing communism within their ranks. (It is important to note that he does *not* recommend this for the whole society inclusive of the economic classes, which will compose the majority of the citizens.) There is no private property and even the communal property is simple and austere, so that no love of personal possessions is likely to arise among these guardians.

Now let's arm our earth-born heroes[1] and lead them forth under the command of their rulers. Let them look around for a site for their encampment, a place where they can best suppress insurrection from within, and also defend themselves against enemies, who like wolves may come down on the fold from without. After they have encamped, let them sacrifice to the appropriate gods and prepare their dwellings. Or should it be otherwise?

Just so, he said.

And their dwellings must be such as will shield them against the cold of winter and the heat of summer.

I suppose you mean houses, he replied.

Yes, I said; but they must be the houses of soldiers, and not of shopkeepers.

What is the difference? he asked.

I'll try to explain it, I replied. To keep watchdogs who, from want of discipline or from hunger, or from some bad habit or other, would turn on the sheep and worry them, behaving not like dogs but like wolves, would be a terrible and dreadful thing in a shepherd, would it not?

Truly dreadful.

Consequently every care must be taken to ensure that our auxiliaries, being stronger than our ordinary citizens, may come to overpower them and become savage tyrants instead of friends and allies?

Yes, we must be careful about that.

And would not a really good education furnish the best safeguard against this?

But they are well educated already, he replied.

---

1   It becomes clear that Socrates has in mind here only the guardians and their auxiliaries.

Let's not be so sure about that, Glaucon, I said. What I am certain of is that they ought to receive the right education, whatever that may be, if they are to have the best chance of being gentle and humane to one another and to those under their protection.

Very true, he replied.

And not only their education, but their dwellings, and all their belongings, should be such that will neither make them less excellent as guardians nor tempt them to prey on the other citizens. Any man of sense must acknowledge that.

He must.

Then let us consider what will be their way of life if they are to have the character we envision for them. In the first place, none of them should have any property of their own beyond the bare necessities; neither should they have a private house or storehouse shut against anyone who has a mind to enter; their provisions should be only such as are required by trained soldiers, who are moderate and brave; they should agree to receive from the citizens a fixed rate of pay, enough to meet the expenses of the year and no more; and they will dine and live together like soldiers in a camp. Gold and silver of the divine sort, we will tell them, they already have from the god within them, and so they have no need of the ordinary metals which are current among people, nor should they pollute the divine by any such earthly mixture; for that ordinary metal has been the source of many unholy deeds, but their own is undefiled. They alone of all the citizens may not touch or handle silver or gold, or be under the same roof with them, or wear them, or drink from them. Living this way they will save themselves and be the saviours of the state.

If they ever acquire homes or lands or money of their own, they will become housekeepers and farmers instead of guardians, enemies and tyrants instead of allies of the other citizens; hating and being hated, plotting and being plotted against, they will pass their whole life in much greater terror of internal than of external enemies, and the hour of ruin, both to themselves and to the rest of the state will be at hand. For all these reasons should we not say that our state shall be ordered in this way, and that these shall be the regulations laid down by us for our guardians regarding their houses and all other matters?

Yes, said Glaucon.

FOR DISCUSSION:

Is there something wrong or perilous about allowing wealthy people to hold public office? Is it possible to allow this and somehow securely protect society against conflicts of interest on the part of its rulers?

Adeimantus now objects that it appears that the guardians and auxiliaries will not be leading very happy lives, even compared to the other classes, since they are allowed no wealth or luxuries, living as they do in the austere communism Socrates has assigned them. This gives Socrates an occasion to rail against the idea that the happiness of the whole city is achieved by maximizing the indolent pleasures of each class; rather, he says, each class should have its own sort of happiness, one which does not interfere with their performing the functions that define them. This applies to the guardians as well, the implication being that a luxurious life-style for them would be incompatible with their job of guarding the laws and the state.

Here Adeimantus interposed a question: How would you answer, Socrates, he said, if someone were to say that you are making these people miserable, and, further, making them the cause of their own unhappiness? The city in fact belongs to them, but they are none the better off for that. Other people acquire property, build large and beautiful houses, provide them with suitable furniture, make private sacrifices to the gods, and entertain guests. Moreover, as you were saying just now, they possess gold and silver and all the things usually thought necessary for a happy life. Your guardians, on the other hand, seem like a bunch of hired mercenaries with nothing better to do than stand around and keep guard all day.

Yes, I said; and you can add that they are only fed and not paid in addition to their food, like other people. Therefore they cannot take pleasure trips; they have no money to spend on girl friends or any other luxuries they dream up, which is what is commonly thought to make people happy. These and many other accusations you are omitting.

Well, take them all to be included in the charge.

So, I said, you are asking for our answer to this?

Yes.

If we keep to our old, familiar path, I said, I think we shall find the answer. We shall say that, though it would not be surprising if, even as they are, our guardians were the happiest of people, still that was not our aim in founding the state, i.e. it was not to make one class happier than all the rest, but to provide the greatest happiness for the whole state. We thought that in a state ordered toward the good of the whole we would be most likely to find justice, and in the ill-ordered state, injustice. Once we had found them, then we could decide the question which has been before us for so long. Right now, I take it, we are constructing the happy state, not bit-by-bit but as a whole, not with a view to the happiness of a few citizens but to that of the whole. Later we will proceed to the opposite sort of state.

Suppose we were painting a statue, and someone came up to us and said, "Why do you not put the most beautiful colours on the finest parts of the body—the eyes ought to be purple, but you have made them black." To him it would be fair to reply: "Sir, surely you wouldn't have us make the eyes so beautiful that they don't look like eyes; rather we should give this and other parts what is appropriate to them so that the whole is beautiful." And so I say to you, do not compel us to assign to the guardians a sort of happiness which will make them anything but guardians; for we could also dress our farmers in royal apparel, set crowns of gold on their heads, and invite them to till the ground just as much as they like and no more. Our potters too might be allowed to lie back on couches and feast by the fireside while passing around the wine; their potter's wheel would be close by, but they could work at it only as much as they wanted to. This way we could make every class happy, and then the entire city would be happy.

Do not put this idea into our heads; for, if we listen to you, the farmer will no longer be a farmer, the potter will cease to be a potter, and none of the classes will retain its distinctive character. In many cases this is of little consequence; if a cobbler gets spoiled and pretends to be what he is not, there is no danger to the state. But when the guardians of the laws and of the government only appear to be guardians and are not really, then see how they turn the state upside-down; and, on the other hand, they alone have the power to give order and happiness to the state. We intend our guardians to be true preservers and not the destroyers of the state; whereas our opponent is thinking of peasants at a festival enjoying a life of revelry, not of citizens in a real city, and so he is speaking of something other than what we call a state.

Consequently we have to consider whether in appointing our guardians we should look to their own greatest happiness, or whether to the happiness that resides in the state as a whole. If the latter, then the guardians and the auxiliaries, and all the others equally as well, must be compelled or induced to do their own work in the best way. In this way the state as a whole will come to be well-ordered, and then each of the different classes will receive the happiness which is appropriate to their natures.

I think you are right about that.

FOR DISCUSSION:

What does it mean to have a "happy" state? Is it anything more than the sum of the happinesses of the individuals that make it up?

Do you think that Plato really thinks that partying and leading a life of indolence is what happiness consists in for most people?

B.5.d: *REPUBLIC* IV

427c-434d[1]

Socrates now proceeds with his program of trying to find justice in the most well-governed state so that then we can go on to something analogous in individuals. In the text below he actually expands his aims to see what in such a state constitutes each of the four main virtues: wisdom, courage, moderation, and justice. It is assumed from the start that there is some sense in speaking about a state or city as being wise, brave, and moderate, and that these terms do not really apply only to individual men and women.

Socrates is talking to Adeimantus.

[*Socrates*:] But where amid all this is justice, son of Ariston, tell me where. Now that we have established our city, light a candle and search, and get your brother [i.e. Glaucon] and Polemarchus and the rest of our friends to help, and let us see where in it we can discover justice and where injustice, and how they differ from each other, and which of them will make a person happy whether or not he is seen as just, or unjust, by gods and humans.

Nonsense, said Glaucon; didn't you promise to search yourself, saying that it would be impious of you not to help justice out in her hour of need?

I do not deny that I said that, so, since you remind me of it, I'll follow through, but you must lend a hand.

We will, he replied.

Well, then, I hope to make the discovery this way: I intend to begin with the assumption that our state, if rightly ordered, is completely good.

---

1 Translated by Jowett, with modifications.

That is certainly the case.

And being completely good, is therefore wise, brave, moderate and just.

That too is clear.

Then, if we find some of these qualities in the state, we can assume that the ones not found are nonetheless present?

Very good.

Now, if there were four things, and we were searching for one of them, wherever it might be, we might get to know that one right away, and then there would be no need to go on; or we might get to know the other three first, and then that would be enough to indicate the one we're after for it would be whatever is left.

Very true, he said.

Now, shouldn't we use a similar method as regards the virtues, which are four in number?

Clearly.

First among these virtues found in the state is wisdom, and here I note a certain peculiarity.

What is that?

The state we have been describing is said to be wise because it is good in its policies?

Very true.

And good policy is clearly a kind of knowledge, for it is not by ignorance but by knowledge that men come to have good policies?

Clearly.

Now there are in the state many sorts of knowledge?

Of course.

There is the knowledge the carpenter has; but is that the sort of knowledge which gives a city a claim to being wise and good in its policies?

Certainly not; that would only give a city the reputation of skill in carpentering.

Then a city is not to be called wise because it possesses a knowledge which gives it the best policies about how to make furniture?

Certainly not.

Nor by reason of a knowledge which makes for policies about brass pots, I said, and likewise for any similar sort of knowledge?

Not by reason of any of them, he said.

Nor yet by reason of a knowledge of how to cultivate the ground; that would just give the city a name for being good at farming?

Yes.

Well, I said, is there any knowledge in our newly founded state among any of the citizens who set policy which concerns not any particular aspect of the state but concerns the whole, and considers how a state can best deal with itself and with other states?

There certainly is.

What is it and where is it to be found? I asked.

It's the knowledge the guardians have, he replied, and resides among those we just now described as guardians in the fullest sense.

And what do we call a city in virtue of having this sort of knowledge?

We call it well-advised and truly wise.

And in our city will there be more of these true guardians or more smiths?[1]

Far more smiths, he said.

Won't the guardians be the smallest of all those classes who take their name from some sort of knowledge?

Much the smallest.

And so it is by reason of the knowledge which resides in the smallest part of the state, the part that takes the lead and rules the state which is established along natural lines, and this state will be called wise; this class, which has the only knowledge worth being called wisdom, has been ordained by nature to be the smallest of all the classes.

Most true.

Here, then, we have somehow or other discovered the nature and seat in the state of one of the four virtues.

And very satisfactorily discovered, in my opinion, he replied.

Again, I said, there is no problem seeing the nature of courage, and in what part that quality resides which gives the name of 'brave' to the state.

How do you mean?

Why, I said, anyone who calls any state brave, or cowardly, will be thinking of the part which fights and goes out to war on the state's behalf.

No one, he replied, would ever think of any other.

The rest of the citizenry may be brave, or may be cowardly, but their courage or cowardice will not, as I see it, tend to make the city either the one or the other.

Certainly not.

The city will be brave in virtue of a portion of itself which preserves under all

---

1   Metal workers.

circumstances that conviction about what is to be feared and what not feared which was inculcated in it by the city's founder; and that character is what you call courage.

Could you please repeat that, for I don't think I entirely understand you.

I mean that courage is a kind of preservative.

Preservative of what?

Of the conviction about what is to be feared, what those things are, which is implanted by the law through education. By the words 'under all circumstances' I mean to indicate that the person in situations of pleasure or pain, or under the influence of desire or fear, does not lose that conviction. Do you want an illustration?

If you please.

You know, I said, that dyers, when they want to dye wool with the colour of true sea-purple, begin by selecting white wool; this they prepare and dress very carefully so that the white ground will absorb the purple dye to the fullest extent. Only then does the dying get underway; and whatever is dyed in this manner holds its colour fast, and no washing either with lye or without it can take away the lustre. But, when the ground has not been properly prepared, you will have noticed how poor the purple, or any other colour, looks.

Yes, he said; it will be faded and look ridiculous.

So now, I said, you will understand what our object was in selecting our soldiers and educating them in music and gymnastic; we were contriving influences which would prepare them to take the colour of our institutions to perfection. Their education and training was to indelibly fix their opinion about what was dangerous, so that it would not be washed away by such potent detergents as pleasure, a far more powerful detergent than any soap or lye; or by sorrow, fear, and desire, the most powerful of all the other detergents. It is this sort of general power of preserving true convictions about what are real and what are pseudo-dangers that I call and maintain to be courage, unless you disagree.

I do agree, he replied; for I suppose you mean to exclude the sort of conviction which arises without education, such as that of a wild beast or a slave; this, in your opinion, is not the courage which comes from our institutions and ought to have another name.

Most certainly.

Then I accept your account of courage.

Good. And if we add to 'courage' the words 'of ordinary citizens' you will not be far wrong.[1] Later, if you like, we will carry the inquiry further, but right now we are looking for justice, not courage, and for these purposes we have said enough.

You are right, he replied.

FOR DISCUSSION:

We do often speak of a wise people, or a brave people, but is this the same as what Socrates means by a wise state, and a brave state?

Why isn't courage just a willingness to take risks?

The virtue of moderation means bringing under restraint just those pleasures and desires which earlier were thought to be such powerful "detergents" and to threaten the stability of the convictions that the brave person must have. But since such desires are far more prevalent in the lower classes of the city Socrates has constructed, the restraint must come from the less numerous but better born and educated class that rules the city. Moderation in this city, then, is the consensus that this latter class should be allowed to rule the others. Note that this is not just violent suppression of the enjoyments of the lower classes by the sophisticated elite, but involves the voluntary acquiescence of the former to the rule of the guardians. If this were not the case, Socrates could hardly call moderation a sort of concord or harmony.

There remain two virtues to be discovered in the state: first moderation, and then justice, the ultimate goal of our search.

Very true.

Now can we locate justice right off without bothering ourselves with moderation?

I don't know how we'd do that, he said, nor do I want justice brought to light without also getting a view of moderation. Consequently I would like you to consider moderation first.

Certainly, I replied, I have no good reason to refuse your request.

Go ahead, then.

I will. So far as I can see right now, moderation seems to have more the nature of concord or harmony than did the earlier ones.

---

1 This is one of a number of places where Plato hints that a superior form of virtue will be described later, viz. the virtue that comes with the sort of knowledge that the guardians will have once they complete their long educational program.

How so? he asked.

Moderation, I replied, is the ordering or restraining of certain pleasures and cravings. This is implied by the common talk of a person being "master of himself", an odd expression, and other ways of speaking point in the same direction.

No doubt, he said.

There is something ridiculous about this expression 'master of himself', for the master is also the servant, and the servant the master, since it is the same person that is being talked about.

Certainly.

What it really means, I think, is that in the human soul there is a better and also a worse principle; and when the better has the worse under control, then a person is said to be master of himself, which is a term of praise. But when, owing to bad education of associations, the better principle, which is also the smaller, is overwhelmed by the greater force of the worse, then the person is castigated and called a slave to himself and self-indulgent.

Yes, that makes sense.

And now, I said, look at our newly created state, and there you will find one of these two conditions realized: the state, you will grant, can rightly be called master of itself, given that the words 'moderation' and 'self-mastery' truly mean the rule of the better part over the worse.

Yes, he said, I see what you say is right.

The mob of diverse and complex pleasures, pains, and cravings is prevalent chiefly in children, women and slaves, and in the so-called freemen of the lowest and more numerous class.

Certainly.

On the other hand, the simple and moderate desires, which with the aid of reason are guided by thought and true opinion, are found only in a few, those who are best born and best educated.

Very true.

These two classes, as you can well see, can be found in our state; and the inferior desires of the many are held down by the superior ones and the wisdom of the few.

I can see that, he said.

So, if any city at all can be described as master of its own pleasures and desires, i.e. master of itself, ours can?

Certainly.

It can also be called moderate, for exactly the same reasons?

Yes.

So, if there be any state where rulers and subjects are agreed as to who gets to rule, that again will be our state?

No doubt about it.

Given then that the citizens are agreed on this among themselves, in which class will moderation be found—in the rulers or in the subjects?

In both, I would imagine.

Do you see that we were not far wrong in guessing that moderation was a sort of harmony?

Why so?

Why, because, unlike courage and wisdom, each of which resides in a single part only, the one making the state wise and the other brave, moderation extends to the whole and runs through all the notes on the scale, producing a harmony of the weaker and the stronger and those in between, whether you suppose them to be stronger or weaker in wisdom or power or numbers or wealth, or whatever you want. We are entirely correct, then, in taking moderation to be the agreement of those naturally superior with those inferior about the right as to who gets to rule, both in states and in individuals.

I am in complete agreement.

FOR DISCUSSION:

What would Plato say if we said that in fact educated people seem no more self-restrained so far as indulgence in ordinary pleasures are concerned than those who are less educated?

Should education aim at producing moderate individuals?

Socrates now closes in on the original object of his inquiry, the nature of justice in the state. The proposal he makes is that it is just the strict division of labour between the three main classes that makes a state just; injustice, on the other hand, arises when members of one class attempt to take on the jobs of the other classes, especially when artisans and tradesmen generally try to move up to the jobs of soldiers, or soldiers to the job of ruler. The arguments he gives are fairly persuasive if the conclusion is that this switching around of duties will be ruinous for the state that Socrates has described, and that this would be considered unjust. Conversely, preservation of the division of labour would tend to maintain the happy order of the state, and so would be considered just. But that does not prove that this perpetuation of the division of labour among the three classes is the *definition* of what justice is in a state, and Socrates admits at the end that this has not as yet been definitively proven.

And so, I said, we can take it that three out of the four virtues have been discovered in the state. Now the last of the qualities which are required for a virtuous state must be justice; we need to say what this is.

Clearly.

So, now, Glaucon, we need to be like hunters surrounding a thicket and keep a sharp lookout so that justice does not get away and escape from right under our eyes; for without doubt she is somewhere in this area. Keep watch, then, and try to catch sight of her, and if you see her first, let me know.

I wish I could! But you had better think of me as more a follower who has eyes only good enough to see what you show him; that is about all I am good for.

Well, offer up a prayer and follow then.

I will, but you have to show the way.

There isn't any path here, I said, and the woods is dark and impenetrable. Still we must push on.

Let's go on.

There, I see something. Hooray! I said, I begin to see a track; I think the quarry will not escape us.

That's good news!

Really, I said, we are completely stupid.

Why's that?

Well, my good man, at the start of our inquiry, ages ago, justice was right there in front of us and we never saw it. Nothing could be more ridiculous! Like people who go around looking for what they have right in their hands, so similarly with us; we looked not at the thing we sought but at what was far off in the distance, and that, no doubt, is why we missed it.

What do you mean?

I mean that in reality for a long time now we have been talking about justice without realizing that we had already begun to disclose its reality.

Would you please bring this to an end and get to the point.

All right, then, tell me, I said, whether I am right or not. You remember the original principle which we insisted on laying down for the construction of the state: that each individual should practise just one thing only, the thing to which he was best suited by nature. Justice is just this principle, or some form of it.

Yes, we often said that an individual should do just one thing.

Further, we affirmed that justice was minding one's own business and not meddling in other people's; we said so again and again, and many others have said the same to us.

Yes, we said that.

Then minding one's own business really appears, in a certain way at least, to be justice. Do you know what makes me infer that?

I don't, but I'd like to be told.

I think that this virtue, the one that remains after we have examined wisdom, courage and moderation, is what makes those other three able to grow in the city and preserves them as long as it is present. You remember that we said that if the other three were discovered by us, justice would be the one left.

That has to be the case.

Moreover, if we are asked to determine which of these four by its presence contributes most to the excellence of the state, whether the agreement of rulers and subject, or the preservation in the soldiers of the conviction that was established about what is to be feared, or wisdom and watchfulness in the rulers, or whether this other I have been mentioning, which is found in children and women, slave and freeman, artisan, ruler, subject—the quality, I mean, of everyone doing his or her own work and not being a busybody— would take the prize, that question would not be so easy to answer.

Certainly, he said, it would be difficult to say which.

But we can say that this principle of each individual in the state doing his or her own work rivals the other three in producing excellence in the state.

Yes.

And wouldn't you say that the only possible competitor to those three is justice?

Exactly.

Here is something else which points to the same conclusion. Wouldn't you assign the responsibility for determining lawsuits to those who are the rulers?

Certainly.

And are these suits decided on any other ground than that a person may neither take what is another's nor be deprived of what is their own?

Yes, that is the principle.

And this is just?

Yes.

Then this indicates too that justice is having and doing what is a person's very own?

Very true.

Again, say whether you agree with me or not. Suppose a carpenter does the job of a cobbler, or a cobbler that of a carpenter; and suppose them to exchange their tools or their positions, or the same person to be doing the work of both, or whatever change you imagine. Do you think that any great harm would result to the state?

Not much.

But when the cobbler or any other person whom nature suited to be an artisan emboldened by wealth or strength or the number of his followers, or any advantage of that sort, tries to force his way into the class of soldiers, or a soldier tries to fill a seat among the guardians, for which he is unfitted, or there is any switching around of tools and duties or one person is an artisan, soldier, and statesman all in one, then I think you will agree with me that this switching around and meddling of one with another is the ruin of the state.

Most true.

Seeing then, I said, that there are these three distinct classes, any meddling of one with another, or change of one into another, is most destructive of the state and an extreme case of evildoing?

Precisely.

And what is most harmful to the state you would say is injustice?

Certainly.

This, then, is injustice; and, on the other hand, when the artisan, the auxiliary, and the guardian each do their own jobs, that is justice, and will make the city just.

I agree with you.

Let's not be too confident about this as yet. But, if we find that this conception of justice is verified in the case of the individual as well as in the state, there will no longer be room for doubt; if it is not verified, then we'll have to start a fresh inquiry.

FOR DISCUSSION:

Does Socrates' conception of justice given above rule out there being a just democratic state? Or a just oligarchic state? Would, in fact, only his ideal state turn out to be just? Would that bother Plato?

What is it for a state to deal justly with its citizens? Is this what makes a state just?

B.5.e: *REPUBLIC* V[1]

(1) 451C-464D

ncient Greek attitudes toward women were deeply ambivalent. Women were not allowed any role in the governing of cities, but they were given a dominant position in the running of many religious festivals. A strain of misogyny infects some of the oldest tales about women, but the works of the tragedians which have come down to us show a great respect for the depth of women's feelings and perceptions about life and political affairs. Plato is one of the few Greek thinkers who challenged the virtually universal exclusion of women from civic affairs, and the text below is where he argues his case in the greatest detail. There is no reason to doubt that Socrates' position here reflects a view Plato took to be a serious proposal of great merit, but it is also important not to equate it with modern-day feminism. Socrates thinks women with talent for soldiering and governing should be allowed into the ranks of guardians and given the sort of education a guardian requires, despite the fact that in all the important tasks of this vocation they are *on average inferior* to men. The important point for him is that nothing about women's distinctive role in sex and reproduction implies that a natural talent for the vocation of soldier, and even ruler, will not be distributed among them just as frequently as it is among men (though the average degree of these talents be lower). In fact he takes this to be obviously the case, so that it is the exclusion of women from these professions, not their inclusion, which is really contrary to nature.

[*Socrates:*] ...The part of the men in this drama has been played out, and now maybe we should go on to the women, especially since you are so insistent.

---

1 Translated by Jowett, with modifications.

For men born and educated like our citizens the only way, in my opinion, to have women and children and treat them is to follow the path on which we originally started. We put the men in the position of watchdogs guarding the flock.

[*Glaucon:*] True.

Let us further suppose the birth and education of our women to be subject to similar or nearly similar regulations; then we shall see if the result suits us or not.

What do you mean?

I mean to put this question: Are dogs divided into males and females, or do they both share equally in hunting and in keeping watch and in the other duties of dogs? Or do we entrust to the males the entire and exclusive care of the flocks, while we leave the females at home, thinking that the bearing and suckling of their puppies is labour enough for them?

No, he said, they share alike; the only difference between them is that the males are stronger and the females weaker.

But can you use different animals for the same purpose without breeding and feeding them in the same way.

You cannot.

Then, if women are to have the same duties as the men, they must have the same nurture and education?

Yes.

The education we gave the men was music and gymnastic.

Yes.

Then women must be taught music and gymnastic and also the art of war, which they must practise like the men?

That follows, I suppose.

Perhaps, I said, several of our proposals, if carried out, would by being so contrary to established custom invite ridicule.

No doubt about that.

Yes, and the most ridiculous thing of all will be the sight of women naked in the wrestling schools, exercising with the men, especially when they are no longer young; they certainly will not be a vision of loveliness, any more than are the enthusiastic old men who despite their wrinkles and ugliness continue to frequent the gymnasia.

Yes, indeed, he said; current ideas about these things would find the whole thing ridiculous.

But then, I said, as we have decided to say what we think, we must not fear the wisecracks which will be directed against this sort of innovation. You can imagine what they will say of women's attainments in both music and gymnastic, and above all about their wearing armour and riding astride horses!

Very true.

Yet having begun setting out rules, we must not shrink from their harsher provisions. At the same time we will ask these clever wits to be serious for once. Not long ago, we'll remind them, the Greeks held the opinion, which is still generally accepted among foreigners, that the sight of a naked man was ridiculous and shameful. When first the Cretans and then the Spartans first introduced the custom, the humorists had, I suppose, a field day.

No doubt.

But when experience showed that it was far better to go naked than to cover up, laughter died down and a practise which reason approved ceased to look ridiculous to the eye. It became clear that it is idle to treat anything as ridiculous other than what is bad, and whoever directs ridicule at any other sight than that of folly and wrongdoing, or tries to judge what is beautiful by any standard other than what is good, is a fool.

Very true, he replied.

First, then, we must find out whether these proposals are at all feasible. And we must open the debate to anyone who, whether in jest or in earnest, wants to raise the question of whether women's nature is capable of sharing either wholly or partly in the activities of men, or not at all. Is the art of war one of the arts in which she can or cannot share? That will be the best way to start the inquiry, and will probably lead to the best conclusion.

That will be by far the best way.

Shall we take the other side first and begin by arguing against ourselves; that way our adversary's position will not go undefended.

Why not? he said.

Then let us put a speech into the mouths of our opponents. They will say:

Socrates and Glaucon, there is no need for opponents to argue against you, for you yourselves, when you first constructed the state, allowed that everybody was to do the one job suited to their own nature.

Certainly, if I am not mistaken, we did indeed allow that.

And do not men and women have very different natures?

We'll reply that, of course, they do.

Shouldn't, then, the tasks assigned to men and to women be different so that they suit their different natures?

Certainly they should.

If that's so, then haven't you fallen into serious inconsistency by saying that men and women should do the same things, even though they have such different natures?

What defence will you construct for us, my good man, against anyone who comes up with this line of attack?

It's not so easy to find one at a moment's notice; all I can do is ask and urge you to make a rebuttal for us, whatever it may be.

These are the objections, Glaucon, and there are lots of others of a similar sort, which I foresaw long ago; they made me afraid and reluctant to deal with any law about the possession of wives and the rearing of children.

By Zeus, he said, the problem is certainly not an easy one!

Yes, I said; but the fact is that when a man is out of his depth, whether he has fallen into a little swimming bath or into mid-ocean, he has to swim all the same.

Very true.

Don't we have to swim and try to reach the shore, while hoping that Arion's dolphin[1] or some other miracle may save us?

I suppose so, he said.

Well then, let us see if we can find some way out. We acknowledged, did we not, that different natures ought to have different pursuits, and that men's and women's natures are different. And now what are we saying? That different natures ought to have the same pursuits—this is the inconsistency we are charged with.

Precisely.

Ah, Glaucon, I said, what glorious power lies in the practice of finding contradictions!

Why do you say that?

Because I think that many people fall into this practice without wanting to. When they think they are reasoning, they are really wrangling; and because they cannot define and analyze so as to be clear about what they are discussing, they pursue mere verbal oppositions and end up practicing disputation[2] rather than dialectic.

Yes, he replied, that often happens, but what has that got to do with us and our argument?

A great deal; for we are in danger of unintentionally falling into a verbal opposition.

---

1   The musician Arion, according to a story related by Herodotus, escaped some murderous sailors by jumping into the sea. He was rescued by a dolphin that carried him to the shore.
2   I.e., "eristic", the kind of debate Socrates charges the sophists with. He claims that "dialectic" is very different from this in that it aims at finding agreement on some conclusion.

In what way?

Why we valiantly and disputatiously insist on the verbal truth that different natures ought to have different pursuits, but we never considered at all what we meant by sameness and difference of nature, or in what respect these natures and pursuits are to be distinguished when we assigned different pursuits to different natures and the same to the same natures.

No, he said, we never considered that.

I said: Suppose, to illustrate the point, we were to ask the question whether there is not an opposition in nature between bald men and hairy men; then, given we admit that, if bald men are cobblers, should we forbid the hairy men from being cobblers, and conversely?

That would be ridiculous.

Yes, ridiculous; but why? Because we never intended when we constructed the state that the opposition of natures was to extend to every difference, but rather only to those differences which were relevant to the pursuit in which the individual was engaged. We meant, for example, that a man and a woman who both have the mind of a physician are to be said to have the same nature.

True.

But a man who is a physician and a man who is a carpenter have different natures?

Certainly.

And if, I said, the male and the female sex appear to differ in their fitness for any art or pursuit, we should say that this pursuit or art ought to be assigned to the one or the other suited to it; but if the difference consists merely in the fact that women bear children and men beget them, this is no proof that a woman differs from a man for our purposes, and we shall continue to hold that our guardians and their women ought to have the same pursuits.

Very true, he said.

Next, we shall ask our opponent in relation to what art or pursuit involved in civic life a woman's nature differs from that of a man's.

Fair enough.

And perhaps he, like yourself, will say that it is not easy to make a reply right away, but given time to reflect there would be no problem.

Yes, perhaps.

Then shall we invite him to join us in the argument, and then we might be able to show him that there is no occupation involved in civic affairs that is peculiarly the province of women?

By all means.

Let us say to him: Come now, and we will ask you a question: When you spoke of a nature gifted or not gifted in some respect, did you mean to say that one person will acquire a thing easily, another with difficulty; a little learning will lead one to discover a great deal, whereas the other, after lots of study and application no sooner learns than forgets; or again did you mean that the one has a body which serves well their mind, while the other's body is a hindrance? Wouldn't these be the sorts of differences that distinguish one who is gifted by nature from one who is not?

No one will deny that.

And can you mention any pursuit of mankind where males have all these gifts and qualities to a higher degree than do the females? Need I waste time speaking about the art of weaving or baking cakes or making preserves, where women do really appear superior and in which a woman would be mortified to be beaten by a man?

You are quite right, he replied, when you maintain the general inferiority of the female sex; even though many women are in many things superior to many men, yet on the whole what you say is true.

If that's right, my friend, I said, there is no particular occupation concerned with civic affairs which a woman has just because she is a woman, or which a man has in virtue of his sex; rather the gifts of nature are spread around in both alike; all the pursuits of men are pursuits of women too; it's just that for all of them women are the weaker of the two.

Very true.

Are we then to assign all the occupations to the men and none to the women?

That will never do.

One woman will have a gift for healing, another not; one has musical talent, another has no music in her nature at all?

That's right.

And one woman has a talent for gymnastic and military exercises, while another is unwarlike and hates gymnastics?

Certainly.

And one woman loves knowledge, while another hates it; one may be high-spirited, while another not?

That too is true.

So one woman will have the temper of a guardian, and another not. Was not the basis for selection of male guardians differences of this sort?

Yes.

Men and women alike possess the qualities which make a guardian; they differ only in their comparative strength or weakness.

Obviously.

And those women who have such qualities should be selected to share the lives and duties of men who have similar qualities and whom they resemble in capacities and character?

Very true.

And shouldn't the same natures have the same pursuits?

They should.

So we come back to where we started: there is nothing contrary to nature in educating the women of our guardians in music and gymnastic.

Certainly not.

The rule we proposed, then, was consonant with nature, and therefore not an impossibility or mere wishful thinking; rather the opposite practice, the one that now prevails, is what really goes against nature.

That appears to be true.

FOR DISCUSSION:

Suppose we found that in fact in some sorts of pursuits women were on average innately superior to men, or men were on average innately superior to women. Would that mean that men, or women, should be excluded from the education needed for those pursuits? Would it have any implications for public policy at all?

Though feasible, the inclusion of women into the warrior and guardian classes might still not be good for the state. But Socrates argues that it is, on the obvious ground that by educating the women naturally suited for those classes they will be producing the best sort of women, and the state cannot help but benefit from this improvement in the quality of its citizenry.

Our first consideration was whether our proposal was feasible, and then secondly whether it would be beneficial?

Yes.

The feasibility has now been acknowledged?

Yes.

So next we have to establish that it is best.

Right.

You will admit that the same education which makes a man a good guardian will also make a woman a good guardian, for their natures are the same?

Yes.

Now I'd like to ask you a question.

What is it?

As for men, do you think that some are better and some worse, or all are alike.

They are certainly not all alike.

Now in the state which we were constructing do you take the guardians who have been brought up in the manner we prescribed to be better men, or the shoemakers whose education has been in shoemaking?

What an absurd question!

I take that to be an answer, I replied. So, can't we go on to say that our guardians are the best of all our citizens?

By far the best.

And the women so educated the best of all women?

Yes, by far the best.

And can there be anything better so far as the interests of the state are concerned than that it produce men and women of the very best type?

Nothing better.

And the education we have prescribed in music and gymnastic will accomplish this end?

Certainly.

So the institution we have prescribed is not only feasible but is in the highest degree beneficial to the state.

True.

Then let the women of our guardians strip, for their virtue will be their robe; they must share in the toils of war and the defence of their country alongside their men and have no other occupation. Except that the lighter duties are to be assigned to the women, owing to their natural weakness, their duties will be the same as those of the men. As for the man who laughs at naked women exercising their bodies because it is best that they should, in his laughter he will be "gathering unripe fruit" and really doesn't know what he is laughing at or where that all leads. For the fairest words ever spoken were these: What is beneficial is beautiful, and what is harmful is foul.

Very true.

As though the inclusion of women in the ruling class would not be controversial enough, Socrates proceeds to something sure to arouse even more vehement opposition. Within the guardian class (in the broad sense inclusive of auxiliaries) he proposes that there be no family units and that in fact no mother or father even know which of the children is theirs, nor the children know who their biological parents are. To effect this he proposes that mating between the male and female guardians be regulated so that it only occurs in a properly sanctified way between pairs joined during the course of one of many periodic marriage festivals. There does not seem to be any idea that once married the pair would cohabit for long, if at all; each of them would, it seems, be available for a new partner at the next festival that the rulers allowed them to be married in. Thus Socrates speaks of the women among the guardians as "held in common" by the men, but in fact the relationship is completely symmetrical, the women are no more "held in common" by the men than the men are by the women.

But this is not all. The rulers surreptitiously arrange the marriages so as to promote a program of eugenics, modelled on the way people breed dogs and birds. The pairs that get to marry are chosen by lot, but the rulers secretly fix this whole process in such a way that the guardians whom they deem the best get to mate with others of the best sort. This scheme has to remain secret, of course, otherwise those who keep losing out on the draw of the lots would feel cheated and rise up in anger.

The offspring of the marriages between the better quality guardians are taken off to a crèche to be raised by nurses. The mothers and fathers never know which among the babies at the crèche are their own, and the mothers evidently suckle whichever infant the attendants hand them. (There is a problem here in that mothers would know the newly born from those born somewhat earlier and be able to make a guess as to which is their own infant, but Socrates does not address this.) Some other arrangements are made for offspring of inferior parents. Mothers in the guardian class are not to spend very much time suckling babies, and no time at all with the other troublesome tasks of child rearing. That is left to special officials assigned the task.

So, then, in our regulations regarding women we have not been swept away and drowned like swimmers fighting a wave for our proposal that the guardians of either sex should have all their pursuits in common; rather our argument turns out to be consistent in that it shows the proposal is both feasible and beneficial.

It was no small wave, either.

Wait till you see the next.

Go ahead. Let's see it.

The law, I said, which follows on everything we have said so far: that all the women of our guardians are to be held in common by all the men and none shall cohabit privately, and their children shall be raised in common, and no parent is to know which child is theirs and no child which parent is theirs.

Yes, he said, that is a much greater wave than the other; and the feasibility as well as the utility of such a law are far more questionable.

I don't think, I said, that there can be much dispute about the very great utility of having women and children in common; the feasibility is quite another matter and will be much disputed.

I think a good many doubts can be raised about both.

You're implying that I need to deal with both questions, I replied. I thought you would admit the utility of the proposal, and then I could escape that question and deal only with the one about feasibility.

Your little attempt has been detected, so you will, please, give a defence of both.

All right, I submit to my fate. Yet grant me a little favour. Let me feast my mind on the dream as day dreamers often do when they walk alone. For before they have discovered any way of realizing their wishes—that is a matter they never trouble about—they would rather not tire themselves out thinking about what is possible and what not; rather they assume that what they desire is already granted to them and proceed with their plan, taking delight in going into the details of what they intend to do when their wish has come true. So do idle minds become still more idle.

Now I am myself giving in to this weakness, and I would like, with your permission, to pass over the question of feasibility for the moment. Assuming, then, the feasibility of our proposal, I shall go on to inquire how the rulers will carry out these arrangements, and I shall show that our plan, if put into effect, will be of the greatest benefit to the state and to the guardians. That is what I want to consider first together with you, and postpone the other topic.

Permission granted. Go on.

First, I think that if our rulers, and their auxiliaries, are to be worthy of the name they bear, there must be the power of command in the one and the willingness to obey in the other. The guardians must themselves obey the laws, and when it comes to the details that are left to their discretion they must imitate the spirit of those laws.

That is right, he said.

You, I said, who are the legislator, having selected the men must now select the women so that they have as far as possible natures like that of the men.

They must all live in common houses and meet at common meals. None of them will have anything that is specially his or her own; they will all live together, be brought up together, and join together in gymnastic exercises. Natural necessity will draw them together to have sex—'necessity' is not too strong a word, I think?

Not geometrical necessity, he said, but the necessity that lovers experience, and which is far more persuasive and forceful than the former for the mass of mankind.

True, I said; but, Glaucon, anything like irregular unions would be considered unholy in a happy city, and will not be allowed.

Yes, he said, and it ought not be permitted.

Clearly we will have to have marriages which are sacred in the highest degree, and it is those that are most beneficial that are sacred.

Exactly.

And how can marriages be made most beneficial? I put that question to you because I see in your house hunting dogs and a number of pedigree cocks. Now, tell me, have you ever noticed something about their mating breeding?

What is that?

In the first place, although they are all of good stock, aren't some better than others?

True.

And do you breed from them all indifferently, or do you take care to breed from the best only?

From the best.

And for breeding do you take the oldest or the youngest, or only those in their prime?

I choose only those in their prime.

And if you did not take care about the breeding, the quality of your dogs and birds would deteriorate?

Certainly.

Does the same hold of horses and animals in general?

Undoubtedly.

Good heavens! my dear friend, I said, if this same principle holds for the human race, what immense skill will be needed in our rulers!

Certainly, the same principle holds; but why does this require a lot of skill?

Because, I said, our rulers will have to resort to many of those drugs we talked about earlier. When patients do not require drugs but need only be put on a diet, then the lesser sort of physician suffices; but when drugs have to be given, we know that a physician of more daring and imagination is needed.

Very true, he said; but what is your point?

I mean, I replied, that our rulers will find it necessary to administer a considerable dose of falsehood and deceit for the good of their subjects. We were saying earlier that resort to all these things regarded as drugs might be of advantage.

And we were very right.

So this lawful use of them seems likely to be often needed in the regulations of marriages and births.

How so?

Why, I said, the principle has been laid down earlier that the best of either sex should be united with the best as often as possible, and the inferior with the inferior as seldom as possible. Also that the offspring of the former sort of union should be reared, but not those of the other, if the flock is to be maintained in first-rate condition. How all this is brought about must be a secret known only to the rulers; otherwise, there will be danger of dissension within our herd of guardians.

Very true.

Wouldn't it be good to appoint certain festivals at which we will bring together the brides and bridegrooms, and sacrifices will be offered and suitable marriage songs composed by our poets? The number of weddings is a matter best left to the discretion of the rulers, whose aim will be to preserve the population at a constant level? There are many other things they will have to consider, such as the effects of wars and diseases and so on, in order as far as possible to keep the state from becoming either too large or too small.

Certainly.

We shall have to invent some ingenious system of drawing lots at the marriage festivals so that the inferior candidates will blame their luck rather than the rulers.

To be sure, he said.

And I think that the young men who excel at war and in other pursuits, besides their other honours and rewards, be given more opportunities for sex with the women. These schemes will provide a ready pretext for making sure they are the ones begetting the most children.

True.

And the proper officials, whether male or female or both, for offices I take it are to be held by women as well as by men—

Yes.

They will take the offspring of the superior parents to a pen or crèche, and there they will be left with certain nurses who live in a separate quarter of the city; but the offspring of the inferior, or even of the better when they happen to be deformed, will be put away in some unknown place that must remain secret.

Yes, he said, if the breed of our guardians is to be kept pure.

They will supervise the nursing of the children and bring the mothers to the crèche when they are full of milk, taking the greatest possible care that no mother recognizes her own child; wet nurses may be engaged as required. Care will also be taken that the process of suckling shall not be too prolonged, and that the mothers will not have to get up at night or take other trouble, but will turn over this sort of thing to the nurses and attendants.

You suppose the women of the guardians to have a very easy time of it when they are having children.

And so they should. Let's, however, get on with our scheme. We were saying that the parents should be in the prime of life?

Very true.

What is the prime of life? Can it not be defined as a period of about twenty years in a woman's life, and thirty in a man's?

Which years are those?

A woman, I said, can at twenty years of age begin to bear children for the state, and go on bearing them until she is forty. A man should begin to beget them when he has passed "the racer's prime in swiftness" and continue until fifty five.

I see, he said, that you mean the years when both men and women are at their best in terms of both mental and physical vigour.

Anyone above or below the prescribed ages who meddles with the procreation of children for the state shall be said to have done an unholy and unjust thing. The child of which he is the father, if its birth escapes detection, will not have been attended by the prayers and sacrifices that the priestesses and priests, and the whole city, offer in order to make the new generation better and more useful than their good and useful parents. Rather this child will have been born in darkness and in lust.

Very true.

The same regulation will apply to any man within the prescribed age limits who has sex with a woman in the prime of life without the sanction of the rulers; we shall say that he has reared a bastard to the state, unsanctioned by the law and by religion.

Very true, he replied.

As soon, however, as the men and women have passed the prescribed ages, we shall leave them free to have sexual relations with whomever they please, except that a man may not marry his daughter or his daughter's daughter, or his mother or his mother's mother; and women, on the other hand, are prohibited from marrying their sons or fathers, or son's sons or father's father, and so on in either direction. And we grant all this on the strict condition that nothing so conceived which may come to be is to see the light of day; and, if a birth is unable to be prevented, the parents must understand that the offspring of such a union cannot be preserved and must be disposed of.

That too, he said, is very reasonable. But how are they going to know who are their fathers and daughters and so on?

They will never know. This is the way it will go: A man will call all male offspring born from the seventh to the tenth month after he was a bridegroom his sons, and all the female ones daughters, and all those offspring will call him father. Likewise, he will call all their offspring his grandchildren, and they will call his group grandfathers and grandmothers. All the children born in the period when their fathers and mothers were procreating will regard each other as brothers and sisters. This should be enough for the prohibitions we mentioned. However, the prohibition on marriage between brothers and sisters is not to be absolute; if the draw of the lots favours their union and the oracle at Delphi agrees, then they are allowed to marry.

Quite right, he said.

FOR DISCUSSION:

Has Plato overlooked some necessary functions which the nuclear family plays that could not be fulfilled by the scheme Socrates outlines above?

Socrates suggests that the rulers will aim at avoiding much population growth or decrease by their marriage arrangements. But would this work if those arrangements apply only to the guardians and not to the economic class?

The reason the above arrangements for the guardians are good for the state as a whole is, according to Socrates, that it promotes their unity by eliminating as much as possible the causes of dissension. By having everything in common, even their family, there is minimal occasion for dispute about what belongs to whom and consequently little chance for what gives pleasure to one guardian not to give it to all the guardians, and likewise with pain. The communism of the guardian class does away with the conflicting interests among its members, and thus allows them to concentrate on their common interest, the preservation of the state.

Such is the scheme, Glaucon, by which the guardians are to have their women and children in common. And now you would have the argument show that this arrangement is consistent with the rest of our institutions and also that nothing could be better, would you not?

Yes, certainly.

Shall we try to reach agreement by asking ourselves what ought to be the chief aim of the legislator in legislating for the state, and what is the greatest good for the state, and what the greatest evil? And then go on to consider whether what we proposed accords with that good and not with that evil?

By all means.

Can there be any greater evil in a city than discord and division, falling into many instead of remaining one? Or is there any greater good than the bond of unity?

There cannot.

And there is unity where there is sharing of pleasures and pains, where the citizens are joyous or grieved together over the same births and deaths?

No doubt.

But where there are no shared feelings but only private ones, the bond is broken—when you have some rejoicing and others are plunged in grief over the same events happening to the city or to the citizens?

Certainly.

Such disunion commonly originates in disagreement about the use of the terms 'mine' and 'not mine', 'another's', and 'not another's'.

Exactly.

And is not the best-ordered state that in which the greatest number of people apply the terms 'mine' and 'not mine' to the same things in the same way?

Quite true.

The best city is the one which is most like an individual person. When one hurts just their finger, the bodily frame is so connected that the event is communicated to the governing element in the soul, and the whole body feels the hurt and shares the pain of the part injured; hence we say that the person has a pain in their finger. We speak the same way about any other part of the body which feels pain when injured or pleasure when injury is relieved.

Very true, he replied; and I agree with you that the best ordered state comes closest to this common feeling you describe.

So when any one of the citizens experiences anything good or bad, the whole state will make that its own, and will either rejoice or sorrow with him?

Yes, he said, that will happen in a well-ordered state.

It's time now to return to our state and see whether its arrangements as opposed to other sorts of arrangements most accord with these conclusions.

Very good.

Our state, like every other, has rulers and subjects?

True.

All of whom call one another citizens?

Of course.

But in other states is there not some other name which people give to their rulers?

Generally they call them masters, but in democratic states they simply call them rulers.

And in our state what other name besides 'citizens' do they apply to the rulers.

They are called preservers and helpers.

And what do the rulers call the people?

Their employers and supporters.

And what do they call them in other states?

Slaves.

And what do the rulers call one another in other states?

Fellow rulers.

And what in ours?

Fellow guardians.

Did you ever know in other states cases where a ruler speaks of one of his colleagues as kin while calling others strangers?

Yes, very often.

And the one he calls kin he describes as a person who is "his own", and the one he calls a stranger he says is not his own?

Exactly.

But in our city would any of our guardians think or speak of any other guardian as a stranger?

They certainly would not. For everyone whom they meet they will regard either as a brother or sister, father or mother, son or daughter, or as the child or parent of those who are related to them in those ways.

Very good! I said. But here is another question for you: Shall they be a family in name only, or shall they behave in the spirit of that name? For example, in the use of the word 'father', would the care of a father be implied and the filial reverence and duty and obedience to him which the law commands; and is the violator of these duties to be regarded as impious and unjust and not likely to receive much good either from the gods or from humans? Are these not the themes which the children will hear repeated in their ears by all the citizens about what is due to parents and other kinfolk?

These, he said, and nothing else; for what can be more preposterous than for them to utter these words without acting in the spirit of them?

In our city, then, more than in any other, when anyone does well, or ill, then the others will respond that it is "with me" that it is well, or it is "with me" that it is ill.

Most true.

And in agreement with this way of thinking and speaking, did we not say that they will have their pleasures and pains in common?

Yes, and so they will.

And they will have a common interest in the same thing which they will all call "my own", and having this common interest they will all share the same feelings of pleasure and pain?

Yes, far more so than in other states.

The reason for this, over and above the general institutions of the state, will be that the guardians hold all their women and children in common?

That will be the chief reason.

And this unity of feeling we admitted to be the greatest good, as was implied by our own comparison of a well-ordered state to the relation of the whole body to its various parts when affected by pleasure or pain?

We agreed to that, and rightly too.

So the holding of wives and children in common is clearly the source of the greatest good to the state?

Certainly.

And this agrees with the other principle which we were affirming,—that the guardians were not to have houses or lands or any other property; their pay was to be their food, which they were to receive from the other citizens, and their expenses will be taken care of in common; for we intend them to preserve their true character of guardians.

Correct.

Do not, then, the former arrangements and these present ones tend to make them more truly guardians? They will not tear the city into pieces by differing about "mine" and "not mine", each man dragging any acquisition he has made into a house of his own, where he has his own separate wife and children and so his own private pleasures and pains. Rather all will be affected as far as possible by the same pleasures and pains because they all share the same conviction about what is near and dear to them, and therefore they all work towards a common goal.

FOR DISCUSSION:

Our own political system is based on competition between rival factions within the ruling class. How can this be justified as against Plato's argument that dissension within that class is just what we most want to avoid?

(2) 471C–474B

Glaucon now challenges Socrates to show that the arrangements for the ideal state that Socrates has described can actually be realized. In response Socrates insists that feasibility should not be a requirement for correctly delineating what is perfect, but Glaucon will hardly be put off by that ploy. Socrates is forced to come up with a way to actually achieve something which at least approximates the arrangements which are the best. With much trepidation he suggests that it is only when the rulers are philosophers that there will be an end to the troubles which beset all the states that are familiar to us. Here Plato broaches his most radical thesis of all: philosophy is the way to true happiness both for the community and for individuals.

Plato's vision of what the philosopher is and what his wisdom consists in is discussed in parts of the *Republic* not given in these selections. It suffices to know that on his view philosophic wisdom is not achieved through careful observation of the physical and social world around us but through a process of examination of the basic ethical notions which we use in guiding our conduct, notions like justice, courage, power, etc. That examination is dialectical, i.e., it is carried out by putting forward definitions and subjecting them to critical scrutiny in the way Socrates does in many of the dialogues generally thought to have been written earlier. The end result is to bring to full consciousness a knowledge which we already have but are only dimly aware of. Plato thinks that the objects of this knowledge, objects which he calls "Forms", have an unchanging and timeless existence in a realm quite separate from the world of ordinary experience. That latter world makes some limited sense only insofar as it imitates the world of the Forms. The philosopher is the person who, once he becomes reacquainted with those Forms, finds them beautiful and sees how the world most people think is the only reality in fact is far less real than the world of Forms. To some extent the political theory of the *Republic* can survive a scrapping of this peculiar view of philosophy as long as we admit that there is some objective science which a few people can become expert in and which is necessary for rulers to know if they are to rule society well. Plato's basic thesis is that expert knowledge of some sort is the key to managing political affairs in a way that maximizes the welfare of the whole community.

[*Glaucon:*] But still, Socrates, I have to say that if we let you go on in this way you will entirely forget the other question which at the very beginning of this discussion you thrust aside: Is such an arrangement of society possible, and how, if at all? For I am quite ready to acknowledge that the plan you propose, given it is feasible, would do all sorts of good for the state. I will add something you omitted, that your citizens will be the bravest of warriors and will never desert their ranks, for they will all know one another, and each will call the other father, brother, son; and if you suppose the women to join their armies, whether in the same rank or in the rear, either to strike terror in the enemy or as auxiliaries in case of need, I know that they will be absolutely invincible. There are as well many domestic benefits which might be mentioned and which I also fully acknowledge; so, given I admit all these advantages and as many more as you please, we need say no more about them, while assuming this state exists. But let us now turn to the question of whether it could exist, and if so, how it could be brought into existence.

What a sudden onslaught this is, I said, showing no tolerance for my shilly-shallying. Here I have hardly escaped the first and second waves and you launch on me this third, the most formidable of them all. When you have seen what it is like and heard my reply, I am sure you will be lenient, and at least acknowledge that my fear and hesitation were quite natural given the paradoxical proposal I am going to put forth for discussion.

The more you go on making excuses like this, he said, the more we will insist that you tell us how such a state is possible. So now please get on with it.

Let me begin by reminding you that we started this whole inquiry by searching after justice and injustice.

True, but so what?

I was only going to ask whether, once we have discovered them, we are to demand that the just man totally accord with this standard of justice in every respect and with no deviation, or can we be satisfied with an approximation and the attainment in him of a greater degree of justice than is found in others?

The approximation will be enough.

We are inquiring into justice itself and into what is a perfectly just man, and into injustice itself and the perfectly unjust man, and we were to look at these in order to judge our own happiness and unhappiness by the standard which they exhibited and the degree to which we resembled them, but not with any view to showing that they actually existed.

True, he said.

Suppose a painter drew with consummate art the pattern of the ideally beautiful human being. Would he be any the less a good painter for being unable to show that such a human actually existed?

He would not.

And were we not in words trying to create the pattern of the ideally good state?

To be sure.

So is our theory any the worse for our being unable to prove the possibility of a city's being organized in the way we described?

Surely not, he replied.

That is the truth of the matter, I said. But if, at your request, I am to try and show how and under what conditions our ideal has the best chance of being realized, I must ask you, having this view, to repeat what you have already admitted.

What is that?

Can anything be realized in fact in the way we describe it in words, or do not words always go beyond the facts, and must not the actual, whatever people think, always in the nature of things fall short of truth compared with words?

I agree.

Then you must not insist on my showing that the actual state agrees with what we described in words. If we just make out how a city can be governed very nearly as we proposed, that will amount to showing the possibility you demand and you will be satisfied. I am sure I will be satisfied; won't you?

Yes, I will.

Next it seems we must try to show what is the fault in states which prevents their being organized in the way we described, and what is the least change which would enable a state to pass over into this type of government. Preferably this will be a change in just one thing, or, if not, two, or at any rate as few things as possible.

Certainly, he replied.

There is one change, then, I said, which I think might be enough, but it is not a small or easy one, although it is possible.

What is it?

I am about, I said, to confront what is the greatest of waves; nevertheless, I say what I have to say, even though the wave drown me in laughter and scorn. So mark my words.

I am all ears.

Unless, I said, philosophers become kings in our states, or those whom we now call kings and rulers become true philosophers, so that political power and philosophic wisdom coincide, and unless those lesser natures who run after one without the other are compulsorily excluded, there can be no end of troubles, Glaucon, in our cities or for all mankind. Only when this happens will the system of governance we have been describing spring to life and see the light of day. Such was the thought, my dear Glaucon, which I shrank from speaking out loud because of its very paradoxical character, for it is hard to see that in no other state can there be happiness, whether private or public.

Socrates, he exclaimed, having delivered yourself of such a pronouncement you must expect a great number of persons, and not at all contemptible ones, to pull off their coats, so to speak, and, seizing any weapon that is at hand, charge at you full tilt intending all sorts of dreadful deeds. If you do not prepare replies with which to escape their assaults, you will learn what it is to be ridiculed and scorned.

You got me into this scrape, I said.

And I was perfectly right; however, I will do all I can to get you out of it. But I can only give you encouragement and good advice, and perhaps I can better answer your questions than someone else—that is all. With that help, you must do your best to convince the unbelievers that you are right.

I am obligated to try, I said, now that you offer such invaluable assistance.

FOR DISCUSSION:

Can it be of any value to propose social institutions which are ideal but utterly unrealizable?

B.5.f: *REPUBLIC* VI

502c-506b[1]

R eturning to the theme of the previous selection, that rulers are needed who are philosophers if we are to get a well governed state, Socrates elaborates on what is required of a ruler and a philosopher, and admits that the whole complex of qualities needed will not often be found in any given individual. In particular quickness of mind and boldness of spirit must be united with a love of knowledge and the ability to pursue the most difficult studies, including the one which leads to the highest form of knowledge, the knowledge of the good. Socrates intimates that the virtues of justice, moderation, courage, and wisdom reach their perfect form only when accompanied by this knowledge, which only a few can possibly attain. It is these enlightened few which must be allowed to rule if things are to go well for the state as a whole. Plato thus stands at the origins of that train of thought which believes political power can be wielded beneficially only when in the hands of a few properly educated and supremely wise individuals. At some point Plato may have thought that his Academy would produce such people and that through their efforts the Greek cities might be delivered from their never ending series of political wars and debacles, but if so, his hopes were doomed to disappointment.

[*Socrates*:] And now we say not only that our arrangements, if they could be enacted, would be for the best, but also that the enactment of them, though difficult, is not impossible.

[*Adeimantus*:] Very good.

---

1   Translated by Jowett, with modifications.

So we have disposed of one set of difficulties. But more remain: How and by what studies and pursuits these preservers of our constitution are to be created, and at what ages will they take up the various studies.

Certainly.

I tried to omit earlier the awkward topics of the possession of women and the procreation of children, and the appointment of rulers, because I knew that business would be controversial and in any case was difficult to attain. But that effort was useless, for I had to discuss them all the same. We have taken care of the women and children, but the matter of the rulers remains, and there we have to make a new beginning. We said, you will recall, that they were to be lovers of their country, that love proven by tests of pleasures and pains to be one which would not fade neither in hardships nor in dangers, nor in any other turn of fortune. Those who failed the tests were to be rejected, but those who always came through flawlessly, like gold tested in the refiner's fire, were to be made rulers and to receive honours and rewards while alive as well as in death. That was what we had said when the argument turned aside and veiled her face so as not to confront the question we now have to take up.

I recall that perfectly, he said.

Yes, my friend, I said, and then I shrank from hazarding the bold proposals we put forward. But now let us find the courage to make the definitive proposal: that it is philosophers who will be established as guardians in the fullest sense.

Yes, let that be granted.

And do not suppose there will be many of them; for the gifts we thought were required rarely come together but are mostly found separated from each other.

What do you mean? he said.

You are aware, I said, that quick intelligence, memory, sagacity, cleverness, and similar qualities, do not often come together with a high-spirited and generous soul; and when they do persons of that sort are not often also disposed to live a quiet, stable, and orderly life. Instead, just because of their quick intelligence they are subject to the whims of chance and lose any steadiness of purpose.

Well said.

On the other hand, those whose temperaments are stable and steadfast, who are manifestly trustworthy, and who in war are imperturbable and hardened against fear, are apt to behave the same way when confronted with studies. They are always in a torpid state and apt to yawn and go to sleep when faced with any intellectual toil.

Quite true.

And yet we said that both qualities were needed in those who were to receive the highest education, receive honours, or engage in ruling.

Certainly, he said.

And don't you think that such a blend will be rarely found?

Yes, indeed.

Then the aspirants must not just be tested in those labours and dangers and pleasures which we mentioned earlier, but there is another kind of test which we did not mention: they must be exercised in many different studies to see whether their souls can endure the highest kind of study, or whether they will faint and flinch under them, as people do in trials and contests of the body.

Yes, he said, you are quite right to test them. But what do you mean by the highest kind of study?

You may recall, I said, that we divided the soul into three parts, and on that basis distinguished justice, moderation, courage and wisdom.

If I had forgotten that, he said, I would not deserve to hear any more.

Now, do you remember the word of caution which preceded the discussion of them?

What do you refer to?

We said, if I am not mistaken, that someone who wanted to see them in the most precise way would have to take a longer and more circuitous route at the end of which they would appear; but we could give a more superficial account of them that accorded with our earlier argument. You said that such an account would be enough for you, and so the inquiry went on in a way which to me did not seem sufficiently precise; whether you were satisfied or not is for you to say.

Yes, he said, I, as well as the others, thought that you gave us a fair measure of truth.

But, my friend, I said, anything which in these matters falls short of the whole truth is not a fair measure; for nothing imperfect is the measure of anything, although people are all too inclined to be contented and think that they need search no further.

Yes, indolence in people is common enough.

And there cannot be any worse fault in a guardian of the state and its laws.

True.

The guardians, then, I said, must be required to take the longer route, and apply themselves to learning as well as gymnastics, or they will never reach that highest knowledge of all, which, as we were just saying, is most peculiarly their own.

What, he said, is there still something higher to be known than justice and the other virtues?

Yes, I said, there is. And as for the virtues too all we have at present is a rough outline, whereas nothing short of a finished picture should satisfy us. When we take great trouble to be as clear and exact as possible with regard to small matters, how ridiculous it would be not to seek the same standard of accuracy as regards things of the greatest moment!

Certainly; but you don't think we're going to let you escape the question what this highest knowledge is, do you?

No, I said; go on and ask it if you want, but I am certain that you have heard the answer many times. So, I guess, you either just don't understand me or, as I suspect, you want to give me some trouble. For you have often been told that the highest object of learning is the Form of the good, and that it is by their relation to it that justice and all the other virtues become useful and beneficial. You can hardly not have realized that it was this that I was about to speak of, this which, as I have often said, we know so little about, and without which any other knowledge of anything will be of no profit, just as possessing something is of no profit without possession of the good. Or do you think there is some profit in possessing everything except what is good, or in knowing things but having no knowledge of what is beautiful and good?

Certainly not.

You are further aware that the mass of people say pleasure is the good, but people of sophistication say it is knowledge.

Yes.

And are you aware that the latter, when asked what knowledge they mean, are in the end forced to say "knowledge of the good"?

How ridiculous!

Yes, I said, that they should begin by criticizing us for not knowing what the good is, but then turn around and say it is knowledge of the good, just as though we already understood what the good is, that is indeed ridiculous.

Absolutely.

Those who treat pleasure as the good are in equal difficulty, for they are compelled to admit that there are bad pleasures as well as good ones.[1]

Certainly.

And so they are forced to admit that the same things are both good and bad.

True.

---

1   This comes out in Socrates' encounter with Callicles in the *Gorgias*. See B.4.b.

Clearly, there are numerous difficulties attending this question.

No doubt.

Further, don't we see that many are happy to do or to have or to seem to be what is just and honourable without the reality; but no one is satisfied with the mere appearance of good; the reality is what they seek, and appearance is held in contempt by everyone.

Very true, he said.

Of this, then, which everyone's soul pursues and treats as the end of all their actions, dimly grasping that it must exist, and yet hesitating because they neither know the nature of this nor can be as certain of it as of other things, and therefore losing whatever good there is in other things, i.e. of something of such supreme importance, the best of men, the ones we want to govern our city, cannot be left in ignorance and darkness.

Certainly not.

I am sure, I said, that those who do not know how the fine and the just relate to the good will not be much in the way of guardians of them; and I suspect that no one ignorant of the good will really know them.

A shrewd suspicion.

And so it will only be when we have a guardian who possesses this knowledge that our state will be perfectly regulated?

Of course, he replied.

FOR DISCUSSION:

Is it necessary to know what goodness is in general if we are to know when any particular institution or way of life is good?

Do we need experts on what is good, i.e., beneficial, and what is bad, i.e., harmful, to the community? Do we actually have such experts? If so, who are they?

B.5.g: *REPUBLIC* VII

(1) 519C-521B[1]

O ne of Plato's ideas most at odds with modern practice in what we now
call democracy is that the whole business of competition for public
office is corrosive of good order in the community. It is better if the
rulers have no love of ruling but would rather be engaged in philosophic inquiry and reflection, which, in Plato's opinion, is a far better way of life. Still it is
just to compel those educated in philosophy to take up the reins of government,
since, in Plato's ideal state at least, their education has been due to the state and
now they owe the community their services in return for that gift.

The passage below immediately follows one in which Plato imagines prisoners chained in a cave where they can never see anything but shadows of
objects projected on a wall of the cave; they take these shadows to be reality.
This dramatic image is meant to be a metaphor for the position most people
find themselves in: they are "chained in the dark", and take the material visible
world to be the only real world, when in fact it's just a very partial and faulty
representation of the invisible but intelligible (to philosophers!) genuine ("upper") reality, the Forms. The Forms exist entirely outside the cave and to be a
philosopher requires making the ascent, difficult and painful though it may
be, out of the cave to that realm. Once accustomed to viewing the Forms the
philosophers take great pleasure in their new knowledge and are very reluctant
to ever return to the cave where most of their fellow citizens still live.

> [*Socrates:*] Then, I said, the business of us who are the founders of the state
> will be to compel the best minds to attain that knowledge which we have

---

1 Translated by Jowett, with modifications.

already shown to be the greatest of all, to scale the heights until they arrive at the good. But once they have ascended and seen enough, we must not allow them to do as they do now.

[*Glaucon:*] What do you mean?

I mean that they remain in the upper world. This must not be allowed; they must be forced to descend again down among the prisoners in the cave, share in their labours and honours, whether they are worth having or not.

But wouldn't that be unjust, he said, to make them live a worse life when they might have a better?

You have again forgotten, my friend, that it was not the intention of the law to make any one class in the state happy above the rest; the happiness was to be in the whole state. It tries to produce harmony by persuasion and compulsion, making them share with one another whatever benefit any of them can bestow on the state. It creates such people not to please themselves, but to be instrumental in binding the state together.

True, he said, I had forgotten that.

Notice, Glaucon, that there will be no injustice in compelling our philosophers to watch over and care for the other citizens. We shall explain to them that in other states it is reasonable that they are not obliged to share in the toil of governing, for there they have sprung up on their own without any favours from the government. Being self-educated they cannot be expected to show any gratitude for the fostering which they have never received. But we have brought you into the world to be rulers of the hive, kings over yourselves and the other citizens, and have educated you far better and more completely than they have been educated, so that you are better able to share both ways of life. Wherefore each of you, when their turn comes, must go down to where the others live and get used to seeing in the dark. Once you are accustomed to that, you will see ten thousand times better than those who always dwell down there, and you will know what the idols and shadows are, what they represent, because you have seen the reality of the beautiful, the just, and the good. You and we, fully awake, will govern our state not in the way other states are governed by men operating in the dark as in a dream, fighting one another over shadows and struggling for power, which they view as some great good. The truth is that the state where the rulers are most reluctant to govern is always the best and most quietly governed, and the state in which they are the most eager is the worst.

Quite true, he replied.

Will our students, when they hear this, refuse to take their turn labouring for the state, when they are allowed to spend most of their time with one another in that purer world?

Certainly not, he answered; for they are just persons and the commands which we impose on them are just. Without any doubt every one of them will take on office as a stern necessity, and not in the way our present rulers do.

Yes, my friend, I said; and there lies the point. You have to contrive for your future rulers another and a better life than that of a ruler, and only then can you have a well-administered state; for only in the state that offers this will those rule who are truly rich, not in silver and gold, but in the wealth that yields happiness, a good and wise life. On the other hand, if they go into administration of public affairs poor and hungering after their own private benefit, thinking that it is this way that they will snatch the good for themselves, there can never be good order. They will be fighting over offices, and the civil and domestic brawls which will result will be the ruin both of the rulers themselves and of the whole state.

Absolutely right, he replied.

And the only life which looks down with scorn on the life of political ambition is that of true philosophy? Can you think of any other?

No, I cannot.

So those who govern ought not to love the task; for, if they do, there will arise rival lovers and they will fight.

No question about it.

FOR DISCUSSION:

If the state has paid for your education, do you think the state has the right to demand from you services that that education prepared you for?

(2)536C-541B[1]

In this final portion of book VII Socrates completes his picture of how the rulers of the ideal state he has been constructing are to be educated. They must, he says, eventually be schooled in dialectic, i.e., the technique of question and response which Socrates uses in so many of the dialogues that Plato wrote, and which Plato thinks is the method to be used when trying to reach an understanding of the real essences of things. What is particularly

---

1 Translated by Jowett, with modifications.

interesting in this passage is Plato's recognition that the technique used in dialectic can be perverted into something which just tricks the unwary into contradictions which they do not know how to avoid. This is to be contrasted, we are told, with the proper and constructive use that leads to a better grasp of truth. The young in their enthusiasm for the technique are especially inclined to misuse it, with dire consequences both for themselves and others.

[*Socrates*:] ...And now let me remind you that, although in our selection of the rulers we chose old men, we must not do so in this. Solon was deluded when he said that a man when he grows old can learn many things, for he can no more learn much than he can run much; youth is the time for extraordinary efforts.

[Glaucon:] Of course.

So arithmetic and geometry and all other indispensable basics that prepare for dialectic, should be introduced to the young; not, however, as something they are forced to do.

Why not?

Because a free person ought not be a slave in the acquisition of knowledge of any kind. Physical exercise, when compulsory, does no harm to the body; but what the mind is forced to learn it will not retain.

Very true.

Then, my good friend, do not use compulsion, but let early education be a sort of amusement; that way you will be better able to see what are the natural bents of the students.

That seems very reasonable.

Do you remember, too, that the children were to be taken to see battles on horseback, and, if there was no danger, they were to be brought close up and like young hounds to be given a taste for blood?

Yes, I remember.

Then those who show the most aptitude in all these labours, studies, and dangers, are to be put on a select list.

At what age?

At the age when compulsory gymnastics are over. The period of two or three years given over to this sort of training is useless for any other purpose; for sleep and exercise are unfavourable to learning, and the test of them in these exercises is of the utmost importance.

Certainly, he replied.

Then at the age of twenty those specially selected will be given greater honours than the others. The separate subjects which they learned in no particular order in their early education will now be brought together so that they can see the connections of them with one another and with reality.

Yes, he said, that is the only kind of knowledge which takes firm root in the mind.

Yes, I said; and the ability to acquire such knowledge is the chief test of talent for dialectic; the mind that can see connections is always a dialectical one, the one that cannot never is.

I agree with you, he said.

These, then, are the qualities you must keep an eye on. Those who possess them in the highest degree and who are most steadfast in their learning as well as in their military and other duties will at the age of thirty have to be chosen by you out of the select class and elevated to higher honour. You must test them in respect of dialectic to see which of them is able to dispense with sight and the other senses and arrive at the place where truth and reality dwell. But at this point, my friend, you must be very careful.

Why?

Don't you notice, I said, how much harm the current practice of dialectic has introduced?

What harm?

The students of the art are filled with lawlessness.

True enough.

But is their behaviour any cause for wonder? Do you have no sympathy for them at all?

Why should I?

I want you, I said, to imagine an adopted son brought up in a large and wealthy family and who has many flatterers. When he reaches adulthood, he learns that his supposed parents are not his real ones, and who the real ones are he cannot discover. Can you guess how he will be likely to behave towards his flatterers and those he supposed to be his parents, first during the time when he is unaware of his false parentage, and then later when he knows? Or shall I guess for you?

Please do.

I would say, then, that while he is ignorant of the truth he will be likely to honour his father and mother and those he supposes are his relations more than he does the flatterers; he will be less inclined to neglect them when in need, or to do or say anything against them; and he will be less willing to disobey them in any important matter.

That he will.

But once he has made the discovery, I imagine he would hold them in less honour and regard, and turn more to the flatterers; their influence on him would grow, and he would now associate with them and adopt their ways, and, unless he were of an unusually good character, he would lose all concern for those he had supposed were his parents or other relations.

Well, that all sounds very likely, but how is this supposed to be applicable to the students of dialectic?

In the following way: You know that we have certain convictions about justice and what is fine, which we were taught as children under the authority of our parents to honour and obey.

That is true.

There are also opposite ways of behaving and pleasurable habits which flatter and seduce the soul, although anyone with a fairly good character will resist their blandishments and continue to honour and obey the convictions of their fathers.

True.

Now, when a person in this condition confronts the question what is the fine and goes on to give the answer which the lawgiver has taught him, and then arguments arise which refute him again and again, he will in the end be reduced to thinking that nothing is fine any more than it is disgraceful, or just and good any more than the reverse, and so on for all the notions he most valued. At this point do you think he will still honour and obey those old convictions?

Impossible.

And once he ceases to think of them as fine and natural in the way he did before, and he fails to discover any true principles, can he be expected to pursue any life other than that which flatters his desires?

He cannot.

And from being a law-abiding person he will have been turned into an outlaw?

Without doubt.

Isn't this just what we find to happen to students of dialectic such as I described, and shouldn't we be lenient with them?

Yes, and we should pity them as well.

So, then, in order that there will be no occasion for pity toward citizens who have reached thirty years of age, we must be very careful about how we introduce them to dialectic.

Certainly.

One precaution is to keep them from tasting the delights of dialectic at too young an age. You will have noticed how youngsters, when they first taste it, argue just for amusement, and are always contradicting and refuting others in imitation of those who refute them; like puppies they delight in pulling and tearing at all who come near them.

Yes, he said, there is nothing they like better.

And when they have won and lost many times in these contests, they rush on to rejecting all that they believed before, and so they discredit not only themselves but the whole business of philosophy in the eyes of the world.

All too true, he said.

But an older person will not engage in such insanity; he will take as his model the dialectician who is seeking truth, and not the one who plays eristic[1] games, contradicting people just for amusement. His greater moderation of character will increase rather than decrease the regard in which the pursuit is held.

Very true, he said.

Weren't all our proposals for requiring that those who are admitted to argumentation be of an orderly and stable nature made with a view to just such precaution, instead of the present practice of admitting anyone whatsoever, no matter how unsuitable?

Very true.

Suppose, I said, the study of dialectic to take the place of gymnastics and to be pursued diligently and earnestly and exclusively for twice the number of years spent in bodily exercise. Will that be enough?

Does that mean six or four years? he asked.

Say five years, I replied. At the end of that time they must be sent down again into the cave and there compelled to take any military or other office which young people are qualified to hold. In this way they will get this sort of experience and not fall short even in that. Also that will provide an opportunity to test whether they will steadfastly resist temptations or flinch and deviate.

How long is this stage to last?

Fifteen years, I answered; and when they have reached fifty, let those who still survive and have distinguished themselves in all their life activities and in every branch of knowledge come at last to the ultimate goal. The time has now

---

1 Confrontationally argumentative.

arrived at which they must raise the eye of the soul to that which sheds its light on everything, the good itself. And when they have viewed this they can use it as the pattern on which they are to arrange the state and the lives of individual citizens, their own lives included. Philosophy will be their chief pursuit, but when their turn comes, they will work away at politics and ruling for the public good, not as though they were performing some heroic action, but just out of a sense of duty. Then, when they have brought up in each generation others like themselves and left them to replace themselves as rulers of the state, they will depart to the Islands of the Blest[1] and dwell there, while the city will give them public memorials and sacrifices, and honour them, if the Pythian oracle[2] consents, as demi-gods, but if not, as in any case blessed and divine.

You are a real sculptor, Socrates; these statues of our rulers are faultless in their beauty.

Yes, Glaucon, and of our ruling women too, for don't suppose that what I have been saying applies just to men and not to women, i.e. the ones endowed with similar natures.

Right you are, he said, since we arranged for the women to share in all things just the same as the men.

So, I said, would you agree that what we have said about the state and its government is not a mere dream, and though difficult is not impossible, but possible only in the way we suggested; which is to say, only when true philosophers, one or more of them come to rule while despising the honours of the present world which they deem petty and worthless, but esteeming above all what is right and the honour that springs from doing what is right, and regarding justice as the greatest and most necessary of all things, and in whose service and maintenance they will reorganize their own city?

How will they go about all this?

They will start by sending all those more than ten years old out into the country. They will take possession of the children and see that they are unaffected by the ways of their parents. They will bring these children up in their own ways and laws, i.e. the laws which we have given them. In this way the state and the government we were speaking about will be realized and happiness obtained, and the country which has a constitution like that will profit the most.

Yes, that will be the best way. And I think, Socrates, that you have described very well how, if ever, such a constitution might come into being.

---

1   A post-mortem paradise reserved for heroes and the virtuous.
2   I.e., the oracle at the temple of Apollo at Delphi.

Enough, then, of this sort of city, and of the person who is its analogue. There is no problem in describing such a person.

No problem at all, he replied; and I agree with you that nothing more need be said.

FOR DISCUSSION:

Do you think we can ever get beyond reliance on childhood training when it comes to our convictions about what is right and wrong, fine and disgraceful? If, yes, how does that happen?

B.5.h: *REPUBLIC* VIII

544c-569c[1]

Plato's ideal state is not immune to the forces of change and decay. Here Plato has Socrates describe its descent through a ranked series of other forms of government, each inferior to the one preceding. At each stage Socrates also draws us a picture of the kind of individual human character that is analogous to the inferior form of political arrangements, endorsing the idea that it is the predominance of such kinds of individuals that perpetrates the process of political degradation. At the same time he places much blame for the rise of such individuals on the inferior kind of education which the state and the older generation provide.

At the beginning Socrates asserts that besides the form of government he and his companions have created for the ideal state, and which is called "aristocracy", there are four other forms: "timocracy" (rule by those seeking honour), oligarchy (rule by the wealthy few), democracy (rule by the mass of people), and tyranny (rule by one man who enslaves everyone else). The first question then is how aristocracy deteriorates into timocracy.[2]

[*Glaucon*:] I am very eager to hear what are the four forms of [defective] government you referred to.

[*Socrates*:] There is no difficulty about that. They all have familiar names.

---

1 Translated by Jowett, with modifications.
2 These names are confusingly used by different authors with different definitions. 'Timocracy' as used by Plato refers to a state in which the rulers' dominant motive is honour; but Aristotle means by that word a state in which the extent of one's political power depends on the amount of property one owns. (The Greek word for 'honour' or 'worth' is '*timē*'.) Also the term 'oligarchy', although literally meaning 'rule by a few' is used by Plato and almost all the ancient authors to mean rule by the rich, who are assumed to be few.

219

First there is that of Crete and Sparta, which is generally admired. Next comes what is called oligarchy, and this meets with less approval and teems with evils. Then comes its antagonist, democracy; and finally there is tyranny, that great and glorious form, going beyond all the others as the fourth and worst disease of the state. I do not know, do you, of any other form of government which can be thought of as a distinct form. There are, of course, hereditary monarchies and states where kingship can be bought and sold, and some other intermediate forms; these can be found equally among Greeks and barbarians.

Yes, he replied, we certainly hear of many curious forms.

Do you know, I said, that governments vary in just the way human characters do, and that there must be as many of the one as of the other? We cannot suppose that states are made out of the proverbial "oak and rock"[1] rather than out of the predominant traits of the human characters which are in them and which, so to speak, tip the scale so that the rest follow.

Yes, he said, they could not come from any other source.

So, if the forms of government are five, then there will also be five types of human soul?

Certainly.

We have already described the type of person who corresponds to aristocracy, and whom we rightly call just and good.

We have.

So let us go on to describe the inferior types: there is the contentious and ambitious sort which corresponds to the Spartan form of government, and then there are the oligarchic, democratic, and tyrannical types. If we then place side by side the most just of these with the most unjust, we shall be able to compare the relative happiness or unhappiness of the life of pure justice compared with that of pure injustice. Then our inquiry will be complete, and we shall know whether we ought to pursue injustice as Thrasymachus advises or go along with the argument we have been developing and prefer justice.[2]

Certainly, he replied, we must do as you say.

Shall we follow our old plan of taking the state first, where things are clearer, and then go on to the individual? And shall we begin with the form of government dominated by a love of honour? I do not know what name to give it; perhaps 'timocracy' or 'timarchy'. We will go on to compare this with the corresponding human character, and, after that, go on to oligarchy and the

---

1   That is, from nature, not human nature. (Quotation from Homer.)
2   This sentence ties the discussion back to earlier parts of the *Republic*. See B.5.a and b.

oligarchic character, and then democracy and the democratic character, and finally tyranny and the tyrant's soul, so as to be able to decide the issue.

That sounds like a reasonable way to go about making a judgement.

First, then, I said, let's inquire how timocracy might arise out of aristocracy. Is it not a fact that revolution originates in dissension within the class of rulers; a united government, no matter how small, cannot be upset?

That's true, he said.

In what way, then, will dissension arise in our city and how will the two classes of auxiliaries and rulers come to be divided against each other and against themselves? Shall we, imitating Homer, pray the Muses to tell us "how discord first arose"? Shall we imagine them to mock us by talking to us in a lofty, tragic style, pretending to be serious while all the while having a joke?

How would they do that?

Something like this:

> A city so constituted is hard to shake, but, seeing that everything which comes to be also is destroyed, even a form of government such as yours will not last forever but will eventually be dissolved. And this is its dissolution: In plants that grow in the earth, as well as in animals that move on the surface of the earth, there are cycles of fertility and barrenness of soul and body, which are short in those that exist but for a short while and long in those that live long. But to attain the knowledge of human fecundity and barrenness all the wisdom and education of your rulers will not suffice; the laws that regulate these matters will not be discovered by reasoning combined with sense perception and will remain hidden from them so that they will bring children into the world when they ought not. Divine procreation has a period which is contained in a perfect number,[1] but the period for mortal procreation involves a number represented by a geometrical figure that determines when is the right or wrong time for births.[2] When your guardians make a mistake about this figure and unite brides and bridegrooms out of season, the offspring will not be well-endowed or fortunate. Even though only the best of them will be appointed by their predecessors, still they will be unworthy

---

1 Probably a number equal to the sum of the numbers which divide into it without remainder, such as 6 or 28. After Pythagoras, there is a strong tradition among the Greeks to see the structures of nature as constituted in terms of basic numerical relations.
2 There is in the Greek text a very obscure description of this number which has been omitted from this translation.

to take their fathers' places, and, when they come to power, they will soon pay insufficient care to us Muses, first by underrating music and then neglecting gymnastic. As a result the education of the young men in your state will suffer. In the succeeding generation rulers will be appointed who have lost the power of testing the metal of your different races, which, like Hesiod's, are of gold and silver and brass and iron. Iron will get mingled with silver, and brass with gold, and from this will arise dissimilarity and inequality and irregularity, which always and in all places are causes of dissension and war.

This is what the Muses affirm to be the origin of discord wherever it arises, and this is their answer to us.

Yes, and we can assume they have given us the right answer.

Of course, they have; they are the Muses, aren't they?

So what do they say next.

When discord arose, the two groups were drawn in different directions. The iron and brass fell to acquiring money and land and houses and gold and silver; but the gold and silver group, not wanting money but having true riches in their own natures, inclined toward virtue and the ancient order of things. There was contention between them, but at last they agreed to distribute their land and houses among individual owners; and then they enslaved their former friends and retainers, whom they had formerly protected as freemen, and made them subjects and servants, while they themselves engaged in warfare and keeping watch over them.

I think you have got it right about the origin of this change.

And the new form of government that has arisen this way will be intermediate between oligarchy and aristocracy?

Very true.

FOR DISCUSSION:

Socrates holds that community of property as against private holdings is a protection against discord. Is he right about that?

The "timocrats," if we may call them that, are men (are women still included?) who are ambitious for the honours and accolades that society bestows on its heroes. They achieve these chiefly through their prowess and success as warriors and so are constantly either at war or preparing for war. What Socrates is describing here is a military caste whose distorted education soon leads them to yearn after wealth as well, and so to accumulate private riches, in contrast to the spirit of the guardians in Plato's ideal city with their strict communism. Corresponding to the domination of the political order by the military is the domination of an individual's soul by the spirited element in it rather than the rational principle.

That is how the change will occur, but after that how will things proceed? Clearly the new state, being in between oligarchy and aristocracy, will follow one in some ways, the other in other ways, while also having some traits of its own.

True, he said.

In the honour given to rulers, in the abstinence of the warrior class from farming, handicrafts, and money-making generally, in the custom of common meals and in the attention paid to gymnastics and military training—in all these respects this state will resemble the former.

True.

On the other hand, it will have some characteristics peculiar to it. It will fear admitting really clever people to power, because the ones available are not simple, straightforward types but ones who are ambivalent. Consequently it turns to passionate and less complicated characters, by nature fitted for war rather than peace. Also it will set great value on military strategies and tricks, and be perpetually waging war.

Yes.

Yes, I said; and such people will be desirous of money, like the people who live in oligarchies; they will have a fierce secret longing for gold and silver, hiding them away in private storehouses and treasuries. They will also build walls around their houses, living in love-nests of their own where at great expense they can lavish their riches on their wives or anyone they please.

Most true, he said.

And they are miserly because they have no way of acquiring the money that they prize; on the other hand, they will be prodigal when it comes to spending someone else's money to gratify their own desires. They run away from the law, their father, because they have been educated not by persuasion but by compulsion, for they have neglected the Muse of philosophy and reason and honoured gymnastic more than music.

This form of government you describe is doubtless a mixture of good and evil.

Indeed, there is a mixture, I said; but one thing, and one only, predominates: the spirit of contention and ambition, and this is due to the prevalence of their passionate or spirited side.

Definitely.

Such is the origin and such the character of this state, which we have described in outline only, since a fuller account is not required for showing the most perfectly just and most perfectly unjust. To go through all the states and the characters of individuals without omitting anything would be an interminable labour.

Very true, he replied.

Now what sort of individual corresponds to this form of government? How did such people come into being and what are they like?

So far as contentiousness goes, said Adeimantus, this person would not be unlike our friend Glaucon here.

Perhaps, I said, he is like him in that one respect, but in other ways he is very different.

What ways are those?

He will be more assertive and less cultivated, although he is a lover of music and fond of listening to speeches though not himself a speaker. Such a person is apt to be rough on slaves, unlike educated people who merely disdain them. He will be courteous to freemen and very submissive to authority; he is a lover of power and a lover of honour, and claims to be a ruler not because he is eloquent, or anything like that, but because of his exploits in war or preparation for war. He also loves gymnastic exercises and hunting.

Yes, that seems to catch the spirit of that form of government.

Such a person will despise riches only when he is young, but as he ages he is more and more attracted to them, because there is something of the avaricious nature in him and his virtue is not pure and single-minded since its best guardian has been lost.

What guardian?

Reason, I said, tempered with music, which dwelling in a person is the only preserver of virtue throughout life.

Good, he said.

Such is the timocratic youth, and he is like the timocratic state.

Exactly.

His origin is as follows: He is often the young son of a brave father, who dwells in an ill-governed city, where he declines honours and offices and avoids law-suits and all that bother; rather he is willing to waive his rights in order to escape trouble.

How does the son develop?

Well, in the first place, he hears his mother complaining that her husband has no place among the rulers and consequently she has no status among other women. Further, when she sees her husband not caring much about money, and instead of battling and railing in the law courts or assembly just accepting quietly whatever happens to him, and when she notices that he is always absorbed in his thoughts, while showing her consideration but not all that much, she is annoyed, and tells her son that his father is only half a man and far too easy-going, and then adds in all the complaints about how ill-treated she is, which are so common among women.

Yes, said Adeimantus, such complaining is all too familiar.

And you know, I said, that the old servants, the ones who are loyal and friendly, from time to time talk privately to the son in the same vein. If they see anyone who owes his father money, or is wronging him in any way, while he fails to prosecute them, they tell the youth that when he grows up he must retaliate on people of this sort and be more a man than his father is. When the son goes out in public he hears and sees the same sort of thing: those who do their own business in the city are called simpletons and held in low repute, while busy-bodies are honoured and applauded. The result is that the young man, hearing and seeing all these things, hearing too the words of his father and having a nearer view of his life so he can make comparisons between him and others, is drawn in opposite directions. While his father is watering and nourishing the rational principle in his soul, the others are encouraging the spirited and appetitive; even though, then, he is not originally of a bad nature, but has just kept bad company, he is brought by these two influences to a compromise in which he turns over the government of his soul to the intermediate principle of ambition and spiritedness, and so becomes arrogant and ambitious.

You describe him and his origins perfectly.

So we have before us now, I said, the second form of government and the second type of character?

We have.

The next form of defective government is oligarchy, in which the few rich people rule for their own benefit over an impoverished multitude. In this society acquiring riches is the chief thing held in honour and anyone who isn't wealthy is disdained. The oligarchs enshrine their own rule by enforcing a strict property qualification on who can participate in the offices of government. The society becomes divided between the small governing class of rich men and the mass of the people, who fall into increasing poverty. This leads to the development of a criminal class—drones with stings, as Socrates calls them—and the rulers have to take care to repress these types by force.

Next, shall we look at another man, who, as Aeschylus might say, "is set over against another state", or rather keep to our plan of describing the state first?

By all means, the city first.

The next one in the series, I believe, is oligarchy.

And what sort of government do you mean by oligarchy?

A government based on a property qualification, where the rich have power and the poor cannot hold office.

I see.

Shouldn't I begin by describing how the timocracy gives way to oligarchy?

Yes.

Well, I said, even a blind person could see how this happens.

How?

The accumulation of gold in the treasuries of private individuals is the ruin of timocracy; they stretch the law in finding new ways of spending their money, for what do they or their wives care about the law?

Yes, indeed.

Each one seeing another grow rich seeks to rival him and thus the greater number of them become lovers of money.

Likely enough.

And as they grow richer and richer, the more they honour riches and the less they honour virtue. Can't we think of the opposition between wealth and virtue as though each lay on opposite sides of a balance?

True.

So to the extent that riches and rich men are honoured in a state to that extent virtue is dishonoured.

Clearly.

And what is honoured is cultivated, and what receives no honour is neglected?

That's obvious.

So, in the end, instead of loving victory and glory, men become lovers of money and profit; they honour and look up to the rich man and make him a ruler, and dishonour the poor person.

That is what they do.

They next proceed to make a law which fixes a sum of money as the qualification for the privilege of being in the ruling class; the sum is higher in one place and lower in another, depending on whether the oligarchy is more or less exclusive; and they allow no one whose property falls below the amount fixed to hold office. This measure is effected by armed force, if terrorism has not already done its work.

Very true.

And that, speaking generally, is how an oligarchy gets established.

Yes, he said; but what are the characteristics of this regime and what are the defects which we said it would have?

First of all, I said, consider this rule which forms its basis. Just think what would happen if pilots were chosen according to how much property they owned, and a poor man were refused permission to steer, even though he were a better pilot.

You mean that they would end up in a shipwreck?

Yes; and is not this true of the government of anything?

I would imagine so.

Except a city? Or would you include a city?

No, he said; it is especially the case with cities, for the rule of a city is the greatest and most difficult of all.

That, then, will be the first great defect of oligarchy?

Clearly.

And here is another defect, which is just as bad.

What is that?

The inevitable division: such a state is not one, but two states, the one of the poor, the other of the rich. They live on the same land and are always conspiring against one another.

By Zeus, that is not a lesser defect!

Another feature that discredits it is that, for the same reason, they are incapable of carrying on any war. Either they arm the masses, and then they are more afraid of them than they are of the enemy, or, if they do not call them out in the hour of battle, the oligarchs find themselves just as few when it comes to fighting as they are few in ruling. And at the same time their fondness of money makes them unwilling to pay the taxes needed.

How reprehensible!

And, as we said before, under this form of government the same persons combine too many occupations; they are farmers, businessmen, and soldiers all in one. Do you think that will work well?

Anything but.

There is still another evil, which is, perhaps, the greatest of all, and which first emerges as a possibility in this state.

What evil is that?

A person is allowed to sell all that he owns and another may acquire all his property; yet after the sale the person may continue to dwell in the city of which he is no longer a part, being neither a businessman, nor an artisan, nor a horseman, nor a foot-soldier, but only a poor, helpless creature.

Yes, that is an evil which first gets its start in this sort of state.

This evil is certainly not prevented there; oligarchies have both the extremes of great wealth and utter poverty.

But think again. In this pauper's earlier days, while he had money to spend, was he any good to the state in the ways I have mentioned? Or did he just seem to be a member of the ruling class, although in truth he was neither ruler nor subject, but just a consumer?

That's what he was. He seemed otherwise, but in fact he was just a spendthrift.

Can we not say that as a drone springs up in a hive, and is a pest in it, so he grows up a drone in his home, a pest to the state.

Just so, Socrates.

God has made the flying drones, Adeimantus, all without stings, while the flightless ones he has made some without stings but others with dreadful stings. In the stingless class we find those who in their old age end up as beggars; from the class with stings come what we call criminals.

Most true, he said.

Clearly, then, whenever you have beggars in a state you will find close by hidden away thieves, cut-purses, robbers of temples, and all sorts of villainous types.

Clearly.

Well, I said, do you not find beggars in oligarchical states?

Yes, he said; nearly everybody is a beggar who is not a ruler.

And shouldn't we assume, then, that there are also lots of criminals in them, rogues who have stings, and whom the authorities take care to put down by force?

A fair assumption.

The existence of such persons is to be attributed to poor education, ill-training, and a bad way of governing the state?

True.

Such, then, is the character and such are the evils that pertain to oligarchy, and there may be still further evils?

Very likely.

FOR DISCUSSION:

Are virtue and riches related as though on opposite sides of a balance so that when one increases the other decreases?

How do you imagine the few rich are able to enforce their rule on the multitude of poor?

Is the prevalence of criminals in society a sure sign that society is not governed well and its educational system is defective?

Turning to the individual personality that corresponds to the oligarchic form of government, Socrates describes a person who is concerned entirely with the amassing of wealth. In the terms set by the tripartite division of the soul, this means turning the rule over to the appetites and making both reason and spirit subservient to the part least deserving of rule. But within the appetites or cravings there are those which are necessary for any sort of life at all and those which demand mere luxuries. The oligarchic personality represses the latter because he sees that they are expensive to satisfy and will endanger his store of money. Among these expensive desires are those of the criminal drones, which the oligarchic type of person generally rejects but without any real awareness of why they are bad. The result is a person who appears very decent and respectable but in fact is kept from criminal conduct only by an obsession with amassing wealth.

So oligarchy, i.e. the form of government in which the rulers are selected on the basis of their wealth, may be dismissed. Let's now go on to consider the character and origin of the individual who corresponds to this state.

By all means.

Does not the timocratic youth turn into an oligarchic type in this way?

What way?

A time comes when the timocratic man has a son, who at first emulates his father and follows his example. But then suddenly he sees his father run afoul of the state and founder like a ship on a sunken reef; he is ruined and all his possessions lost. Perhaps he was a general or some other high office holder who has been brought into court by some informers and either put to death, or exiled, or deprived of his privileges as a citizen, and all his property taken from him.

Nothing more likely.

Once the son has seen and suffered all this, he is a ruined man, and the experience teaches him to throw out the ambition which once sat in the throne and ruled him. Humbled by poverty he takes to money-making and by petty miserliness and hard work he amasses a fortune. Is not such a person likely to place the money-loving spirit of appetite on the vacant throne and allow it to play the role of the Great King[1] within him, girt with tiara, golden chain, and scimitar.

Absolutely, he replied.

And when he has made reason and spirit sit down on the ground obediently on either side of their ruler, and taught them to know their place, he compels the one to think only of how lesser sums may be turned into larger ones, and will not allow the other to worship and admire anything but riches and rich men, or to be ambitious for anything so much as for the acquisition of wealth and the means of acquiring it.

No change, he said, is so speedy and so sure as this conversion of the ambitious youth into the avaricious one.

So this is the oligarchic youth?

Yes, he said; at any rate the individual from whom he evolved is like the state from which oligarchy came.

Let us see, then, whether there is any likeness between them.

Very good.

First, then, they are alike in the value they set on wealth?

Certainly.

Also the individual is given to thrift and hard work. He only satisfied his necessary desires, confining his expenditures to them; the other desires he represses, under the idea that they are unprofitable.

True.

He is a squalid fellow, who is always looking to turn a profit and add to his hoard—the sort of person who is much admired by ordinary people. Is he not a close likeness of the state he is analogous to?

He seems to me to be; at any rate both he and that state put great value on money.

He is clearly not one who has prized the cultivation of his mind, I said.

I don't imagine so, he said; had he been educated he would never have put a blind god[2] in charge of his chorus, or given him top honours.

Excellent! I said. Let's go further. Don't we have to admit that owing to this want of education we'll find in him the cravings of the drones, those whom we classified as either beggars or criminals, though his habitual self-control will keep them in check.

True.

---

1 The reference is to the king of Persia.
2 Ploutos, the god of wealth, was blinded by Zeus so that he would not favour the virtuous in his distributions.

Do you know where you will have to look if you want to uncover his criminal tendencies?

Where?

Look at him when he has some great opportunity to act dishonestly, as in the guardianship of an orphan.

Right.

It will be clear enough then that in his ordinary dealings, which give him a reputation for honesty, he represses his criminal desires and practices only a coerced moderation. He does not make himself see that these desires are wrong or tame them by reason; rather they are held down by fear because he trembles for his possessions.

To be sure.

Yes, by Zeus, my dear friend, you will discover that the desires of the drone are there all the time once he has other people's money to spend.

Yes, and they will be strong in him too.

This person, then, will be at war with himself; he will really be two persons, not one; but, in general, his better desires will be found to prevail over the worse.

True.

For these reasons this person will present a more respectable appearance than most, yet the true virtue of a soul in peace and harmony with itself will flee far away and never come near him.

I agree.

And surely this stingy person will not be much of a competitor for victory honours or other prizes in the city, for he is not prepared to spend his money on contests and competitions, so afraid is he of awakening his expensive cravings by inviting them to participate in the struggle. In true oligarchic fashion he fights with only a small part of his resources with the result that he loses the prize but saves his money.

Very true.

Can there be any doubt, then, that the miser and money-maker corresponds to the oligarchic state?

None at all.

FOR DISCUSSION:

What are the sources of an obsessive desire for wealth according to Plato? Do you think he adequately treats this topic?

Why does Plato think a person would do better in competitions if they enlisted the support of cravings for unnecessary things? Is he right about this?

The descent continues with the oligarchic regime giving way to a democracy. What the Greeks, and particularly the Athenians, understood by democracy is very unlike the sort of government we call democratic today. The ultimate governing body was the assembly of all the citizens and the various officers of the state were chosen from the body of citizens by lot, not by elections. So democracy did indeed mean government by the citizens and of the citizens, not government by elected representatives of the citizen body. Plato sees this form of government arising from the oligarchy's own concentration on increasing the wealth of the rulers while driving the general populace into poverty by enticing them into usurious loans. Eventually the poor see that they have the strength to overwhelm the pampered oligarchs and their associates by force, and so they set up a regime in which all citizens have equal rights and access to political power.

Next comes democracy; we have yet to consider its origin and nature, and then we will inquire into the ways of democratic type persons and bring them up for judgement.

That, he said, accords with our method.

Well, I said, how does the change from oligarchy to democracy come about? Isn't this the way of it? The good at which the oligarchic state aims is to become as rich as possible, a desire which is insatiable?

What then?

The rulers, aware that their power rests on their wealth, refuse to enact laws curtailing the extravagance of the spendthrift youths, because those rulers gain by the ruin that ensues. They hope to lend them money on their property and then buy up their estates and so increase their own wealth and importance.

To be sure.

There can be no doubt that the love of wealth and the spirit of moderation cannot exist together in citizens of the same city to any considerable extent; one or the other must be disregarded.

That's pretty clear.

And in oligarchic states the general spread of riotous living and extravagance often leads to men of good upbringing falling into utter poverty?

Yes, that often happens.

But these people still remain in the city, loaded with debt and even disenfranchised; they hate and conspire against those who have taken their property, and against the rest of society, and are eager for revolution.

How true.

On the other hand, the money-makers go about with their heads down intent on their business and seemingly unaware of the existence of these people. Instead, they insert their sting, their money, into someone else who is not on guard against them, and then by usury they multiply their funds while also multiplying the number of drones and paupers.

Yes, those people certainly do multiply.

When this evil bursts into flame, they will refuse to extinguish it either by passing a law which forbids a person squandering his own property, or by another remedy.

What other remedy?

The one which is next best and has the advantage of compelling citizens to pay attention to their virtue. Let there be a general law that everyone shall enter into voluntary contracts at their own risk; then there will be less of this scandalous pursuit of money and the evil we were speaking of would be a lot less.

Yes, it would be.

As it is, the rulers motivated in the way I have described treat their subjects badly. At the same time they and their associates, especially the young men of the ruling class, become accustomed to a life of luxury and idleness, avoiding any effort of either body or mind, and so become incapable of resisting either pleasure or pain.

Very true.

And don't they themselves in their habit of caring for nothing besides the pursuit of money become just as indifferent to virtue as are the poverty-stricken?

Yes, just as indifferent.

Given that is the condition into which they have fallen, what will happen when the rulers and subjects happen to come together, whether on a military march or as fellow-travellers by sea to some festival, and they observe one another's behaviour in a moment of danger? At that moment there is no likelihood that the rich will scorn the poor; on the contrary, the wiry, sunburnt poor man placed in battle beside a pampered wealthy one, panting from his exertions while carrying an undue burden of flesh, will hardly avoid drawing the conclusion that men like these are rich only because no one has the guts to take it away from them; and when the poor get together the word will go round that these men are good for nothing and ready for a fall.

Yes, he said, I know very well that that is the way they talk.

And, just as a body which is unhealthy will at the slightest external shock fall into illness, or even when there is no external cause fall into internal disorder, so also, whenever there is weakness in a state, it is likely to fall sick at the slightest occasion and go to war with itself as soon as one faction brings in oligarchic allies from outside and the other democratic ones. Sometime civil war will break out even without help from outside.

Quite true.

And so democracy arises once the poor have conquered their opponents, slaughtered some, banished others, while to those left they give an equal share in civil rights and government. In this form of government the magistrates are usually chosen by lot.

Yes, he said, that is how democracy gets established, whether the change has been brought about by force of arms, or fear has caused the opposing party to withdraw.

FOR DISCUSSION:

Are there ways Plato does not mention by which the oligarchs could perpetuate their power? How do the wealthy in our own society safeguard their access to political power?

H.L. MENCKEN, FROM "THE POLITICIAN":[1]

The truth, to the overwhelming majority of mankind, is indistinguishable from a headache.

Plato seems to think that freedom, meaning the absence of any external constraints on what one does or says, necessarily accompanies the equality which defines the democratic regime. Each person lives as pleases him or her, and, as a result, there is huge variety in the ways people conduct their lives. There is also a good deal of disregard of the law and tolerance for people convicted of crimes. Socrates' words drip with sarcasm as he describes the "charms" of the democratic regime.

And now what will this regime be like? What will be the way of life it supports? Clearly the way this state governs itself will show something about the democratic type of person.

---

1   Lecture, Columbia University, 4 January 1940. Collected in *Mencken Chrestomathy* (New York: Knopf, 1949).

Obviously, he said.

First of all the people are free. Doesn't the city resound with freedom and free speech? And isn't everybody allowed to do just as they please?

That's the way it is, he replied.

Given this freedom, isn't the individual able to arrange for himself his own life just as he pleases?

Clearly.

So in this kind of state there will be the greatest variety of types of people? There will.

This, then, seems likely to be the fairest of states, being like an embroidered robe which is spangled with every sort of flower. And just as women and children think a variety of colours to be what is most delightful of all, so to many men this sort of state, spangled with the manners and characters of all mankind, may well appear the fairest regime of all.

Yes.

In fact, there will be no better place in which to look for forms of government.

Why is that?

Because of the freedom which reigns there—they have an example of every sort of constitution. He who intends to establish a state, in the way we have been doing, ought to go to a democracy as to a bazaar where they sell them and pick out the one which suits him best. Having made his choice, he can then found his state.

He will find plenty to choose from.

There won't be any necessity, I said, for you to govern in this state, even if you have the competence, or to be governed, unless that's what you like, or to go to war when the rest do, or be at peace when the rest are, unless that's what suits you. That some law forbids your holding office or being a juror does not at all prevent you from doing so, if the fancy strikes you. Surely a most pleasant way of life, for the moment.

For the moment, perhaps.

And is not the leniency shown to condemned criminals in some case really quite charming? Have you not noticed how, in a democracy, many persons, even though they have been sentenced to death or exile, just stay put where they are and walk around in public, parading like a hero, and nobody sees or cares?

Many times.

Note too the permissive spirit of democracy, its superiority to petty considerations and its disregard for all the fine principles we solemnly laid down at the foundation of the city, as, for example, when we said that, except in the cases of rarely gifted natures, no one will ever turn out to be a good man who has not from his childhood been used to playing with beautiful things and pursuing what is fine and good. How grandly does democracy trample all these fine ideas under her feet, exhibiting utter indifference to the way a person has previously conducted himself before entering public office and promoting to honour anyone who claims to be the people's friend.

A magnificent spirit, indeed.

These and other features are distinctive of democracy and make it a charming form of government, full of variety and disorder, and dispensing equality to equals and unequals alike.

We know her well.

FOR DISCUSSION:

Do the egalitarian political arrangements of Greek democracy inevitably lead to the freedom Socrates describes, and even to a sort of anarchy?

In our own notion of the term "democracy," is freedom, or at least some freedoms, an essential element?

After giving us an explanation of the distinction between necessary and unnecessary desires and pleasures, Socrates pictures the "democratic" man as differing from his oligarchic father by allowing the unnecessary desires and pleasures equal space in his life with the necessary, whereas the old oligarch concentrated all his efforts on the latter. The "drones", which we have seen to be a potent class of idlers in the oligarchic state, encourage the growth of profligacy in the youth, and the war between his desire for the self-indulgent life and his lingering respect for the values of his parent bring on a turmoil which ends only when he decides to give preference to neither sort of pleasure but just take whatever ones offer themselves up. Consequently his soul lacks all discipline and becomes, like the state it corresponds to, a site where a chaotic variety of forms of governance may be observed.

Now consider the individual character. Or shall we start by saying how he comes into existence, as we did in the case of the state?

Yes.

Isn't this how it goes? He is the son of a stingy, oligarchic father, who has trained him in his own habits.

Exactly.

And, like his father, he deprives himself by force of the pleasures which accompany spending money rather than getting it, those which are called unnecessary?

Obviously.

Shall we, in order to be absolutely clear, define which are the necessary and which are the unnecessary pleasures?

Please do.

Are not the necessary pleasures those we cannot get rid of and also those whose enjoyment is a benefit to us? It is right to call them necessary, because we are made by nature to desire both what is beneficial and what is necessary, and we cannot help it.

True.

So we were not wrong to call them "necessary"?

No.

On the other hand, those that we can get rid of if we take pains from youth up to do so, and which bring us no benefit, even in some cases bring harm, isn't it right to call all these "unnecessary"?

Yes, certainly.

Let's pick an example of each kind so we can get at the general idea of them.

Very good.

Will not the desire to eat, that is to eat simple, plain food of the sort required for health and strength, be in the necessary class?

That seems right.

The desire to eat bread is necessary in two ways: it does us good and it is essential to the continuance of life?

Yes.

But the desire for meat is necessary only in so far as it is good for health?

Certainly.

But the desires which go beyond this, for other varieties of food, or other luxuries, ones that could be got rid of with proper training in youth, and are harmful to the body, as well as to the soul in its pursuit of wisdom and virtue, these are rightly called unnecessary?

Very true.

Can't we say that these desires are wasteful, while the others are profitable since they help a person with their work?

Certainly.

And the same holds for the sexual desires, and all the others?

Yes.

And the men we referred to as drones, weren't they the type who are just buzzing with unnecessary pleasures and desires, and are enslaved to them, while he who is governed by the necessary ones alone was the stingy and oligarchic type?

Very true.

Now let's see how the democratic type grows out of the oligarchic. This I suspect is the usual way it goes.

How's that?

When a young man who has been brought up in the way we were just now describing, i.e. in an uncultured and miserly way, has tasted the drones' honey and come to associate with fierce and crafty types who are able to indulge him in all sorts of refinements and varieties of pleasure, then, as you can well imagine, the oligarchic form of governance within his soul will start changing into the democratic?

Inevitably.

Just as in the city revolution was brought about by a party within the state calling on allies without who were of like mind, so the young man is changed by desires from without coming to the assistance of kindred desires within his soul?

Certainly.

Then, if there is an ally that aids the oligarchic principle within him, perhaps a father or some other kin who advise and rebuke him, there arises in his soul opposing factions and he comes to be at war with himself.

That must happen.

Sometimes, I suppose, the democratic principle gives way to the oligarchic, and some of his desires are extinguished, others banished, and a sense of shame gains ground in his soul and order is restored.

Yes, sometimes that happens.

Then again, sometimes, after the old desires have been driven out, fresh ones spring up, akin to the old ones; and, because his father knows nothing of education, they are allowed to increase in strength and number.

Yes, he said, that is often the way it is.

These new desires draw him back to his old associates, whom he meets with secretly, and a whole new brood of desires is hatched.

Very true.

In the end they seize the very citadel of the young man's soul, finding it empty of all studies, fine pursuits and true discourse, which are the best watchmen and sentinels in the souls of people who are dear to the gods.

There are none better.

False and boastful conceits and words charge forward and take their place.

They are certain to do so.

And so the young man returns to the land of the lotus-eaters[1] and openly takes up residence there. If any help be sent by his kin to the oligarchic side of him, those boastful conceits shut the gates against them. No embassy is allowed to enter the castle's keep, nor will they receive or listen to the fatherly counsel of older persons. In the ensuing battle they win the day, and so modesty, which they call naïveté, they drive away in dishonour. Moderation becomes unmanly weakness and is trampled in the muck and cast out. Frugality and restrained living they treat as boorish stinginess, and so by the help of a rabble of harmful appetites they drive all else outside the borders.

They certainly do.

And when they have emptied and swept clear the soul of this man who is now in their power and whom they are initiating into great mysteries, the next thing is to bring in a procession[2] of insolence, anarchy, waste, and impudence, all in bright array with garlands on their heads and accompanied by a crowd hymning their praises and calling them sweet names: insolence they call breeding, anarchy liberty, waste magnificence, and impudence courage. And so the young man departs from his original character, that was trained in the school of necessity, into the freedom and libertinism of useless and unnecessary pleasures.

Yes, he said, it's easy to see those changes.

After this he lives on, spending his money, efforts and time on unnecessary pleasures just as much as on the necessary ones; but, if he is lucky enough not to be too disordered in his mind, when he grows older the turmoil will subside, and then he may re-admit some part of the exiled virtues and expel some of their successors, so that he balances his pleasures and lives in a sort of equilibrium, allowing himself to be governed by whichever pleasure happens to come up first and, when tired of that, on to another; he despises none of them, but encourages them all equally.

Very true, he said.

But he doesn't allow into the citadel any true word of advice. If anyone says to him that some pleasures come from satisfying good and fine desires, while

---

1 A reference to the story in the *Odyssey*, ix 94-97, of a land where people eat the fruit of the lotus, which makes them drugged, lazy, and forgetful of everything, never wanting to leave.
2 Plato is here likening what happens in the young man's soul to the evening procession of images and worshippers that was part of the celebration of the Eleusinian mysteries.

others base desires, and that he ought to honour and enjoy the former while restraining and subduing the latter, whenever he hears this he just shakes his head and says that they are all alike, and that one is just as good as another.

Yes, he said, that's what he does.

Yes, I said, he lives from day to day indulging the desire of the moment: one day he is into drinking and listening to the flute; the next he is a water-drinker and goes on a diet to lose weight; then he takes a turn at gymnastics, only to lapse into idleness and lethargy; or perhaps the life of a philosopher appeals to him, but more often he is busy with politics, getting to his feet and saying and doing anything whatsoever that comes into his head; and if he is admiring of someone who is a warrior, off he goes in that direction, or if of business men, then in that. There is no law or order to his life, and this sort of undisciplined existence he terms joy, bliss, freedom, and so he continues on.

Yes, he said, that's a perfect description of the person who insists on equality.

Yes, I said, his life is full of variety, just as the democratic state was a spangled epitome of all types of constitutions. Many men and women look to him for their model, since he contains within himself all sorts of forms of governance and qualities.

Exactly.

So, let him correspond to democracy; he may truly be called the democratic man.

That's the way to categorize him.

FOR DISCUSSION:

What do we mean by 'natural' if we say that the necessary desires and pleasures are natural and the unnecessary ones unnatural?

Do you think that Plato is arguing for complete abstinence from the unnecessary pleasures? If not, what is he arguing for?

Is the pleasure of philosophizing an unnecessary one? What would Plato say?

SIGMUND FREUD, FROM *INTRODUCTORY LECTURES ON PSYCHOANALYSIS*:[1]

We believe that civilization has been created under the pressure of the exigencies of life at the cost of satisfaction of the instincts; and we believe that civilization is to a large extent being constantly created

---

1   Translated by James Strachey in the edition published by W.W. Norton & Co., New York, 1965.

anew, since each individual who makes a fresh entry into human society repeats this sacrifice of instinctual satisfaction for the benefit of the whole community. Among the instinctual forces which are put to this use, the sexual impulses play an important part; in this process they are sublimated—that is to say, they are diverted from the sexual aims and directed to others that are socially higher and no longer sexual. But this arrangement is unstable; the sexual instincts are imperfectly tamed, and in the case of every individual who is supposed to join in the work of civilization, there is a risk that his sexual instincts may refuse to be put to that use.

━━━━━━━━━━━━━━━━━━━━━━━━━━━━━━━━━━━━━━━

When Socrates comes to describe the decline of democracy into tyranny, it is once again the "drones" who instigate the transition. In a democracy they become dominant politically and take advantage of their power to plunder the rich while keeping the goodwill of the populace by redistributing land and wealth. Eventually the wealthy class tries to reassert itself, but then they are charged with being oligarchs and wanting to destroy the democracy. The mass of the people are alarmed and agree to make one of the more ruthless drones their protector. Conflict ensues. The rich plot revolution and assassination. The "protector" demands a bodyguard, and with the mob behind him kills or exiles his opponents. Having tasted the power over life and death he now wields, he turns into a full-fledged tyrant.

> Last of all comes the finest of all, whether we are talking of a form of government or an individual man, tyranny and the tyrant.
>
> Of course.
>
> Come now, my friend, tell me how tyranny arises. It's pretty clear that it is an outgrowth of democracy.
>
> Clearly.
>
> Does it, then, in a sense, arise out of democracy in the same way that democracy arose from oligarchy?
>
> How's that?
>
> Was not the good and chief aim of oligarchy the acquisition of wealth?
>
> Yes.
>
> And this insatiable desire after wealth to the neglect of all other things for the sake of money-making was also the ruin of oligarchy?
>
> True.

And is not the passion of democracy for what it defines as the criterion of the good what leads to its downfall too?

What criterion is that?

Freedom, I replied. This they tell you in a democracy is the grandest possession of the state, the one which makes it the only fit place for a person with a free spirit to live.

Yes, that's what everyone says.

I was about to note that this insatiable desire for this one good and the neglect of everything else is what leads to revolution and brings on a demand for tyranny.

How so?

Why, when a democracy is thirsting for freedom but has bad wine stewards presiding over the feast and has consequently drunk too deeply of the undiluted wine of freedom, then, unless the rulers have been utterly unstinting in their provision of this freedom, she calls them to account and punishes them, saying that they are cursed oligarchs.

Yes, he replied, that's a common occurrence.

People who obey the rulers are reviled as slaves and men of no merit; democracy would have subjects who are like rulers and rulers who are like subjects; these are the people whom she praises and honours both in public and in private. Now, in such a state can freedom have any limit?

Certainly not.

By degrees anarchy finds its way into the private homes and ends up infecting even the animals.

What do you mean?

I mean the father falls into the habit of behaving like the child, and the child like the father, showing no respect for either parent and considering this to be freedom. The foreign resident is on equal footing with the citizen and the citizen with the foreign resident, while the complete stranger is as good as either.

Yes, he said, that is the way it goes.

And these are not the only evils. There are several lesser ones: In a society like this the teacher fears and flatters his students, and the students despise their masters and tutors; young and old copy each other, the young competing with the old in speeches and actions while the old, fearing to be thought disagreeable tyrants, descend to a youthful level of gaiety and joking.

How true, he said.

The ultimate in public liberty is reached when slaves, whether male or female, who have been purchased are just as free as the person who bought them. And I almost forgot to mention the spirit of freedom and equality that is found in the relation between the sexes.

Well, to quote Aeschylus, we might as well "utter the word which rises to our lips."

I'll do just that. I have to add that no one who hasn't seen it would believe how much greater is the freedom the domestic animals have in a democracy as compared with any other state. Truly the bitches confirm the proverb "like mistress, like dog", and the horses and donkeys have a way of marching along with all the rights and dignities of freemen; they will run into anybody who gets in their way, if he does not leave the road clear for them. Freedom is truly bursting out all over.

I have memories of just such things. They are what I experience often when I take a walk out into the country.

The result of all these things put together is that the citizens become hypersensitive and resent even the least hint of authority; in the end, as you know, they will have no one over them and come to disregard the laws, written or unwritten.

Yes, I know that all too well.

Such, my friend, I said, is the fair and lively root out of which springs tyranny.

Lively it certainly is! But what comes next?

Ruin. The same fault which destroyed oligarchy, when intensified by liberty overwhelms democracy. The truth is that an excess in anything usually brings on a reaction in the opposite direction; this holds not just in the weather or in plants and animals but especially in political regimes.

True.

An excess of freedom, whether in states or in individuals, seems to pass over into slavery.

Yes, that's likely.

And so tyranny naturally arises out of democracy, and the most extreme form of tyranny and slavery out of the most extreme form of freedom?

As we might expect.

That, however, was not I believe your question. Rather what you wanted to know is what the disorder is which occurs in both oligarchy and democracy and is the ruin of both?

That's right, he replied.

I have in mind that class of idle spendthrifts, of whom the bolder are the leaders and the more timid just follow along. These are the ones we compared to drones, some of whom are stingless but others equipped with stings.

A good comparison.

These two classes are plagues in every city where they occur, being what phlegm and bile[1] are to the body. The good physician and the good lawgiver in a state should, like a wise beekeeper, keep them at a distance and prevent, if possible, their ever getting in. But if they do somehow find a way in, then they and their cells should be cut out as quickly as possible.

Yes, by all means.

Now, to see more clearly what we are about let's imagine democracy to be divided, as in fact it is, into three classes. In the first place, freedom creates many more drones in the democratic state than there were in the oligarchic.

That's true.

And in the democracy they become much more powerful.

How so?

Because in the oligarchy they are disqualified and driven from office, and so they stay weak from lack of exercise. But in a democracy they become almost completely dominant; the keenest among them make speeches and take actions, while the others buzz around the rostrum preventing any opposition from getting in a word. The result is that in democracies almost everything is managed by the drones.

Very true, he said.

Then there is another class which is constantly being set apart from the mass of people.

What class is that?

They are the disciplined class, which usually becomes the richest.

That's to be expected.

Here is an abundant source of honey which the drones can squeeze out of these people.

Certainly very little will be squeezed out of those who have little.

These people are called "the rich", and they become a pasture for the drones.

That is pretty much what happens, he said.

The third class will be the "people" and consists of those who patiently cultivate what little property they have; they are not interested in politics, but when assembled they form the largest and most powerful class in a democracy.

True, he said; but then the populace is seldom willing to come together unless they get a little share of the honey.

---

1   Two of the four bodily "humours" whose imbalance was thought to result in disease. An excess of phlegm was associated with sluggish apathy; an excess of bile with anger and irritability.

And don't they get a share? I said. Don't their leaders deprive the rich of their estates and distribute them among the people, while all along making sure that the larger portion is reserved for themselves?

Yes, he said, they do get a share to that extent.

And so those whose property is plundered this way are compelled to defend themselves with speeches before the Assembly and whatever actions they can take?

What else can they do?

And then, although they have no real desire for a revolution, others charge them with plotting against the people and being reactionary oligarchs.

True.

Finally, when they see that the people, not intentionally but through ignorance induced by deceptive slanderers, are out to do them wrong, they are then forced to become real oligarchs. They would rather not be, but the evil results from being tormented by the stings of the drones.

Exactly.

Then come impeachments, judgements and trials, in which each party arraigns the other.

True.

The people always find some champion to protect their interests, and they nurse him into greatness.

Yes, that's what they do.

This and nothing else is the root from which a tyrant springs; he first sprouts up as a protector.

Yes, that is clear.

How then does a protector change into a tyrant? Clearly when he does what the man is said to do in the legend of the shrine of Lycaean Zeus in Arcadia.

What legend?

The story is that he who has tasted the flesh of a single human victim minced up with that of other sacrificial victims is destined to become a wolf. Did you never hear it?

Oh yes.

It describes the people's protector. With the mob fully backing him, he feels free to shed the blood of kinsmen; with that favourite method of false accusation he brings them into court and so murders them, blotting out a person's life and with unholy tongue and lips tasting the blood of his fellow citizen. Some he kills, others he banishes, while all the while hinting at abolishing debts and redistributing estates. After this, what will be his destiny? Must he not either perish at the hands of his enemies, or turn from being a human being into a wolf, in other words, a tyrant?

Inevitably.

This, I said, is the person who organizes the faction that opposes the rich?

He is.

If, after a while, he is driven out, but then comes back despite the opposition, he will be a full grown tyrant.

That is clear.

If the opposition cannot get him expelled or condemned to death by publicly accusing him, they conspire to assassinate him.

That's the way it usually goes.

Then comes the well-known request for a bodyguard, the device of all those who have got this far in their tyrannical career; "Don't let the people's friend," they say, "fall victim to them."

Exactly.

The people readily agree; in their alarm over his fate they don't have any fear for themselves.

Very true.

At this point any rich man who is accused of being an enemy of the people had better heed the words of the oracle said to Croesus:

Flee—flee along the pebbled beach of Hermus;

Stay not, nor be ashamed to be a coward.

If he doesn't, he won't have any second chance to be ashamed.

So if he's caught he dies.

Of course.

And this protector of whom we spoke is to be seen not, like Hector's charioteer,[1] "measuring his towering length in dust" but rather himself overthrowing many and standing up in the chariot of the state with the reins in his hand, no longer a protector, but now an absolute tyrant.

No doubt, he said.

FOR DISCUSSION:

Do you think Plato puts too much emphasis on the democratic origins of tyranny? Could not tyranny just as well arise directly out of oligarchy?

The tyrant's precarious hold on power forces him into increasingly unpopular measures such as wars, and he can subdue his opposition only by murder and other outrages until he has cleaned out all the decent people

---

1   *Iliad*, xvi, 776.

who might dare to challenge his rule. In the end he relies on a military force composed mostly of foreigners and former slaves to keep in subjection the citizens of the city. Plato is obviously speaking from his own observations of the course tyrants had taken in some of the cities of Greece in his own time. It is a grim picture, but not one utterly unfamiliar to us today.

Now let us consider the happiness of the man and also of the state in which such a creature has come to exist.

Yes, let's go on to that.

At first, in the early days of his power, he is all smiles and greets everyone he meets. No tyrant he; rather he makes all sorts of generous promises in both public and private. He cancels debts, distributes land to the people and his followers; in general he assumes a mild and gracious air towards everybody.

Of course, he said.

But once he has disposed of foreign enemies either by conquest or by treaties so that there is nothing to fear from them, then he is always stirring up some war or other in order that the people may feel the need for a leader.

To be sure.

And doesn't he have another aim in mind? He wants the people to be impoverished by taxes and so forced to devote their time to meeting their basic wants and so less likely to conspire against him?

Clearly.

And if he suspects any of them of having ideas about freedom and of resisting his authority, he will have a good excuse to destroy them by putting them at the mercy of the enemy; for all these reasons the tyrant must always be provoking wars.

He must.

Now he begins to lose popularity.

It's inevitable.

Then some of those who joined in setting him up and still have some influence speak their mind to him and to each other; the bravest will criticize him to his face.

Yes, that can be expected.

Now the tyrant, if he is to continue in power, must get rid of them, and the purge must continue until there is not a person of worth who remains as either his friend or foe.

It must.

Consequently he must look around him and see who is brave, who high-minded, who wise, and who wealthy. This happy man must be the enemy of them all, whether he wants to or not, until he has purged them all from the state.

Yes, he said; and what a purgation that is!

Yes, I said, not the sort of purgation physicians do to the body, for they take away the worse and leave the better; he does the reverse.

If he wants to keep ruling, that, I suppose, is what he has to do.

What a happy situation for him! He is compelled either to dwell only with lots of bad people and to be hated by them, or not to live at all!

Yes, that's the choice he has.

And the more detestable his actions are to the citizens, the more he will have to recruit trustworthy men for his bodyguard?

Certainly.

And who would they be, and where will he procure them?

They will flock to him, he said, of their own accord as long as he pays them enough.

By the dog! I said; here come more drones, all sorts of them and from foreign lands.

Yes, those are the ones I had in mind.

But how about the locals? Would he not raid the domestic market?

How do you mean?

He will rob the citizens of their slaves, set them free, and enrol them in his bodyguard.

Right, of course, he said; they will be the most trustworthy of all.

What a wonderfully happy creature, I said, this tyrant must be. Having put to death his other supporters, he now has these for his trusted friends.

Yes, he said, these will be the ones he treats as his own.

Yes, I said, and these are the new citizens he has called into existence, who admire him and are his companions, while good people hate and avoid him.

Of course.

Well, then, it is not for nothing that tragedy is deemed wise and Euripides a great tragic poet.

Why is that?

Because it is he who wrote this perceptive line: "Tyrants are wise by their converse with the wise." He clearly meant to say that the people we have just been describing as associates of the tyrant are wise.

Yes, he said, and he also praises tyranny as godlike. He and the other poets say lots of things of this sort.

So, I said, the tragic poets, being wise men, will forgive us and any others who fashion states like ours if we do not allow them into our state on the grounds that they eulogize tyranny.

Yes, he said, those with any sense will no doubt forgive us.

But they will continue to make the rounds of other cities and attract mobs and hire actors with powerful, beautiful and persuasive voices, who will draw those cities toward tyranny or democracy.

True enough.

Moreover, they get paid for this and are celebrated. The greatest honour they receive is from tyrants, as we would expect, and the next greatest from democracies. But the higher they ascend the scale of constitutions the more their reputation suffers and seems from shortness of breath unable to proceed any further.

True.

But we digress. Let's return now and inquire how the tyrant will maintain that fair and numerous and variegated and ever-changing bodyguard of his.

If, he said, there are sacred treasures in the city, he will confiscate and spend them as long as they last, and then there is the property of those he has ruined, and with this he will be able to refrain from the taxes which he otherwise would have been forced to levy on the people.

And when those sources fail?

Well, clearly, he said, he will have to support his drinking companions and mistresses on what he can take from his father's estate.

You mean to say that the very people who gave him existence will maintain him and his comrades?

Inevitably.

But what if the people become outraged and say a grown-up son ought not to rely on his father for support, but rather should be supporting his father? His parents did not bring him into the world, or set him up in life, in order that when the son became an adult they should be the slaves of their own slaves and should support him and his rabble of slaves and minions; rather the son should be protecting them so that by his help they might be liberated from rule by the rich and the aristocrats, as they are called. So they tell him and his companions to leave, just as any parents would drive out of the house a riotous son and his gang of undesirables.

By heaven, he said, then those parents will find out what a monster they have been fostering in their bosom; when they want to drive him out they will find that they are weak and he is strong.

Why, do you mean to say that the tyrant will resort to violence? Even beat his own father if he opposes him?

Yes, he will, once he has disarmed him.

Then he is a parricide, and a cruel guardian of an aged parent. Make no mistake about it, this is real tyranny. As the saying goes, the people who are trying to escape the smoke which is slavery to freemen have now fallen into the fire which is tyranny under slaves. Thus freedom, breaking all the bonds of order and reason turns into the harshest and bitterest form of slavery.

True, he said.

Very well. May we not rightly say that we have sufficiently discussed what tyranny is like and how the transition from democracy to tyranny occurs?

Yes, we've said quite enough about that.

B.5.i: *LAWS* V

742c-744a[1]

T he *Laws* was quite possibly the last of Plato's works and has been left unfinished. It is a second attempt by him at describing a utopian state, but, in contrast to the utopia of the *Republic*, the one in the *Laws* strives to be much more practically attainable. Also, whereas in the *Republic* much emphasis is placed on developing ideal rulers, here in the *Laws* great weight is placed on proper legislation. The short excerpt below states what the proper aim of legislation is. There are three characters in the dialogue: Cleinias, a Cretan; Megillus, a Spartan; and an unnamed Athenian. It is the last who presents Plato's ideas and who is speaking here.

The best way to appreciate that these are the best policies for a state to follow is to examine them in the light of the fundamental aim. Now we maintain that the aim of a statesman who knows what he's about is not in fact the one which most people say the good legislator should have. They'd say that if he knows what he's doing his laws should make the state as huge and as rich as possible; he should give the citizens gold mines and silver mines, and enable them to control as many people as possible by land and sea. And they'd add, too, that to be a satisfactory legislator he must want to see the state as good and as happy as possible. But some of these demands are practical politics, and some are not, and the legislator will confine himself to what can be done, without bothering his head with wishful thinking about impossibilities. I mean, it's pretty well inevitable that happiness and virtue should come hand in hand (and this is the situation the legislator will want to see), but virtue and great wealth are quite incompatible, at any rate great wealth as generally understood (most people

---

1 Translated by Saunders, pp. 212-14.

would think of the extreme case of a millionaire, who will, of course, be a rogue into the bargain). In view of all this, I'll never concede to them that the rich man can become really happy without being virtuous as well: to be extremely virtuous and exceptionally rich at the same time is absolutely out of the question. "Why?" it may be asked. "Because," we will reply, "the profit from using just *and* unjust methods is more than twice as much as that from just methods alone, and a man who refuses to spend his money either honestly or dishonestly spends only half the sum laid out by honest people who are prepared to spend on honest purposes too. So anyone who follows the opposite policy[1] will never become richer that the man who gets twice as much profit from half the expenditure. The former is a good man; the latter is not actually a rogue so long as he uses his money sparingly, but on some occasions he is an absolute villain; thus, as we said, he is *never* good. Ill-gotten and well-gotten gains plus expenditure that is neither just nor unjust, when a man is also sparing with his money, add up to wealth; the absolute rogue, who is generally a spendthrift, is quite impoverished. The man who spends his money for honest ends and uses only just methods to come by it, will not easily become particularly rich or particularly poor. Our thesis is therefore correct: the very rich are not good; and if they are not good, they are not happy either."

The whole point of our legislation was to allow the citizens to live supremely happy lives in the greatest possible mutual friendship. However, they will never be friends if injuries and lawsuits arise among them on a grand scale, but only if they are trivial and rare. That is why we maintain that neither gold nor silver should exist in the state, and there should not be much money made out of menial trades and charging interest, nor from prostitutes; the citizens' wealth should be limited to the products of farming, and even here a man should not be able to make so much that he can't help forgetting the real reason why money was invented (I mean for the care of the soul and body, which without physical and cultural education respectively will never develop into anything worth mentioning). That's what has made us say more than once that the pursuit of money should come last in the scale of value. Every man directs his efforts to three things in all, and if his efforts are directed with a correct sense of priorities he will give money the third and lowest place, and his soul the highest, with his body coming somewhere between the two. In particular, if this scale of values prevails in the society we're now describing, then it has been equipped with a good code of laws. But if any of the laws subsequently passed is found giving pride of place to health in the state rather than the virtue of moderation, or to wealth rather

---

1   I.e., of spending on good objects and confining his receipts to those obtainable by honest methods.

than health and habits of restraint, then quite obviously its priorities will be wrong. So the legislator must repeatedly try to get this sort of thing straight in his own mind by asking "What do I want to achieve?" and "Am I achieving it, or am I off target?" If he does that, perhaps he'll complete his legislation by his own efforts and leave nothing to be done by others. There's no other way he could possibly succeed.

FOR DISCUSSION:

Is Plato right here in thinking that to have a good state the citizens should live in mutual friendship? Is he right that an emphasis on securing wealth among the citizens will undermine that friendship?

B.6: ARISTOTLE

ristotle was born in the town of Stagira in northern Greece in 384 BCE, the son of a physician who sometimes served in that capacity in the Macedonian court. At the age of 17 Aristotle went to Athens and joined the Academy where he studied under Plato for 20 years until the master's death in 348. During that time Aristotle is known to have written dialogues defending Plato's philosophy, but, once Plato was gone and it was clear that Plato's nephew Speusippus would take over the school, Aristotle left and settled in Assos and then Lesbos on the coast of Asia Minor. It was probably there that he engaged in empirical research in zoology and allowed his ideas to float free of the Platonic framework in directions more favorable to empirical science.

Around 342 he is said to have been invited by Philip, then king of Macedon, to come to Pella, the capital of Macedon, and tutor his son, the young Alexander. After winning the battle of Chaironeia in 338, Philip proceeded to subdue the Greek city states, and it must have been with Macedonian support that Aristotle was brought back to Athens and encouraged to establish his own school there, the Lyceum. Since the earlier dialogues he wrote have not survived except in a few fragments, it is the work he produced in the Lyceum on which his reputation now rests. This consists of treatises rather than dialogues, and some of it seems to be more lecture notes than finished work. Strange to say, this material itself was lost for a time, and people in the second century BCE and early first seem to have known Aristotle entirely from his earlier dialogues. But the treatises were recovered in the first century, brought to Rome and edited by Andronicus of Rhodes, who is responsible for the arrangement of the material and some of the titles. In this way the ideas of the mature Aristotle were recovered and became the basis for a revival of the Aristotelian school as something clearly distinct from Platonism.

Philip was assassinated in 337, bringing Alexander to the throne, who then embarked on his campaigns of conquest in the East. In 323 Alexander died, and Athens rebelled against Macedonian rule. This seems to have forced Aristotle to flee, and he died the next year in Euboea, although the Macedonians soon restored their control over the city from which he had fled. The Lyceum continued under the direction of Aristotle's student Theophrastus.

Aristotle's inquiries into the governance of societies is much more empirically oriented than Plato's. Aristotle's school collected the constitutions of many Greek states and the histories of their development. What Aristotle finds is that the conflict between rich and poor is present just about everywhere and threatens the survival of any form of governance. Although he sees that in actuality the most frequent ways of governing are "deviant", i.e., really not genuine constitutions at all, since they operate for the good of the rulers rather than the good of the whole society, he spends much time on analyzing what maintains and what undermines such governments. He is also keenly aware that proposals for reform of constitutional arrangements must be suitable for the condition of the state and the people living in it. Aristotle's approach is to start from where things are, but with an eye to what is better.

Another prominent feature of Aristotle's theory is the naturalness of the "*polis*", i.e., the city-state. Human beings naturally tend toward this sort of social arrangement, he says, because the good life for humans in all its fullness is achievable only in that size and sort of society. This doctrine ties his discussion of politics back to his work, the *Nicomachean Ethics*, where it is laid out in a general way what the good life (= happiness, *eudaimonia*) is. Aristotle's view is very different from theories, not unknown to him, in which the state exists for some much more limited end, such as peaceful co-existence. What is more, on his view, part of the good life just *is* political activity, i.e., taking part in the ruling of the *polis*. A person may benefit in other ways from just living within the realm of a state, but political activity in a just state is a major way of living the good life.

B.6.a: SELECTIONS FROM THE *NICOMACHEAN ETHICS*

Below are some matters treated in the *Ethics* which are important for discussions that occur in the *Politics*. That such passages exist is hardly surprising, given that Aristotle barely distinguishes the two inquiries, and the *Ethics* is treated as an introductory preamble to the study of the political art.

(1) BK.V, CH.7[1]

Justice is, of course, crucial for communities. Here Aristotle makes his own distinction between "natural justice" and "legal justice". Note that Aristotle's concept of the former allows that it is variable. Just what might he mean by that?

Of political justice part is natural, part legal: natural, that which everywhere has the same force and does not exist by people's thinking this or that; legal, that which is originally indifferent, but when it has been laid down is not indifferent, e.g., that a prisoner's ransom shall be a mina, or that a goat and not two sheep shall be sacrificed, and again all the laws that are passed for particular cases, e.g., that sacrifice shall be made in honour of Brasidas,[2] and the provisions of decrees. Now some think that all justice is of this sort, because that which is by nature is unchangeable and has everywhere the same force (as fire burns both here and in Persia), while they see change in the things recognized as just. This, however, is not true in this unqualified way, but is true in a sense; or rather, with the gods it is perhaps not true at all, while with us there is something that is just even by nature, yet all of it is changeable; but still some is by

---

1 Translated by Ross.
2 A famous Spartan general who during the war with Athens fell defending the city of Amphibolis. Afterwards, every year the city had games and sacrifices in his honour.

nature, some not by nature. It is evident which sort of thing, among things capable of being otherwise, is by nature, and which is not but is legal and conventional, assuming that both are equally changeable. And in all other things the same distinction will apply; by nature the right hand is stronger, yet it is possible that all men should come to be ambidextrous. The things which are just by virtue of convention and expediency are like measures; for wine and corn measures are not everywhere equal, but larger in wholesale and smaller in retail markets. Similarly, the things which are just not by nature but by human enactment are not everywhere the same, since constitutions also are not the same, though there is but one which is everywhere by nature the best.

(2) Bκ.VIII, chs.9-11[1]

Where there is some form of justice it becomes possible to have a corresponding form of friendship. Aristotle insists on the importance of friendship for bonding people into communities; justice is not the whole of what is needed. The possibilities for both justice and friendship are affected by the type of governance that exists in a society; there are more possibilities in the non-corrupt forms of government, viz., monarchy, aristocracy, and timocracy (which Aristotle also calls "polity"[2]) and less in the deviant forms, viz., tyranny, oligarchy and democracy.

9. Friendship and justice seem, as we have said at the outset of our discussion, to be concerned with the same objects and exhibited between the same persons. For in every community there is thought to be some form of justice, and friendship too; at least men address as friends their fellow voyagers and fellow soldiers, and so too those associated with them in any other kind of community. And the extent of their association is the extent of their friendship, as it is the extent to which justice exists between them. And the proverb 'what friends have is common property'[3] expresses the truth; for friendship depends on community.[4]

Now brothers and comrades have all things in common, but the others to whom we have referred have definite things in common—some more things, others fewer; for of friendships, too, some are more and others less truly friendships. And the claims of justice differ too; the duties of parents to children, and those of brothers to each

1 Translated by Ross.
2 Also in Greek called 'politeia'. Hence the term has two meanings, the narrow one mentioned here and a broader one covering all forms of government.
3 In Greek 'koina'.
4 In Greek 'koinōnia', derived from 'koinōneō' meaning to share.

other are not the same, nor those of comrades and those of fellow citizens, and so, too, with the other kinds of friendship. There is a difference, therefore, also between the acts that are unjust towards each of these classes of associates, and the injustice increases by being exhibited towards those who are friends in a fuller sense; e.g., it is a more terrible thing to defraud a comrade than a fellow citizen, more terrible not to help a brother than a stranger, and more terrible to wound a father than anyone else. And the demands of justice also seem to increase with the intensity of the friendship, which implies that friendship and justice exist between the same persons and have an equal extension.

Now all forms of community are like parts of the political community; for men journey together with a view to some particular advantage, and to provide something that they need for the purposes of life; and it is for the sake of advantage that the political community too seems both to have come together originally and to endure, for this is what legislators aim at, and they call just that which is to the common advantage. Now the other communities aim at advantage bit by bit, e.g., sailors at what is advantageous on a voyage with a view to making money or something of the kind, fellow-soldiers at what is advantageous in war, whether it is wealth or victory or the taking of a city that they seek, and members of tribes and demes[1] act similarly (Some communities seem to arise for the sake or pleasure, viz. religious guilds and social clubs; for these exist respectively for the sake of offering sacrifice and of companionship. But all these seem to fall under the political community; for it aims not at present advantage but at what is advantageous for life as a whole),[2] offering sacrifices and arranging gatherings for the purpose, and assigning honours to the gods, and providing pleasant relaxations for themselves. For the ancient sacrifices and gatherings seem to take place after the harvest as a sort of first fruits, because it was at these seasons that people had most leisure. All the communities, then, seem to be parts of the political community; and the particular kinds friendship will correspond to the particular kinds of community.

10. There are three kinds of constitution, and an equal number of deviation-forms—perversions, as it were, of them. The constitutions are monarchy, aristocracy, and thirdly that which is based on a property qualification,[3] which it seems appropriate to call timocratic,[4] though most people are wont to call it polity. The best of these is monarchy, the worst timocracy. The deviation from monarchy is tyranny; for both

---

1   A deme was a unit of local government in ancient Attica.
2   The bracketed sentences seem to be an interpolation from some alternative version of the text.
3   In Greek a property assessment was called a '*timēma*'.
4   In Greek '*timokratikē*', from the same root as '*timēma*'.

are forms of one-man rule, but there is the greatest difference between them; the tyrant looks to his own advantage, the king to that of his subjects. For a man is not a king unless he is sufficient to himself and excels his subjects in all good things; and such a man needs nothing further; therefore he will not look to his own interests but to those of his subjects; for a king who is not like that would be a mere titular king. Now tyranny is the very contrary of this; the tyrant pursues his own good. And it is clearer in the case of tyranny that it is the worst deviation-form; but it is the contrary of the best that is worst. Monarchy passes over into tyranny; for tyranny is the evil form of one-man rule and the bad king becomes a tyrant. Aristocracy passes over into oligarchy by the badness of the rulers, who distribute contrary to equity what belongs to the city—all or most of the good things to themselves, and office always to the same people, paying most regard to wealth; thus the rulers are few[1] and are bad men instead of the most worthy. Timocracy passes over into democracy; for these are coterminous, since it is the ideal even of timocracy to be the rule of the majority, and all who have the property qualification count as equal. Democracy is the least bad of the deviations; for in its case the form of constitution is but a slight deviation. These then are the changes to which constitutions are most subject; for these are the smallest and easiest transitions.

One may find resemblances to the constitutions and, as it were, patterns of them even in households. For the association of a father with his sons bears the form of monarchy, since the father cares for his children; and this is why Homer calls Zeus 'father'; it is the ideal of monarchy to be paternal rule. But among the Persians the rule of the father is tyrannical; they use their sons as slaves. Tyrannical too is the rule of a master over slaves; for it is the advantage of the master that is brought about in it. Now this seems to be a correct form of government, but the Persian type is perverted; for the modes of rule appropriate to different relations are diverse. The association of man and wife seems to be aristocratic; for the man rules in accordance with his worth, and in those matters in which a man should rule, but the matters that befit a woman he hands over to her. If the man rules in everything the relation passes over into oligarchy; for in doing so he is not acting in accordance with their respective worth, and not ruling in virtue of his superiority. Sometimes, however, women rule, because they are heiresses; so their rule is not in virtue of excellence but due to wealth and power, as in oligarchies. The association of brothers is like timocracy; for they are equal, except in so far as they differ in age; hence if they differ much in age, the friendship is no longer of the fraternal type. Democracy is found chiefly in masterless dwellings (for here every one is on an equality), and in those in which the ruler is weak

---

1   In Greek 'oligoi', hence 'oligarchy'.

and every one has licence to do as he pleases.

11. Each of the constitutions may be seen to involve friendship just in so far as it involves justice. The friendship between a king and his subjects depends on an excess of benefits conferred; for he confers benefits on his subjects if being a good man he cares for them with a view to their well-being, as a shepherd does for his sheep (whence Homer called Agamemnon[1] 'shepherd of the peoples'). Such too is the friendship of a father, though this exceeds the other in the greatness of the benefits conferred; for he is responsible for the existence of his children, which is thought the greatest good, and for their nurture and upbringing.

These things are ascribed to ancestors as well. Further, by nature a father tends to rule over his sons, ancestors over descendants, a king over his subjects. These friendships imply superiority of one party over the other, which is why ancestors are honoured. The justice therefore that exists between persons so related is not the same on both sides but is in every case proportioned to merit; for that is true of the friendship as well. The friendship of man and wife, again, is the same that is found in an aristocracy; for it is in accordance with virtue the better gets more of what is good, and each gets what befits him; and so, too, with the justice in these relations. The friendship of brothers is like that of comrades; for they are equal and of like age, and such persons are for the most part like in their feelings and their character. Like this, too, is the friendship appropriate to timocratic government; for in such a constitution the ideal is for the citizens to be equal and fair; therefore rule is taken in turn, and on equal terms; and the friendship appropriate here will correspond.

But in the deviation-forms, as justice hardly exists, so too does friendship. It exists least in the worst form; in tyranny there is little or no friendship. For where there is nothing common to ruler and ruled, there is not friendship either, since there is not justice; e.g., between craftsman and tool, soul and body, master and slave; the latter in each case is benefited by that which uses it, but there is no friendship nor justice towards lifeless things. But neither is there friendship towards a horse or an ox, nor to a slave qua[2] slave. For there is nothing common to the two parties; the slave is a living tool and the tool a lifeless slave. Qua slave then, one cannot be friends with him. But qua man one can; for there seems to be some justice between any man and any other who can share in a system of law or be a party to an agreement; therefore there can also be friendship with him in so far as he is a man. Therefore while in tyrannies friendship and justice hardly exist, in democracies they exist more fully; for where the citizens are equal they have much in common.

---

1 The leader of the Greek expedition to Troy.
2 = *considered just insofar as he is a.*

(3) Bk.X, ch.9[1]

The following chapter is the last in the *Nicomachean Ethics* and clearly serves as an introduction to Aristotle's treatise *Politics*. In it Aristotle defends legislation as a way of improving people, given the fact that most human beings have not been well brought-up and must be forced into correct behaviour. Legislation also deals with the nurture of the youth and the occupations assigned to people so that by habituation they are brought to some measure of excellence. He defends as well the need for a political art, an expertise which involves knowledge of general truths (universals), if legislation is to be done well, while also acknowledging the importance of experience and knowledge of particular cases. Finally, he announces that the inquiry to follow will study a variety of actual constitutions and societies in order to arrive at whatever general conclusions are possible, and to give advice that is suited to the peculiarities of different communities. Aristotle and his school are known to have collected a large number of such constitutions and amassed quite a wealth of data on the history, laws and customs of the Greek city states.

If these matters and the virtues, and also friendship and pleasure, have been dealt with sufficiently in outline, are we to suppose that our programme has reached its end? Surely, as the saying goes, where there are things to be done the end is not to survey and recognize the various things, but rather to do them; with regard to virtue, then, it is not enough to know, but we must try to have and use it, or try any other way there may be of becoming good. Now if arguments were in themselves enough to make men good, they would justly, as Theognis[2] says, have won very great rewards, and such rewards should have been provided; but as things are, while they seem to have power to encourage and stimulate the generous-minded among our youth, and to make a character which is gently born, and a true lover of what is noble, ready to be possessed by virtue, they are not able to encourage the many to nobility and goodness. For these do not by nature obey the sense of shame, but only fear, and do not abstain from bad acts because of their baseness but through fear of punishment; living by passion they pursue their own pleasures and the means to them, and the opposite pains, and have not even a conception of what is noble and truly pleasant, since they have never tasted it. What argument would remould such people? It is hard, if not impossible, to remove by argument the traits that have long since been incorporated

---

1   Translated by Ross.
2   Theognis of Megara, a poet of the sixth century BCE.

in the character; and perhaps we must be content if, when all the influences by which we are thought to become good are present, we get some tincture of virtue.

Now some think that we are made good by nature, others by habituation, others by teaching. Nature's part evidently does not depend on us, but as a result of some divine causes is present in those who are truly fortunate; while argument and teaching, we may suspect, are not powerful with all men, but the soul of the student must first have been cultivated by means of habits for noble joy and noble hatred, like earth which is to nourish the seed. For he who lives as passion directs will not hear argument that dissuades him, nor understand it if he does; and how can we persuade one in such a state to change his ways? And in general passion seems to yield not to argument but to force. The character, then, must somehow be there already with a kinship to virtue, loving what is noble and hating what is base.

But it is difficult to get from youth up a right training for virtue if one has not been brought up under right laws; for to live temperately and hardily is not pleasant to most people, especially when they are young. For this reason their nurture and oc-cupations should be fixed by law; for they will not be painful when they have become customary. But it is surely not enough that when they are young they should get the right nurture and attention; since they must, even when they are grown up, practise and be habituated to them, we shall need laws for this as well, and generally speaking to cover the whole of life; for most people obey necessity rather than argument, and punishments rather than the sense of what is noble.

This is why some think that legislators ought to stimulate men to virtue and urge them forward by the motive of the noble, on the assumption that those who have been well advanced by the formation of habits will attend to such influences; and that punishments and penalties should be imposed on those who disobey and are of inferior nature, while the incurably bad should be completely banished. A good man (they think), since he lives with his mind fixed on what is noble, will submit to argument, while a bad man, whose desire is for pleasure, is corrected by pain like a beast of burden. This is, too, why they say the pains inflicted should be those that are most opposed to the pleasures such men love.

However that may be, if (as we have said) the man who is to be good must be well trained and habituated, and go on to spend his time in worthy occupations and neither willingly nor unwillingly do bad actions, and if this can be brought about if men live in accordance with a sort of reason and right order, provided this has force,—if this be so, the paternal command indeed has not the required force or compulsive power (nor in general has the command of one man, unless he be a king or something similar), but the law has compulsive power, while it is at the same time a rule proceeding from a sort of practical wisdom and reason. And while people hate men who oppose their impulses, even if they oppose them rightly, the law in its ordaining of what is good is not burdensome.

In the Spartan state alone, or almost alone, the legislator seems to have paid attention to questions of nurture and occupations; in most states such matters have been neglected, and each man lives as he pleases, Cyclops-fashion, 'to his own wife and children dealing law'.[1] Now it is best that there should be a public and proper care for such matters; but if they are neglected by the community it would seem right for each man to help his children and friends towards virtue, and that they should have the power, or at least the will, to do this.

It would seem from what has been said that he can do this better if he makes himself capable of legislating. For public control is plainly effected by laws, and good control by good laws; whether written or unwritten would seem to make no difference, nor whether they are laws providing for the education of individuals or of groups—any more than it does in the case of music or gymnastics and other such pursuits. For as in cities laws and prevailing types of character have force, so in households do the injunctions and the habits of the father, and these have even more because of the tie of blood and the benefits he confers; for the children start with a natural affection and disposition to obey. Further, private education has an advantage over public, as private medical treatment has; for while in general rest and abstinence from food are good for a man in a fever, for a particular man they may not be; and a boxer presumably does not prescribe the same style of fighting to all his pupils. It would seem, then, that the detail is worked out with more precision if the control is private; for each person is more likely to get what suits his case.

But the details can be best looked after, one by one, by a doctor or gymnastic instructor or anyone else who has the general knowledge of what is good for every one or for people of a certain kind (for the sciences both are said to be, and are, concerned with what is universal); not but what some particular detail may perhaps be well looked after by an unscientific person, if he has studied accurately in the light of experience what happens in each case, just as some people seem to be their own best doctors, though they could give no help to anyone else. None the less, it will perhaps be agreed that if a man does wish to become master of an art or science he must go to the universal, and come to know it as well as possible; for, as we have said, it is with this that the sciences are concerned.

And surely he who wants to make men, whether many or few, better by his care must try to become capable of legislating, if it is through laws that we can become good. For to get anyone whatever—anyone who is put before us—into the right con-

---

1   *The Odyssey*, ix, 114.

dition is not for the first chance comer; if anyone can do it, it is the man who knows, just as in medicine and all other matters which give scope for care and prudence.

Must we not, then, next examine whence or how one can learn how to legislate? Is it, as in all other cases, from statesmen?[1] Certainly it was thought to be a part of statesmanship. Or is a difference apparent between statesmanship and the other sciences and arts? In the others the same people are found offering to teach the arts and practising them, e.g., doctors or painters; but while the sophists profess to teach politics, it is practised not by any of them but by the politicians, who would seem to do so by dint of a certain skill and experience rather than of thought; for they are not found either writing or speaking about such matters (though it were a nobler occupation perhaps than composing speeches for the law-courts and the assembly), nor again are they found to have made statesmen of their own sons or any other of their friends. But it was to be expected that they should if they could; for there is nothing better than such a skill that they could have left to their cities, or could prefer to have for themselves, or, therefore, for those dearest to them.[2] Still, experience seems to contribute not a little; else they could not have become politicians by familiarity with politics; and so it seems that those who aim at knowing about the art of politics need experience as well.

But those of the sophists who profess the art seem to be very far from teaching it. For, to put the matter generally, they do not even know what kind of thing it is nor what kinds of things it is about; otherwise they would not have classed it as identical with rhetoric or even inferior to it, nor have thought it easy to legislate by collecting the laws that are thought well of; they say it is possible to select the best laws, as though even the selection did not demand intelligence and as though right judgement were not the greatest thing, as in matters of music. For while people experienced in any department judge rightly the works produced in it, and understand by what means or how they are achieved, and what harmonizes with what, the inexperienced must be content if they do not fail to see whether the work has been well or ill made—as in the case of painting. Now laws are as it were the 'works' of the political art; how then can one learn from them to be a legislator, or judge which are best? Even medical men do not seem to be made by a study of textbooks. Yet people try, at any rate, to state not only the treatments, but also how particular classes of people can be cured and should be treated—distinguishing the various habits of body; but while this seems useful to experienced people, to the inexperienced it is valueless. Surely, then, while collections of laws, and of constitutions also, may be serviceable to those who can study them and judge what is good or bad and what enactments suit what circumstances, those who

1 The word in Greek is '*politikos*', i.e., a person skilled in directing a *polis*.
2 These remarks echo those of Socrates in the *Protagoras*.

go through such collections without a practised faculty will not have right judgement (unless it be as a spontaneous gift of nature), though they may perhaps become more intelligent in such matters.

Now our predecessors have left the subject of legislation to us unexamined; it is perhaps best, therefore, that we should ourselves study it, and in general study the question of the constitution, in order to complete to the best of our ability our philosophy of human nature. First, then, if anything has been said well in detail by earlier thinkers, let us try to review it; then in the light of the constitutions we have collected let us study what sorts of influence preserve and destroy states, and what sorts preserve or destroy the particular kinds of constitution, and to what causes it is due that some are well and others ill administered. When these have been studied we shall perhaps be more likely to see with a comprehensive view, which constitution is best, and how each must be ordered, and what laws and customs it must use, if it is to be at its best. Let us make a beginning of our discussion.

FOR DISCUSSION:

What is it of the political art that can be formally taught and what of it can only come with experience? Is Aristotle right in his view that the political art contains both components?

Is it possible to have a precise science of political affairs?

Is it a major purpose of legislation to make the citizens morally better than they would be without legislation? Can the laws educate people into moral virtue?

EDMUND BURKE, FROM *REFLECTIONS ON THE REVOLUTION IN FRANCE:*[1]

The science of constructing a commonwealth, or renovating it, or reforming it, is like every other experimental science, not to be taught a priori.[2] Nor is it a short experience that can instruct us in that practical science, because the real effects of moral causes are not always immediate; that which in the first instance is prejudicial may be excellent in its remoter operation, and its excellence may arise even from the ill effects it produces in the beginning.

---

1   Original publication: London, 1790. Now widely available in contemporary editions, including one edited by L.G. Mitchell (Oxford: Oxford UP, 1993).

2   = by reasoning from the supposed causes of what we observe, as opposed to trying to infer the causes from the observed phenomena.

B.6.b: *POLITICS* I

Chs. 1-6[1]

ommunities of humans differ in size, of course, but Aristotle does
not think that this is the only way they differ; rather there is also a
difference in the ends for which they exist as well. The *polis* or state
is a community whose end is "living well", not just survival (the end of the
family), and hence it is a community which is "self-sufficient" for human
well-being. Humans are "political animals" because what it is for them to
live well requires living in the kind of community which is a *polis*, and
thus the *polis* is natural for human beings. This does not mean that human
beings automatically organize themselves into states, or have always lived
in states, but where they are not so organized the need for the state is always
present simply because human well-being requires it.

1. We see that every state[2] is a community of some sort, and that every community is
established for the sake of some good (for everyone performs every action for the sake
of what he takes to be good). Clearly, then while every community aims at some good,
the community that has the most authority of all and encompasses all the others aims
highest, that is to say, at the good that has the most authority of all. This community
is the one called a state, the community that is political.

Those, then, who think that the positions of statesman,[3] king, household manager,
and master of slaves are the same, are not correct. For they hold that each of these
differs not in kind, but only in whether the subjects ruled are few or many; that if, for

---

1 Translated by Reeve, pp. 1-11, with some modifications.
2 In Greek '*polis*', meaning the sort of city-state exemplified by the Greek cities of Athens,
   Thebes, Corinth, etc.
3 In Greek '*politikos*', meaning someone skilled in directing the affairs of a *polis*.

example, someone rules few people, he is a master; if more, a household manager; if still more, he has the position of statesman or king, the assumption being that there is no difference between a large household and a small state. As for the positions of statesman and king, they say that someone who is in charge by himself has the position of king, whereas someone who follows the principles of the appropriate science, ruling and being ruled in turn, has the position of statesman. But these claims are not true. What I am saying will be clear, if we examine the matter according to the method of investigation that has guided us elsewhere. For, as in other cases, a composite has to be analyzed until we reach things that are incomposite, since these are the smallest parts of the whole, so if we also examine the parts that make up a state, we shall see better both how these differ from each other, and whether or not it is possible to gain some expertise in connection with each of the things we have mentioned.

2. If one were to see how these things develop naturally from the beginning, one would, in this case as in others, get the best view of them. First, then, those who cannot exist without each other necessarily form a couple, as female and male do for the sake of procreation (they do not do so from deliberate choice, but, like other animals and plants, because the urge to leave behind something of the same kind as themselves is natural), and as a natural ruler and what is naturally ruled do for the sake of survival. For if something is capable of rational foresight, it is a natural ruler and master, whereas whatever can use its body to labor is ruled and is a natural slave. That is why the same thing is beneficial for both master and slave.

There is a natural distinction, of course, between what is female and what is servile. For, unlike the blacksmiths who make the Delphian knife,[1] nature produces nothing skimpily, but instead makes a single thing for a single task, because every tool will be made best if it serves to perform one task rather than many. Among non-Greeks, however, a woman and a slave occupy the same position. The reason is that they do not have anything that naturally rules; rather their community consists of a male and a female slave. That is why our poets say "it is proper for Greeks to rule non-Greeks,"[2] implying that non-Greek and slave are in nature the same.

The first thing to emerge from these two communities is a household, so that Hesiod is right when he said in his poem, "First and foremost: a house, a wife, and an ox for the plow."[3] For an ox is a poor man's servant. The community naturally constituted to satisfy everyday needs, then, is the household; its members are called

---

1 A multi-purpose knife.
2 E.g., Euripides in *Iphigenia in Aulis*, 1266, 1400.
3 *Works and Days*, 405.

"meal sharers" by Charondas[1] and "manger sharers" by Epimenides the Cretan.[2] But the first community constituted out of several households for the sake of satisfying needs other than everyday ones is a village.

As a colony or offshoot from a household, a village seems to be particularly natural, consisting of what some have called "sharers of the same milk," sons and the sons of sons. That is why states were originally ruled by kings, as nations still are. For they were constituted out of people who were under kingships; for in every household the eldest rules as a king. And so the same holds in the offshoots, because the villagers are blood relatives. This is what Homer is describing when he says: "Each one lays down the law for his own wives and children."[3] For they were scattered about, and that is how people dwelt in the distant past. The reason all people say that the gods too are ruled by a king is that they themselves were ruled by kings in the distant past, and some still are. Human beings model the shapes of the gods on their own, and do the same to their way of life as well.

A complete community constituted out of several villages, once it reaches the limit of total self-sufficiency, practically speaking, is a state. It comes to be for the sake of living, but it remains in existence for the sake of living well. That is why every state exists by nature, since the first communities do. For the state is their end, and nature is an end; for we say that each thing's nature—for example, that of a human being, a horse, or a household—is the character it has when its coming-into-being has been completed. Moreover, that for the sake of which something exists, that is to say, its end, is best, and self-sufficiency is both end and best.

It is evident from these considerations, then, that a state is among the things that exist by nature, that a human being is by nature a political animal, and that anyone who is without a state, not by luck but by nature, is either a poor specimen or else superhuman. Like the one Homer condemns, he too is "clanless, lawless, and homeless."[4] For someone with such a nature is at the same time eager for war, like an isolated piece in a board game.[5]

It is also clear why a human being is more of a political animal than a bee or any other gregarious animal. Nature makes nothing pointlessly, as we say, and no animal has speech except a human being. An utterance is a signifier of what is pleasant or painful, which is why it is found existing among other animals (for their nature goes this far: they do not only perceive what is pleasant or painful but signify it to each other). But speech is for making clear what is beneficial or harmful, and hence also

---

1   A legislator of the sixth century BCE.
2   A poet and religious teacher of the sixth century BCE.
3   *Odyssey,* ix, 114-15.
4   *Iliad,* ix, 63-64.
5   The piece would be vulnerable and thus constantly in battle.

what is just or unjust. For it is peculiar to human beings, in comparison to the other animals, that they alone have perception of what is good or bad, just or unjust, and the rest. And it is community in these that makes a household and a state.

The state is also prior in nature to the household and to each of us individually, since the whole is necessarily prior to the part. For if the whole body is dead, there will no longer be a foot or a hand, except homonymously,[1] as one might speak of a stone "hand" (for a dead hand will be like that); rather everything is defined by its function and by its capacity, so that in such condition they should not be said to be the same things but homonymous ones. Hence that the state is natural and prior in nature to the individual is clear. For, if an individual is not self-sufficient when separated, he will be like all other parts in relation to the whole. Anyone who cannot form a community with others, or who does not need to because he is self-sufficient, is no part of a state; he is either a beast or a god. Hence, though an impulse toward this sort of community exists by nature in everyone, whoever first established one was responsible for the greatest of goods. For as a human being is the best of the animals when perfected, so when separated from law and justice he is worst of all. For injustice is harshest when it has weapons, and a human being grows up with weapons for virtue and practical wisdom to use, which are particularly open to being used for opposite purposes. Hence he is the most unrestrained and most savage of animals when he lacks virtue, as well as the worst where food and sex are concerned. But justice is a political matter; for justice is the organization of a political community, and justice decides what is just.

FOR DISCUSSION:

Is Aristotle saying that an individual separated from a state is a human being only in the way a dead hand is a hand? Why would he say that?

Aristotle knows that states are often formed by people getting together and drawing up a constitution. How would he square that with the claim that the state is natural for human beings?

THOMAS PAINE, FROM *COMMON SENSE*:[2]

Society is produced by our wants, and government by our wickedness; the former promotes our happiness positively by uniting our affections, the latter negatively by restraining our vices.

---

1   I.e., in different senses of the words 'foot' and 'hand' than they have when used of living parts.

2   Originally published as an anonymous pamphlet, Philadelphia, 1776. Widely available in contemporary editions, including one from Dover (New York: 1997).

Ch.3 announces that the inquiry undertaken here will have to examine the parts from which a state is composed, namely households. The household is based on three relationships: master to slave, husband to wife, and father to children; and corresponding to each of these will be some sort of "science", i.e., expertise, and these altogether with the art of "wealth acquisition" compose the art of household management. In those of the succeeding chapters given here the main topic is that first relationship, where the question of whether slavery can possibly be just, is taken up.

3. Since it is evident from what parts a city-state is constituted, we must first discuss household management, for every city-state is constituted from households. The parts of household management correspond in turn to the parts from which the household is constituted, and a complete household consists of slaves and free. But we must first examine each thing in terms of its smallest parts, and the primary and smallest parts of a household are master and slave, husband and wife, father and children. So we shall have to examine these three things to see what each of them is and what features it should have. The three in question are [1] mastership, [2] "marital" science (for we have no word to describe the union of woman and man), and [3] "procreative" science (this also lacks a name of its own). But there is also a part which some believe to be identical to household management, and others believe to be its largest part. We shall have to study its nature too. I am speaking of what is called *wealth acquisition*.

But let us first discuss master and slave, partly to see how they stand in relation to our need for necessities, but at the same time with an eye to knowledge about this topic, to see whether we can acquire some better ideas than those currently entertained. For, as we said at the beginning, some people believe that mastership is a sort of science, and that mastership, household management, statesmanship, and the science of kingship are all the same. But others believe that it is contrary to nature to be a master (for it is by law[1] that one person is a slave and another free, whereas by nature[2] there is no difference between them), which is why it is not just either; for it involves force.

In the next chapter Aristotle defines what a slave is, viz., the inanimate tool of the master. It is particularly interesting in view of modern robotics that Aristotle sees that there would be no need for slaves if there were tools that moved themselves and could take instructions from a human craftsman.

---

1 I.e., *nomōi*, which can mean mere convention.
2 I.e., *phusei*. We are dealing here with the contrast between what is natural and what is conventional, which is also found in Callicles' speech in selection **B.4.b**. A pupil of the sophist Gorgias, Alcidamas, is said to have claimed that "nature never made any man a slave".

4. Since property is part of the household, the science of property acquisition is also a part of household management (for we can neither live nor live well without the necessities). Hence, just as the specialized crafts must have their proper tools if they are going to perform their tasks, so too does the household manager. Some tools are inanimate, however, and some are animate. The ship captain's rudder, for example, is an inanimate tool, but his lookout is an animate one; for where crafts are concerned every assistant is classed as a tool. So a piece of property is a tool for maintaining life; property in general is the sum of such tools; a slave is a piece of animate property of a sort; and all assistants are like tools for using tools. For, if each tool could perform its task on command or by anticipating instructions, and if like the statues of Daedalus[1] or the tripods of Hephaestus[2]—which the poet describes as having "entered the assembly of the gods of their own accord"[3]—shuttles wove cloth by themselves, and picks played the lyre, a master craftsman would not need assistants, and masters would not need slaves.

What are commonly called tools are tools for production. A piece of property, on the other hand, is for *action*.[4] For something comes from a shuttle beyond the use of it, but from a piece of clothing or a bed we get only the use. Besides, since action and production differ in kind, and both need tools, their tools must differ in the same way as they do. Life consists in action, not production. Therefore, slaves too are assistants in the class of things having to do with action. Pieces of property are spoken of in the same way as parts. A part is not just a part of another thing, but is *entirely* that thing's. The same is also true of a piece of property. That is why a master is just his slave's master, not his unqualifiedly, while a slave is not just his master's slave, he is entirely his.

It is clear from these considerations what the nature and capacity of a slave are. For anyone who, despite being human, is by nature not his own but someone else's is a natural slave. And he is someone else's when, despite being human, he is a piece of property; and a piece of property is a tool for action that is separate from its owner.

FOR DISCUSSION:

If a person sells a certain amount of his labour time to an employer, does that make him a temporary "slave" of the employer, given Aristotle's understanding of what a slave is?

---

1   The legendary craftsman whose skill at producing lifelike statues eventually went to the point of making statues that moved themselves mechanically.
2   The Greek divinity in charge of fire and working with metals by fire.
3   *Iliad*, xviii, 376.
4   In Greek: *praxis*, which is intentionally undertaken activity. Here Aristotle uses the term narrowly so as to exclude "makings", which are undertaken to produce some physical object.

Aristotle next tackles the question of what would have to be the case for someone to be a "natural" slave. This leads to his distinguishing different sorts of rule. The sort of rule that mastership over a slave involves is so stringent that the conditions under which it could be natural turn out to be quite extreme.

5. But whether anyone is really like that by nature or not, and whether it is better or just for anyone to be a slave or not or whether all slavery is against nature—these are things we must investigate next. And it is not difficult either to determine the answer by argument or to learn it from actual events. For ruling and being ruled are not only necessary, they are also beneficial, and some things are distinguished right from birth, some suited to rule and others to being ruled. There are many kinds of rulers and ruled, and the better the ruled are, the better the rule over them always is; for example, rule over humans is better than rule over beasts. For a task performed by something better is a better task, and where one thing rules and another is ruled, they have a certain task. For whenever a number of constituents, whether continuous with one another or discontinuous, are combined into one common thing, a ruling element and a subject element appear. These are present in living things, because this is how nature as a whole works. (Some rule also exists in lifeless things: for example, that of a harmony. But an examination of that would perhaps take us too far afield.)

Soul and body are the basic constituents of an animal: the soul is the natural ruler; the body the natural subject. But of course one should examine what is natural in things whose condition is natural, not corrupted. One should therefore study the human being too whose soul and body are in the best possible condition; one in whom this is clear. For in depraved people, and those in a depraved condition, the body will often seem to rule the soul, because their condition is bad and unnatural.

At any rate, it is, as I say, in an animal that we can first observe both rule of a master and rule of a statesman. For the soul rules the body with the rule of a master, whereas understanding rules desire with the rule of a statesman or with the rule of a king. In these cases it is evident that it is natural and beneficial for the body to be ruled by the soul, and for the affective part to be ruled by understanding (the part that has reason), and that it would be harmful to everything if the reverse held, or if these elements were equal. The same applies in the case of human beings with respect to the other animals. For domestic animals are by nature better than wild ones, and it is better for all of them to be ruled by human beings, since this will secure their safety. Moreover, the relation of male to female is that of natural superior to natural inferior, and that of ruler to ruled. But, in fact, the same holds true of all human beings.

Therefore those people who are as different from others as body is from soul or beast from human, and people whose task, that is to say, the best thing to come from them, is to use their bodies are in this condition—those people are natural slaves. And it is better for them to be subject to this rule, since it is also better for the other things we mentioned. For he who can belong to someone else (and that is why he actually does belong to someone else), and he who shares in reason to the extent of understanding it, but does not have it himself (for the other animals obey not reason but feelings), is a natural slave. The difference in the use made of them is small, since both slaves and domestic animals help provide the necessities with their bodies.

Nature tends, then, to make the bodies of slaves and free people different too, the former strong enough to be used for necessities, the later useless for that sort of work, but upright in posture and possessing all the other qualities needed for political life—qualities divided into those needed for war and those for peace. But the opposite often happens as well: some have the bodies of free men; others the souls. This, at any rate, is evident: if people were born whose bodies alone were as excellent as those found in the statues of the gods, everyone would say that those who were substandard deserved to be their slaves. And if this is true of the body, it is even more justifiable to make such a distinction with regard to the soul; but the soul's beauty is not so easy to see as the body's.

It is evident, then, that there are some people, some of whom are naturally free, others naturally slaves, for whom slavery is both just and beneficial.

FOR DISCUSSION:

What could Aristotle mean by being able to understand reason, but not have it? Is anyone actually in this condition? Why would such a person benefit from being someone's slave?

Although Aristotle allows that there are cases like those just described, he holds that in many cases slavery occurs not by nature but by law (i.e., convention). In the next chapter Aristotle shows he is unconvinced that such cases are either beneficial or just to the parties concerned, except where they in fact bring into the master–slave relationship people who are in fact naturally so related. Aristotle must have been aware that the majority of cases of enslavement are of the sort backed only by convention, so rather than his position being a qualified endorsement of the practice, it in fact turns out to be a minimally qualified criticism of it.

6. But it is not difficult to see that those who make the opposite claim are also right, up to a point. For slaves and slavery are spoken of in two ways: for there are also

slaves—that is to say, people who are in a state of slavery—by *law*. The law is a sort of agreement by which what is conquered in war is said to belong to the victors. But many of those conversant with the law challenge the justice of this. They bring a writ of illegality against it, analogous to that brought against a speaker in the assembly.[1] Their supposition is that it is monstrous if someone is going to be the subject and slave to whatever has superior power and is able to subdue him by force. Some hold the latter view, others the former; and this is true even among the wise.

The reason for this dispute, and for the overlap in the arguments, is this: virtue, when it is equipped with resources, is in a way particularly adept in the use of force; and anything that conquers always does so because it is outstanding in *some* good quality. This makes it seem that force is not without virtue, and that only the justice of the matter is in dispute. For one side believes that justice is benevolence, whereas the other believes that it is precisely the rule of the more powerful that is just. At any event, when these accounts are disentangled, the other arguments have neither force nor anything else to persuade us that the one who is more virtuous should not rule or be master.

Then there are those who cleave exclusively, as they think, to justice of a sort (for law is justice of a sort), and maintain that enslavement in war is just. But at the same time they imply that it is not just. For it is possible for wars to be started unjustly, and no one would say that someone is a slave if he did not deserve to be one; otherwise, those regarded as the best born would be slaves or the children of slaves, if any of them were taken captive and sold. That is why indeed they are not willing to describe *them,* but only non-Greeks, as slaves. Yet in saying this, they are seeking precisely the natural slave we talked about in the beginning. For they have to say that some people are slaves everywhere, whereas others are slaves nowhere.

The same holds of noble birth. Nobles regard themselves as well born wherever they are, not only when they are among their own people, but they regard non-Greeks as well born only when they are at home. They imply a distinction between a good birth and freedom that is unqualified and one that is not unqualified. As Theodectes' Helen[2] says: "Sprung from divine roots on both sides, who would think that I deserve to be called a slave?" But when people say this, they are in fact distinguishing slavery from freedom, well born from low born, in terms of virtue and vice[3] alone. For they think that good people come from good people in just the way that human comes

---

1   A speaker who proposed something already against existent law could have such a writ passed against him.

2   Theodectes was a playwright who studied with Aristotle and evidently wrote a play in which Helen of Troy is a character.

3   I.e., in terms of excellences of character and defects of character.

from human, and beast from beast. But often, though nature does have a tendency to bring this about, it is nevertheless unable to do so.

It is clear, then, that the objection with which we began has something to be said for it, and that the one lot are not always natural slaves, nor the other naturally free. But it is also clear that in some cases there is such a distinction—cases where it is beneficial and just for the one to be master and the other to be slave, and where the one ought to be ruled and the other ought to exercise the rule that is natural for him (so that he is in fact a master), and where misrule harms them both. For the same thing is beneficial for both part and whole, body and soul; and a slave is a sort of part of his master—a sort of living but separate part of his body. Hence, there is a certain mutual benefit and mutual friendship for such masters and slaves as deserve to be by nature so related. When their relationship is not that way, however, but is based on law, and they have been subjected to force, the opposite holds.

FOR DISCUSSION:

Can you in fact think of any sort of case where it might be beneficial to both of two humans for one to be the master of the other? Can it be just and beneficial to both the dog and the dog's master for the dog to be the "slave" of the master? If yes, then why can't the same be true between two humans? If no, what mistake are most of us making who keep dogs for useful purposes?

B.6.c: *POLITICS* III

Chs. 6-13[1]

Aristotle recognizes that states can be organized in different ways. The organization of how the offices of the state are to be arranged and filled is a "constitution", and it is this that legislators, Aristotle holds, should be primarily concerned with. The most important constitutional question is that of who is to be given the ultimate authority, but in any event rule should be exercised for the benefit of the ruled, not the rulers, and any constitution which violates this principle must be considered "deviant". As we shall see, Aristotle is fully aware that deviant constitutions predominate among the Greek city-states as well as among foreign communities, and lawgivers must often work within such deviant frameworks.

6. Since these issues have been determined, the next thing to investigate is whether we should suppose that there is just one kind of constitution or several, and, if there are several, what they are, how many they are, and how they differ.

A constitution is an organization of a state's various offices but, particularly, of the one that has authority over everything. For the government has authority in every state, and the constitution is a government. I mean, for example, that in democratic states the people have authority, whereas in oligarchic ones, by contrast, the few have it, and we also say the constitutions of these are different. And we shall give the same account of the other constitutions as well.

First, then, we must set down what it is that a state is constituted for, and how many kinds of rule deal with human beings and communal life. In our first discussions, indeed, where conclusions were reached about household management and rule

---

1 Translated by Reeve, pp. 75-91, with some modifications.

by a master, it was also said that a human being is by nature a political animal. That is why, even when they do not need one another's help, people no less desire to live together, although it is also true that the common benefit brings them together to the extent that it contributes some part of living well to each. This above all is the end, then, whether of everyone in common or of each separately. But human beings also join together and maintain political communities for the sake of life by itself. For there is perhaps some share of what is noble in life alone, as long as it is not too overburdened with the hardships of life. In any case, it is clear that most human beings are willing to endure much hardship in order to cling to life, as if it had a sort of joy inherent in it and a natural sweetness.

But surely it is also easy to distinguish at least the kinds of rule people talk about, since we as well often discuss them in our own exoteric works.[1] For rule by a master, although in truth the same thing is beneficial for both natural masters and natural slaves, is nevertheless rule exercised for the sake of the master's own benefit, and only by happenstance for that of the slave. For rule by a master cannot be preserved if the slave is destroyed. But rule over children, wife, and the household generally, which we call household management, is either for the sake of the ruled or for the sake of something common to both. Essentially, it is for the sake of the ruled, as we see medicine, physical training, and the other arts to be, but by happenstance it might be for the sake of the rulers as well. For nothing prevents the trainer from sometimes being one of the athletes he is training, just as the captain of a ship is always one of the sailors. Thus a trainer or a captain looks to the good of those he rules, but, when he becomes one of them himself, he shares by happenstance in the benefit. For the captain is a sailor, and the trainer, though still a trainer, becomes one of the trained.

Hence, in the case of political office too, where it has been established on the basis of equality and similarity among the citizens, they think it right to take turns at ruling. In the past, as is natural, they thought it right to perform public service when their turn came, and then to have someone look to *their* good, just as they had earlier looked to his benefit when they were in office. Nowadays, however, because of the profits to be had from public funds and from office, people want to be in office continuously, as if they were sick and would be cured by being always in office, for it is perhaps in just that way that they seek office.

It is evident, then, that those constitutions that look to the common benefit turn out, according to what is unqualifiedly just, to be correct, whereas those which look only to the benefit of the rulers are mistaken and are deviations from the correct

---

1   = works meant for the general public, as opposed to 'esoteric' works like the current one, which amounts to a sophisticated treatise. It is known that Aristotle wrote exoteric works in dialogue form, but hardly anything of these survives.

constitutions. For they are like rule by a master, whereas a state is a community of free people.

Ch.7 presents Aristotle's basic classification of constitutions. Having distinguished between the "correct" ones, those in which rule is for the benefit of the ruled, and the "deviant" ones, those in which rule is for the benefit of the rulers, he then divides the correct ones roughly according to the number of those allowed to rule: where only one person rules (i.e., a monarchy) the constitution is a "kingship", where a few rule it is an "aristocracy", and where the mass of the people rule it is a "polity". The deviant constitutions are then obtained by imagining the corruption of each of the correct types; the corruption of kingship is tyranny, that of aristocracy is oligarchy, and that of polity is democracy.

7. Now that these matters have been determined, we must next investigate how many kinds of constitutions there are and what they are, starting first with the correct constitutions. For once they have been defined, the deviant ones will also be made evident.

Since constitution and government signify the same thing, and the government is the authoritative element in any state, and the authoritative element must be either one person, or few, or many, then whenever the one, the few, or the many rule for the common benefit, these constitutions must be correct. But if they aim at the private benefit, whether of the one or the few or the multitude, they are deviations (for either the participants should not be called citizens, or they should share in the benefits).

A monarchy that looks to the common benefit we customarily call a kingship; and rule by a few but more than one, an aristocracy (either because the best[1] people rule, or because they rule with a view to what is best for the state and those who share in it). But when the multitude governs for the common benefit, it is called by the name common to all constitutions, namely 'polity'.[2] Moreover, this happens reasonably. For, while it is possible for one or a few to be outstandingly virtuous, it is difficult for a larger number to be accomplished in every virtue, but it can be so in military virtue in particular. That is precisely why the class of defensive soldiers, the ones who possess the weapons, has the most authority in this constitution.

Deviations from these are tyranny from kingship, oligarchy from aristocracy, and

---

1   In Greek '*aristoi*'.
2   In Greek '*politeia*', which in another sense means constitution.

democracy from polity. For tyranny is rule by one person for the benefit of the monarch, oligarchy is for the benefit of the rich, and democracy is for the benefit of the poor. But none is for their common profit.

In fact the Greek city-states were most often either oligarchies or democracies, and Aristotle spends much effort making clear how these should be defined. Oligarchy is basically rule by the rich for the rich, and is rule by a few only because everywhere the rich are few in comparison with the poor. Democracy is rule by the poor for the poor, and is called rule by the people only because everywhere the majority of the people are poor. The reader should be aware that what Aristotle and the Greek thinkers in general mean by democracy is not what we mean. In a Greek democracy the citizens filled the offices either by taking turns or being chosen by lot. They were not elected, as they are in what we call a democracy. In other words, in a Greek democracy every citizen was directly involved in government at least for some portion of his life. (One should be aware too that women were not considered citizens and thus had no part in governing. Also, every Greek state had quite a number of slaves and foreigners residing in its borders, and these groups had no rights of citizenship either.)

8. We should say a little more about what each of these constitutions is. For certain problems arise, and when one is carrying out any investigation in a philosophical manner, and not merely with a practical purpose in view, it is appropriate not to overlook or omit anything, but to make the truth about each clear.

A tyranny, as we said, exists when a monarchy rules the political community like a master; in an oligarchy those in authority in the constitution are the ones who have property. A democracy is the opposite; those who do not possess much property, and are poor, are in authority. The first problem concerns this definition. Suppose that the majority were rich and had authority in the state; yet there is a democracy whenever the majority has authority. Similarly, to take the opposite case, suppose the poor were fewer in number than the rich, but were stronger and had authority in the constitution; yet when a small group has authority it is said to be an oligarchy. It would seem, then, that these constitutions have not been well defined. But even if one combines being few with being rich in one case, and being a majority with being poor in the other, and describes the constitutions accordingly (oligarchy as that in which the rich are few in number and hold the offices, and democracy as that in which the poor are many and hold them), another problem arises. For what are we to call the constitutions we just described, those where the rich are a majority and the poor a minority, but each has authority in its own constitution, given that there is indeed no further constitution besides those just mentioned?

What this argument seems to make clear is that it is by happenstance that the few have authority in oligarchies and the many in democracies, a result of the fact that everywhere the rich are few and the poor many. That is why, indeed, the reasons just mentioned are not the reasons for the differences. What does distinguish democracy and oligarchy from one another is poverty and wealth: whenever some, whether a minority or a majority, rule because of their wealth, the constitution is necessarily an oligarchy; and whenever the poor rule, it is necessarily a democracy. But it turns out, as we said, that the former are in fact few and the latter many. For only a few people are rich, but all share in freedom; and these are the reasons they both dispute over the constitution.

According to Aristotle the defenders of oligarchy and the defenders of democracy each claim that their respective arrangements are just, with the former talking about treating unequals (in wealth) unequally (which is just *for unequals*) and the latter about treating equals (in freedom) equally (which is just *for equals*), but none of this is just in an unqualified sense. One has to understand that a true state is not concerned merely with protecting property nor merely with living together, but rather with living *well*, and this means that it must be concerned with virtue. This leads Aristotle to distinguish sharply between a state and an alliance; the latter has limited goals compared to the goal of the state. Justice, then, in the unqualified sense deals with what is required for this larger goal of living well, i.e., with morally virtuous behaviour. The whole question of who should rule concerns, on this account, a mere part of that broader sort of justice.

What follows in the ensuing chapters is Aristotle's exploration of this question about who justly rules, and it is clear that he is not about to give a single answer that will work for all constitutions. The whole matter is complicated too by the possibility that rather than persons ruling it should be the laws that rule, but then that leads to the question of what laws are just, and this too cannot be determined apart from relation to a constitution.

9. The first thing one must grasp, however, is what people say the defining marks of oligarchy and democracy are, and what oligarchic and democratic justice are. For they all grasp justice of a sort, but they go only to a certain point and do not discuss the whole of what is just in the most basic sense. For example, justice seems to be equality, and it is, but not for everyone, only *for equals*. Justice also seems to be inequality, since

indeed it is, but not for everyone, only *for unequals*. They disregard the 'for whom', however, and judge badly. The reason is that the judgement concerns themselves, and most people are pretty poor judges about what is their own.

So since what is just is just *for certain people*, and consists in dividing things and people in the same way (as we said earlier in the *Ethics*), they agree about what constitutes equality in the thing but disagree about it in the people.[1] This is largely because of what was just mentioned, that they judge badly about what concerns themselves, but also because, since they are both speaking up to a point about justice of a sort, they think they are speaking about what is unqualifiedly just. For one lot thinks that if they are unequal in one respect (wealth, say) they are wholly unequal, whereas the other lot thinks that if they are equal in one respect (freedom, say) they are wholly equal. But about the most basic considerations they do not speak.

For suppose people constituted a community and came together for the sake of property; then their participation in a state would be proportional to their property, and the oligarchic argument would as a result seem to be a powerful one. (For it is not just that someone who has contributed only one mina to a sum of one hundred minas should have equal shares in that sum, whether of the principal or of the interest, with the one who has contributed all the rest.) But suppose they do not do so only for the sake of life, but rather for the sake of living well, since otherwise there could be a state of slaves or animals, whereas in fact there is not, because these share neither in happiness nor in a life guided by deliberative choice.

And suppose they do not do so for the sake of an alliance to safeguard themselves from being wronged by anyone, nor to facilitate exchange and mutual assistance, since otherwise the Etruscans and the Carthaginians, and all those who have treaties with one another would virtually be citizens of one state. To be sure, they have import agreements, treaties about refraining from injustice, and formal documents of alliance, but no offices common to all of them have been established to deal with these matters; instead each state has different ones. Nor are those in one state concerned with what sort of people the others should be, or that none of those covered by the agreements should be unjust or vicious in any way, but only that neither state acts unjustly toward the other. But those who are concerned with good government give careful attention to political virtue and vice. Hence it is quite evident that the state (at any rate, the one truly so called and not just for the sake of argument) must be concerned with virtue. For otherwise the community becomes an alliance that differs only in location from other alliances in which the allies live far apart, and law becomes an agreement, "a

---

1   Justice is discussed in *Nicomachean Ethics* V.

guarantor of just behavior toward one another," as the sophist Lycophron[1] said, but not such as to make the citizens good and just.

It is evident that this is right. For even if one were to bring their territories together into one, so that the state of the Megarians was attached to that of the Corinthians by walls, it still would not be a single state. Nor would it be so if their citizens intermarried, even though this is one of the forms of community characteristic of states. Similarly, if there were some who lived separately, yet not so separately as to share nothing in common, and had laws against wronging one another in their business transactions (for example, if one were a carpenter, another a farmer, another a cobbler, another something else of that sort, and their number were ten thousand), yet they shared nothing else in common besides such things as exchange and alliance, not even in this case would there be a state.

What, then, is the reason for this? Surely, it is not because the communities are not close to each other. For suppose they joined together while continuing to share in that way, but each nevertheless treated his own household like a state, and the others like a defensive alliance formed only to provide aid against wrongdoers. Even then this still would not be thought a state by those who make a precise study of such things, if indeed they continued to associate with one another in the same manner when together as when separated.

Evidently, then, a state is not a sharing of a common location, and does not exist for the purpose of preventing mutual wrongdoing and exchanging goods. Rather, while these must be present if indeed there is to be a state, when all of them are present, there is still not yet a state, but rather only when households and families live well as a community whose end is a complete and self-sufficient life. But this will not be possible unless they do inhabit one and the same location and practice intermarriage. That is why marriage connections arose in states, as well as brotherhoods, religious sacrifices, and the leisured pursuits of living together. For things of this sort are the result of friendship, since the deliberative choice of living together constitutes friendship. The end of the state is living well, then, but these other things are for the sake of the end. And a state is the community of families and villages in a complete and self-sufficient life, which we say is living happily and nobly.

So political communities must be taken to exist for the sake of noble actions, and not for the sake of living together. Hence those who contribute most to *this* sort of community have a larger share in the state than those who are equal or superior in freedom or family but inferior in political virtue, and than those who surpass in wealth but are surpassed in virtue.

---

1 Very likely a pupil of the famous sophist Gorgias.

It is evident from what has been said, then, that those who dispute about constitutions all speak about a *part* of justice.

FOR DISCUSSION:

If the purpose of a genuine state is to enable the citizens to live well and virtuously, should the government of the state be expected to tell all the citizens how to live their lives?

10. There is a problem as to what part of the state is to have authority, since surely it is either the multitude, or the rich, or excellent people, or the one who is best of all, or a tyrant. But all of these apparently involve difficulties. How so? If the poor, because they are the greater number, divide up the property of the rich, isn't that unjust? "No, by Zeus, it isn't, since it seemed just to those in authority." What, then, should we call extreme injustice? Again, if the majority, having seized everything, should divide up the property of the minority, they are evidently destroying the state. But virtue certainly does not ruin what has it, nor is justice something capable of destroying a state. So it is clear, then, that this law cannot be just. Besides, everything done by a tyrant must be just as well; for he, being stronger, uses force, just as the multitude do against the rich.

But is it just, then, for the rich minority to rule? If they too act in the same way, plundering and confiscating the property of the multitude, and this is just, the other case is as well. It is evident, therefore, that all these things are bad and unjust.

But should excellent people rule and have authority over everything? In that case, everyone else must be deprived of honors by being excluded from political office. For offices are positions of honor, we say, and when the same people always rule, the rest must necessarily be deprived of honors.

But is it better that the one who is best should rule? But this is even more oligarchic, since those deprived of honors are more numerous.

Perhaps, however, someone might say that it is a bad thing in general for a human being to have authority and not the law, since he at any rate has the passions that beset the soul. But if law may be oligarchic or democratic, what difference will that make to our problems? For the things we have just described will happen just the same.

11. As for the other cases, we may let them be the topic for a different discussion. But the view that the multitude rather than the few best people should be in authority would seem to be held, and while it involves a problem, it perhaps also involves some truth. For the many, who are not as individuals excellent people, nevertheless can, when they have come together, be better than the few best people, not individually but collectively, just as feasts to which many contribute are better than feasts provided

at one person's expense. For being many, each of them can have some part of virtue and practical wisdom, and when they come together the multitude is just like a single human being, with many feet, hands, and senses, and so too for their character traits and wisdom. That is why the many are better judges of works of music and of the poets. For one of them judges one part, another another, and all of them the whole thing.

It is in this way that excellent people differ from each of the many, just as beautiful people are said to differ from those who are not beautiful, and as things painted by craft are superior to real things: they bring together what is scattered and separate into one, although, at least if taken separately, this person's eye and some other feature of someone else will be more beautiful than the painted ones.

Whether this superiority of the many to the few excellent people can exist in the case of every people and every multitude is not clear. Though, presumably, by Zeus, it is clear that in some of them it cannot possibly do so, since the same argument would apply to beasts. For what difference is there, practically speaking, between some people and beasts? But nothing prevents what has been said from being true of *some* multitude.

By means of these considerations, too, one might solve the problem mentioned earlier and also the related one of what the free should have authority over, that is to say, the multitude of the citizens who are not rich and have no claim whatsoever arising from virtue. For it would not be safe to have them participate in the most important offices, since, because of their lack of justice and practical wisdom, they would inevitably act unjustly in some instances and make mistakes in others. On the other hand, to give them no share and not to allow them to participate at all would be cause for alarm. For a state in which a large number of people are excluded from office and are poor must of necessity be full of enemies. The remaining alternative, then, is to have them participate in deliberation and judgment, which is precisely why Solon and some other legislators arrange to have them elect and inspect[1] officials, but prevent them from holding office alone.

For when they all come together their perception is adequate, and, when mixed with their betters, they benefit their states, just as a mixture of roughage and pure food concentrate is more useful than a little of the latter by itself.[2] Taken individually, however, each of them is an imperfect judge.

But this organization of the constitution raises problems itself. In the first place,

---

1   In Athens and some other Greek cities government officials were required at the end of their term to submit to an audit of their activities while in office, and could be held responsible for any corrupt practices they may have engaged in.
2   Aristotle is thinking of mixing in bran with pure flour.

it might be held that the same person is able to judge whether or not someone has treated a patient correctly, and to treat patients and cure them of disease when it is present, namely, the doctor. The same would also seem to hold in other areas of experience and other crafts. Therefore, just as a doctor should be inspected by doctors, so others should also be inspected by their peers. But 'doctor' applies to the ordinary practitioner of the art, to a master artisan, and thirdly, to someone with a general education in the art. For there are people of this third sort in (practically speaking) all the arts. And we assign the task of judging to generally educated people no less than to experts.

Moreover, it might be held that election is the same way, since choosing correctly is also a task for experts: choosing a geometer is a task for expert geometers, for example, and choosing a ship's captain is a task for expert captains. For even if some lay people are also involved in the choice of candidates in the case of some tasks and arts, at least they do not play a larger role than the experts. According to this argument, then, the multitude should not be given authority over the election or inspection of officials.

But perhaps not all of these things are correctly stated, both because according to the earlier argument the multitude may not be too servile, since each may be a worse judge than those who know, but a better or no worse one when they all come together; and because there are some arts in which the maker might not be either the only or the best judge: the ones where those who do not possess the art nevertheless, have knowledge of its products. For example, the maker of a house is not the only one who has some knowledge about it; the one who uses it is an even better judge (and the one who uses is the household manager). A captain, too, judges a rudder better than a carpenter, and a guest, rather than the cook, the feast.

This problem might be held to be adequately solved in such a way. But there is another connected with it. For it is held to be absurd for inferior people to have authority over more important matters than excellent people do. But inspections and elections of officials are very important things. And in some constitutions, as we said, these are assigned to the people, since the assembly has authority over all such matters. And yet those with low property assessments and of whatever age participate in the assembly, and in deliberation and decision, whereas those with high property assessment are the treasurers and generals and hold the most important offices.

But one can, in fact, also solve this problem in the same way. For perhaps these things are also correctly organized. For it is neither the individual juror, nor the individual councilor, nor the individual assemblyman who is ruling, but the court, the council, and the people, whereas each of the individuals mentioned is only a part of these. (By 'part' I mean the councilor, the assemblyman, and the juror.) Hence it is just for the multitude to have authority over the more important matters. For the people, the council, and the court consist of many individuals, and their collective property assessment is greater than the assessment of those who, whether individually or in small groups, hold the important offices. So much for how these matters should be determined.

As to the first problem we mentioned,[1] it makes nothing else so evident as that the laws, when correctly established, should be in authority, and that the ruler, whether one or many, should have authority over only those matters on which the laws cannot pronounce with precision, because it is not easy to make universal declarations about everything.

It is not yet clear, however, what correctly established laws should be like, and the problem stated earlier[2] remains to be solved. For the laws must necessarily be bad or good, and just or unjust, at the same time in the same way as the constitutions. Still, at least it is evident that the laws must be established to suit the constitution. But if this is so, it is clear that laws that accord with the correct constitutions must be just, and those that accord with the deviant constitutions not just.

FOR DISCUSSION:

Under what circumstances is it better to let the multitude of people decide matters rather than a few acknowledged experts?

12. Since in every science and art the end is a good, the greatest and best good is the end of the science or art that has the most authority of all of them,[3] and this is the political capacity. But the political good is justice, and justice is the common benefit. Now everyone holds that what is just is some sort of equality, and up to a point, at least, all agree with what has been determined in those philosophical works of ours dealing with ethical issues.[4] For justice is something to someone, and they say it should be something equal to those who are equal. But equality in what and inequality in what, should not be overlooked. For this involves a problem and political philosophy.

Someone might say, perhaps, that offices should be unequally distributed on the basis of superiority in any good whatsoever, provided the people did not differ in their remaining qualities but were exactly similar, since, where people differ, so does what is just and what accords with merit. But if this is true, then those who are superior in complexion, or height, or any other good whatsoever will get more of the things with

---

1   I.e., the question of who should hold authority in the state.
2   At the end of ch.10.
3   I.e., what is called the "master art" in *Nicomachean Ethics* I, 1.
4   For example, *Nicomachean Ethics* V.

which political justice is concerned. And isn't this plainly false? The matter is evident in the various sciences and capacities. For among flute players equally proficient in the art, those who are of better birth do not get more or better flutes, since they will not play the flute any better if they do. It is the superior performers who should also get the superior instruments. If what has been said is somehow not clear, it will become so if we take it still further. Suppose someone is superior in flute playing but is very inferior in birth or in beauty; then, even if each of these (I mean birth and beauty) is a greater good than flute playing, and is proportionately more superior to flute playing than he is superior in flute playing, he should still get the outstanding flutes. For the superiority in wealth and birth would have to contribute to the performance, but in fact they contribute nothing to it.

Besides, according to this argument every good would have to be commensurable with every other. For if being a certain height counted more, height in general would be in competition with both wealth and freedom. So, if one person is more outstanding in height than another is in virtue, and if height in general is of more weight than virtue, then all goods would be commensurable. For if a certain amount of size is better than a certain amount of virtue, it is clear that some amount of the one is equal to some amount of the other. Since this is impossible, it is clear that in political matters, too, it is reasonable not to dispute over political office on the basis of just any sort of inequality. For if some are slow runners and others fast, this is no reason for the latter to have more and the former less; it is in athletic competitions that such a difference wins honor. The dispute must be based on the things from which a state is constituted. Hence the well-born, the free, and the rich reasonably lay claim to office. For there must be both free people and those with assessed property, since a state cannot consist entirely of poor people any more than entirely of slaves. But if these things are needed in a state, so too, it is clear, are justice and political virtue, since a state cannot be managed without these. Rather, without the former a state cannot exist, and without the latter it cannot be well managed.

FOR DISCUSSION:

Is it possible *objectively* to rank in value all the different goods, such as the ones Aristotle mentions? Or is any such ranking inevitably just a matter of personal preference?

13. As regards the existence of a state, all, or at any rate some, of these would seem to have a correct claim in the dispute. But as regards the good life, education and virtue

would seem to have the most just claim of all in the dispute, as was also said earlier.[1] But since those equal in one thing only should not have equality in everything, nor inequality if they are unequal in only one thing, all constitutions of this sort[2] must be deviant.

We said before that all dispute somewhat justly, but that not all do so in an unqualifiedly just way. The rich have a claim due to the fact that they own a larger share of the land, and the land is something common, and that, in addition, they are usually more trustworthy where contracts are concerned. The free and the well-born have closely related claims, for those who are better born are more properly citizens than those of ignoble birth, and good birth is honored at home by everyone. Besides, they have a claim because better people are likely to come from better people, since good birth is excellence of family. Similarly, then, we shall say that virtue has a just claim in the dispute, since justice, we say, is a communal virtue, which all the other virtues necessarily accompany. But the majority too have a just claim against the minority, since they are stronger, richer, and better, when taken as the majority in relation to the minority.

If they were all present in a single state, therefore (I mean, for example, the good, the rich, the well-born, and a political multitude in addition), will there be a dispute as to who should rule or not? Within each of the constitutions we have mentioned, to be sure, the decision as to who should rule is indisputable, since these differ from one another because of what is in authority; for example, because in one the rich are in authority, in another the good men, and each of the others differs in the same way. But be that as it may, we are investigating how the matter is to be determined when all these are present simultaneously. Suppose, for example, that those who possess virtue are extremely few in number, how should the matter be settled? Should their fewness be considered in relation to the task? To whether they are able to manage the state? Or to whether there are enough of them to constitute a state by themselves?

But there is a problem that faces all who dispute over political office. Those who claim that they deserve to rule because of their wealth could be held to have no justice to their claim at all, and similarly those claiming to do so because of their family. For it is clear that if someone is richer again than everyone else, then, on the basis of the same justice, this one person will have to rule them all. Similarly, it is clear that someone who is outstanding when it comes to good birth should rule those who

---

1 At the end of ch. 9.
2 I.e., of the sort which give to those equal in one thing only equality in everything, and to those unequal in one thing only inequality in everything. For example, democracy gives to those equal just in freedom equality in access to all political offices, and oligarchy gives to those unequal just in wealth greater access to all political offices.

dispute on the basis of freedom. Perhaps the same thing will also occur in the case of virtue where aristocracies are concerned. For if one man were better than the others in the government, even though they were good men, then, on the basis of the same justice, this man should be in authority. So, if the majority too should be in authority because they are superior to the few, then, if one person, or more than one but fewer than the many, were superior to the others, these should be in authority rather than the multitude. All this seems to make it evident, then, that none of the definitions on the basis of which people claim that they themselves deserve to rule, whereas everyone else deserves to be ruled by them, is correct. For the multitude would have an argument of some justice even against those who claim that they deserve to have authority over the government because of their virtue, and similarly against those who base their claim on wealth. For nothing prevents the multitude from being sometimes better and richer than the few, not as individuals but collectively.

Hence the problem that some people raise and investigate can also be dealt with in this way. For they raise the problem of whether a legislator who wishes to establish the most correct laws should legislate for the benefit of the better citizens or that of the majority, when the case just mentioned occurs. But what is correct must be taken to mean what is equitable; and what is equitable in relation to the benefit of the entire state, and the common benefit of the citizens. And a citizen generally speaking is someone who participates in ruling and in being ruled, although in each constitution he is someone different. It is in the best one, however, that he is the one who has the capacity and who deliberately chooses to be ruled and to rule with an eye to the virtuous life. But, if there is one person or more than one (though not enough to make up a complete state) who is so outstanding by reason of his superior virtue that neither the virtue nor the political capacity of all the others is commensurable with his (if there is only one) or theirs (if there are a number of them), then such people can no longer be regarded as part of the state. For they would be treated unjustly if they were thought to merit equal shares, when they are so unequal in virtue and political capacity. For anyone of that sort would reasonably be regarded as a god among human beings. Hence it is clear that legislation too must be concerned with those who are equals both in birth and in capacity, and that for the other sort there is no law, since they themselves are the law. For, indeed, anyone who attempted to legislate for them would be ridiculous, since they would presumably respond in the way Antisthenes[1] tells us the lions did when the hares acted like popular leaders and demanded equality for everyone.[2]

---

1   A follower of Socrates and founder of the Cynic school.
2   According to Aesop the lion's reply was: "Where are your claws and teeth?"

That is why, indeed, democratically governed states introduce ostracism.[1] For of all states these are held to pursue equality most, and so they ostracize those held to be outstandingly powerful (whether because of their wealth, their many friends, or any other source of political capacity), banishing them from the state for fixed periods of time. The story goes, too, that the Argonauts[2] left Heracles behind for this sort of reason: the Argo[3] refused to carry him with the other sailors on the grounds that his weight greatly exceeded theirs. That is also why those who criticize tyranny or the advice that Periander[4] gave Thrasybulus[5] should not be considered to be unqualifiedly correct in their censure. For they say that Periander said nothing to the messenger who had been sent to him for advice, but leveled a cornfield by cutting off the outstandingly tall ears. When the messenger, who did not know why Periander did this, reported what had happened, Thrasybulus understood that he was to get rid of the outstanding men.

This advice is not beneficial only to tyrants, however, nor are tyrants the only ones who follow it. The same situation holds too in oligarchies and democracies. For ostracism has the same sort of effect as cutting down the outstanding people, i.e. sending them into exile. But those in control of power treat states and nations in the same way. For example, as soon as Athens had a firm grip on its imperial rule, it humbled Samos, Chios, and Lesbos,[6] in violation of treaties it had with them; and the king of the Persians often cut the Medes and Babylonians down to size, as well as any others who had grown presumptuous because they had once ruled empires of their own.

The problem is a general one that concerns all constitutions, even the correct ones. For, though the deviant constitutions use such methods with an eye to the private benefit, the position is the same with those that aim at the common good. But this is also clear in the case of the other arts and sciences. For no painter would allow an animal to have a disproportionately large foot, not even if it were an outstandingly beautiful one, nor would a shipbuilder allow this in the case of the stern or any of the other parts of the ship, nor will a chorus master tolerate a member of the chorus who has a louder and more beautiful voice than the entire chorus. So, from this point of view, there is nothing to prevent monarchs from being in harmony with the state they rule when they resort to this sort of practice, provided their rule benefits their state. Where acknowledged sorts of superiority are concerned, then, there is some political

---

1   In Athens and elsewhere, a citizen could be punished (preemptively and without trial) by banishment from the state for ten years.
2   The legendary band headed by Jason that set off in search of the Golden Fleece.
3   Jason's ship which had been equipped by Athena with a board that talked.
4   A tyrant who ruled Corinth from 625-585.
5   Another tyrant, who ruled Miletus.
6   Island city-states that had allied themselves with Athens in the war against Sparta.

justice to the argument in favor of ostracism.

It would be better, certainly, if the legislator established the constitution in the beginning so that it had no need for such a remedy. But the next best thing is to try to fix the constitution, should the need arise, with a corrective of this sort. This is not what actually tended to happen in states, however. For they did not look to the benefit of their own constitutions, but used ostracism for purposes of faction. It is evident, then, that in each of the deviant constitutions ostracism is privately advantageous and just, but it is perhaps also evident that it is not unqualifiedly just.

In the case of the best constitution, however, there is a considerable problem, not about superiority in other goods, such as capacity or wealth or having many friends, but when there happens to be someone who is superior in virtue. For surely people would not say that such a person should be expelled or banished, but neither would they say that they should rule over him. For that would be like claiming that they deserved to rule over Zeus, dividing the offices [so that he ruled and was ruled in turn]. The remaining possibility, and it seems to be a natural one, is for everyone to obey such a person gladly, so that those like him will be permanent kings in their states.

FOR DISCUSSION:

Is it at all possible for there to be someone so wise and just that it would be better to be ruled by their decrees than by established law?

Is it ever the case that people with outstanding abilities for wise political leadership should be excluded from political office?

B.6.d: *POLITICS* IV

Chs. 8-12[1]

Perhaps Aristotle's most original contribution to the question of constitutions is his mention of "polity" as a genuine option and a correct (i.e., non-deviant) arrangement. The polity seems to result from combining features of two deviant constitutions, oligarchy and democracy, and is proposed by Aristotle as a possible solution to the chief conflict that bedeviled Greek states in his time and earlier: the tension between the rich and the poor.

8. It remains for us to speak about so-called polity and about tyranny. We have adopted this arrangement because, even though neither polity nor the aristocracies just mentioned are deviant, in truth they do fall short of the most correct constitution and thus are counted among the deviant forms, the deviant forms being deviations from them, as we mentioned in the beginning. On the other hand, it is reasonable to treat tyranny last, since it is least of all a constitution, and our inquiry is about constitutions. So much for the reason for organizing things in this way.

But we must now set forth our views on polity. Its nature should be more evident now that we have determined the facts about oligarchy and democracy. For polity, to put it simply, is a mixture of oligarchy and democracy. It is customary, however, to call those mixtures that lean toward democracy polities, and those that lean more toward oligarchy aristocracies, because education and good birth more commonly accompany those who are richer. Besides, the rich are held to possess already what unjust people commit injustice to get, which is why the rich are referred to as noble-and-good men, and as notables. So, since aristocracies strive to give superiority to the best citizens,

---

1 Translated by Reeve, pp. 114-23, with some modifications.

oligarchies too are said to consist primarily of noble-and-good men. And it is held to be impossible for a state to be well governed if it is not governed aristocratically but by bad people, and equally impossible for a state that is not well governed to be governed aristocratically. But good government does not exist if the laws, though well established, are not obeyed. Hence we must take good government to exist in one way when the established laws are obeyed, and in another way when the laws that are in fact obeyed are well established (for even badly established laws can be obeyed). The second situation can come about in two ways: people may obey either the best laws possible for them, or the unqualifiedly best ones.

Aristocracy is held most of all to exist when offices are distributed on the basis of virtue. For virtue is the defining mark of aristocracy, wealth of oligarchy, and freedom of democracy. But majority opinion is found in all of them. For in oligarchy and aristocracy and in democracies, the opinion of the major part of those who participate in the constitution has authority. Now in most states the kind of constitution is wrongly named, since the mixture aims only at the rich and the poor, at wealth and freedom. For among pretty much most people the rich are taken to occupy the place of noble-and-good men. But there are in fact three grounds for claiming equal participation in the constitution: freedom, wealth, and virtue. (The fourth, which they call good birth, is a consequence of two of the others, since good birth is a combination of old money and virtue.) Hence it is evident that the mixture of the two, the rich and the poor, ought to be called polity, whereas a mixture of the three deserves most of all the others (except for the true and first kind) to be called an aristocracy.

We have said, then, that there are other kinds of constitutions besides monarchy, democracy, and oligarchy. And it is evident what they are, how aristocracies differ among themselves, and polities from aristocracy; and that they are not far apart from one another.

9. After what has been said, let us next discuss how, in addition to democracy and oligarchy, so-called polity arises, and how it should be established. At the same time, however, the defining principles of democracy and oligarchy will become clear. For what we must do is get hold of the division of these, and then take, as it were, a token[1] from each to put together.

There are three defining principles of the combination and mixture: One is to take legislation from both constitutions. For example, in the case of deciding court cases, oligarchies impose a fine on the rich if they do not take part in deciding court cases,

---

1   A token (*symbolon*) was a half of a coin which had been broken so that it could then be used to vouch for the identity of the possessor to the person possessing the other half.

but provide no payment for the poor, whereas democracies pay the poor but do not fine the rich. But what is common to both constitutions and an intermediate between them is doing both. And hence this is characteristic of a polity, which is a mixture formed from both. This, then is one way to conjoin them.

Another [defining principle] is to take the intermediate between the organizations of each. In democracies, for example, membership in the assembly is either not based on a property assessment at all or on a very small one, whereas in oligarchies it is based on a large property assessment. The common position here is to require neither of these assessments but the one that is an intermediate between the two of them.

A third [defining principle] is to take elements from both organizations, some from oligarchic law and others from democratic law. I mean, for example, it is held to be democratic for officials to be chosen by lot, and oligarchic by election; democratic not on the basis of a property assessment, oligarchic on such a basis. It is aristocratic, therefore, and characteristic of polity to take one element from one and another from the other, by making officials elected, as in an oligarchy, but not on the basis of a property assessment, as in a democracy.

This, then, is the way to mix them. But the defining principle of a good mixture of democracy and oligarchy is when it is possible to speak of the same constitution both as an oligarchy and as a democracy. For it is clear that speakers speak of it in this way because the mixture is a good one. The intermediate, too, is like this, since each of the extremes is visible in it. This is precisely how it is with the Spartan constitution; for many people attempt to speak of it as if it were a democracy, because it has many democratic elements in its organization. First, for example, there is the way sons are brought up. Those of the rich are brought up like those of the poor, and are educated in a way that the sons of the poor could be. Similarly, at the next age, when they have become men, it is the same way. For nothing distinguishes a rich person from a poor one; the food at the messes is the same for everyone, and the rich wear clothes that any poor person could also provide for himself. A further democratic element is that of the two most important offices, the people elect candidates to one and share in the other; for they elect the senators and share in the overseership. But other people call the Spartan constitution an oligarchy on account of its having many oligarchic elements. For example, all the officials are chosen by vote and none by lot; a few have authority to impose death and exile; and there are many other such elements. In a constitution that is well mixed, however, both elements should be held to be present—and neither; and it should survive because of itself and not because of external factors, and because of itself, not because a majority wishes it (since that could happen in a bad constitution too), but because none of the parts of the state as a whole would even want another constitution.

We have now described how a polity should be established and likewise those constitutions that are termed aristocracies.

10. It remained for us to speak about tyranny, not because there is much to say about it, but so that it can take its place in our inquiry, since we assign it too a place among the constitutions. Now we dealt with kingship in our first discussions[1] (when we investigated whether the kind of kingship that is most particularly so called is beneficial for states or not beneficial, who and from what source should be established in it, and in what manner). And we distinguished two kinds of tyranny while we were investigating kingship, because their power somehow also overlaps with kingship, owing to the fact that both are based on law. For some non-Greeks choose autocratic monarchs, and in former times among the ancient Greeks there were people called dictators who became monarchs in this way. There are, however, certain differences between these; but both were kingly inasmuch as they were based on law, and involved monarchical rule over willing subjects; but both were tyrannical, inasmuch as the monarchs ruled like masters in accord with their own judgment. But there is also a third kind of tyranny, which is held to be tyranny in the highest degree, being a counterpart to absolute kingship. Any monarchy is necessarily a tyranny of this kind if the monarch rules in an unaccountable fashion over people who are similar to him or better than him, with an eye to his own benefit, not that of the ruled. It is, therefore, rule over unwilling people, since no free person willingly endures such rule.

The kinds of tyranny are these and this many, then, for the aforementioned reasons.

Polity, Aristotle believes, is for most people the best constitution that is achievable, but it depends crucially on the existence of a middle class that is neither poor nor very rich. Aristotle has the idea that this class can, if it is sufficiently large, prevent the rich from dominating the poor and establishing an oligarchy, as well as the poor from dominating the rich and establishing a democracy.

11. What is the best constitution, and what is the best life for most states and most human beings, judging neither by an excellence that is beyond the reach of ordinary people, nor by a kind of education that requires natural gifts and resources that depend on luck, nor by the ideal constitution, but by a life that most people can share and a constitution in which most states can participate? For the constitutions

---

1   In Bk.iii, 14-17. Not included in these selections.

called aristocracies, which we discussed just now, either fall outside the reach of most states or border on so called polities (that is why the two have to be spoken about as one).

Decision about all these matters depends on the same elements. For if what is said in the *Ethics* is right, and a happy life is the one that expresses virtue and is without impediment, and virtue is a mean, then the middle life, the mean that each sort of person can actually achieve, must be best. These same defining principles must also hold of the virtue and vice of a state or a constitution, since a constitution is a sort of life of a state.

In all states there are three parts of the state: the very rich, the very poor, and a third, those in between the former. So, since it is agreed that what is moderate and in a mean is best, it is evident that possessing a middle amount of goods of luck is also best. For it most readily obeys reason, whereas whatever is exceedingly beautiful, strong, well born, or wealthy, or conversely whatever is exceedingly poor, weak, or lacking in honor, has a hard time obeying reason. For the former sort tend more toward arrogance and major vice, whereas the latter tend too much toward malice and petty vice; and wrongdoing is caused in the one case by arrogance and in the other case by malice. Besides, the middle classes are least inclined either to avoid ruling or to pursue it, both of which are harmful to states.

Furthermore, those who are superior in the goods of luck (strength, wealth, friends, and other such things) neither wish to be ruled nor know how to be ruled (and this is a characteristic they acquire right from the start at home while they are still children; for, because of their luxurious lifestyle they are not accustomed to being ruled, even in school). Those, on the other hand, who are exceedingly deprived of such goods are too humble. Hence the latter do not know how to rule, but only how to be ruled in the way slaves are ruled, whereas the former do not know how to be ruled in any way, but only how to rule as masters rule. The result is a state consisting not of free people but of slaves and masters, the one group full of envy and the other full of arrogance. Nothing is further removed from a friendship and a community that is political; for community involves friendship, since enemies do not wish to share even a journey in common. But a state, at least, tends to consist as much as possible of people who are equal and similar, and this condition belongs particularly to those in the middle. Consequently, this state, the one constituted out of those from which we say the state is naturally constituted, must of necessity be best governed. Moreover, of all citizens, those in the middle survive best in states; for neither do they desire other people's property as the poor do, nor do other people desire theirs, as the poor desire that of the rich. And because they are neither plotted against nor engage in plotting, they live out their lives free from danger. That is why

Phocylides[1] did well to pray: "Many things are best for those in the middle. I want to be in the middle in a state."

It is clear, therefore, that the political community that depends on those in the middle is best too, and that states can be well governed where those in the middle are numerous and stronger, preferably than both of the others, or, failing that, than one of them. For it will tip the balance when added to either and prevent the opposing extremes from arising. That is precisely why it is the height of good luck if those who are governing own a middle or adequate amount of property, because when some people own an excessive amount and the rest own nothing, either extreme democracy arises or unmixed oligarchy or, as a result of both excesses, tyranny. For tyranny arises from the most vigorous kind of democracy and oligarchy, but much less often from middle constitutions or those close to them. We will give the reason for this later when we discuss changes in constitutions.

That the middle constitution is best is evident, since it alone is free from faction. For conflicts and dissensions seldom occur among the citizens where there are many in the middle. Large states are also freer from faction for the same reason, namely that more are in the middle. In small states, on the other hand, it is easy to divide all the citizens into two, so that no middle is left and pretty well everyone is either poor or rich. Democracies are also more stable and longer lasting than oligarchies because of those in the middle (for they are more numerous in democracies than in oligarchies and share in office holding more), since, when the poor predominate without these, failure sets in and they are quickly ruined. The fact that the best legislators have come from the middle citizens should be regarded as evidence of this. For Solon was one of these, as is clear from his poems, as were Lycurgus[2] (for he was not a king), Charondas,[3] and pretty well most of the others.

It is also evident from these considerations why most constitutions are either democratic or oligarchic; for, because the middle class in them is often small, whichever of the others preponderates (whether the property owners or the people), those who overstep the middle way conduct the constitution to suit themselves, so that it becomes either a democracy or an oligarchy. In addition to this, because of the conflicts and fights that occur between the people and the rich, whenever one side or the other happens to gain more power than its opponents, they establish neither a common constitution nor an equal one, but take their superiority in the constitution as a reward of their victory and make in the one case a democracy and in the other an oligarchy. Then, too, each of those who achieved dominance in Greece has looked

---

1   A poet of the sixth century BCE.
2   According to legend he created the Spartan constitution.
3   A legislator in southern Macedonia in the sixth century BCE.

to their own constitutions and established either democracies or oligarchies in states, aiming not at the benefit of these states but at their own. As a consequence of all this, the middle constitution either never comes into existence or does so rarely and in few places; for among those who have previously held positions of leadership only one man[1] has ever been persuaded to introduce this kind of organization, and it has now become customary for those in states not even to wish for equality, but either to seek rule or to put up with being dominated.

What the best constitution is, then, and why it is so is evident from these considerations. As for the other constitutions (for there are, as we say, several kinds of democracies and of oligarchies), which of them is to be put first, which second, and so on in the same way, according to whether it is better or worse, is not hard to see now that the best has been determined. For the one nearest to this must of necessity always be better and one further from the middle worse, provided one is not judging on the basis of certain assumptions. I say "on the basis of certain assumptions" because it often happens that, while one constitution is more choiceworthy, nothing prevents a different one from being more beneficial for some.

FOR DISCUSSION:

Is Aristotle right in thinking that, generally speaking, people of moderate wealth are better both at ruling and being ruled than either the rich or the poor?

12. The next thing to go through after what has been said is which constitution and which kind of it is beneficial for which and which kind of people. First, though, a general point must be grasped about all of them, namely, that the part of a state that wishes the constitution to continue must be stronger than any part that does not. Every state is made up of both quality and quantity. By 'quality' I mean freedom, wealth, education, and good birth; by 'quantity' I mean the superiority of size. But it is possible that the quality belongs to one of the parts of which a state is constituted, whereas the quantity belongs to another. For example, the low-born may be more numerous than the well-born, or the poor more numerous than the rich, but yet the one may not be as superior in quantity as it is inferior in quality. Hence these have to be judged in relation to one another. Where the multitude of poor people is superior in the proportion mentioned, there it is natural for a democracy to exist, with each particular kind of democracy corresponding to the superiority of each particular kind of the people. For example, if the multitude of farmers is predominant, it will be the

---

1   It is not known to whom Aristotle refers.

first kind of democracy;[1] if the vulgar craftsmen and wage earners are, the last kind;[2] and similarly for the others in between these. But where the multitude of those who are rich and notable is more superior in quality than it is inferior in quantity, there an oligarchy is natural, with each particular kind of oligarchy corresponding to the superiority of the multitude of oligarchs, in the same way as before.

But the legislator should always include the middle in his constitution: if he is establishing oligarchic laws, he should aim at those in the middle, and if democratic ones, he must bring them in by these laws. And where the multitude of those in the middle outweighs either both of the extremes together or even only one of them, it is possible to have a stable constitution. For there is no fear that the rich and the poor will conspire together against these, since neither will ever want to serve as slaves to the other; and if they look for a constitution that is more common than this, they will find none. For they would not put up with ruling in turn, because they distrust one another; and an arbitrator is most trusted everywhere, and the middle person is an arbitrator. The better mixed a constitution is the more stable it is. But many of those who wish to establish aristocratic constitutions make the mistake not only of granting more to the rich but also of deceiving the people. For sooner or later false goods inevitably give rise to a true evil; for the acquisitive behavior of the rich does more to destroy the constitution than that of the poor.

FOR DISCUSSION:

Should the government of a state strive as much as possible to increase the size of the middle class by reducing the numbers both of the rich and of the poor?

---

1 This is a kind where the law is put in charge and there are few deliberative assemblies.
2 This is a kind where rule by assemblies is preferred to rule by laws.

B.6.e: *POLITICS* VII

(1) Chs. 1-3[1]

The constitution which is unqualifiedly best, not merely best for a certain people or community, is the one which most facilitates the state's pursuit of the best sort of life for its citizens, both individually and collectively. We know from the *Ethics* that Aristotle thinks this best sort of life is one that manifests the excellences, particularly the moral virtues and practical wisdom. (The place of excellences such as philosophic wisdom, i.e., a full knowledge of the nature of the cosmos, in theoretical as opposed to practical thought, is left unclear in the *Politics*.)

1. Anyone who intends to investigate the best constitution in the proper way must first determine which life is most choiceworthy, since if this remains unclear, what the best constitution is must also remain unclear. For it is appropriate for those to fare best who live in the best constitution their circumstances allow, provided nothing contrary to reasonable expectation occurs. That is why we should first come to some agreement about what the most choiceworthy life is for practically speaking everyone, and then determine whether it is the same for an individual as for a community, or different.

Since, then, I consider that I have already expressed much that is adequate about the best life in the exoteric works, I propose to make use of them here as well. For since, in the case of one division at least, there are three groups: external goods, goods of the body, and goods of the soul, surely no one would raise a dispute and say that not all of them need be possessed by those who are blessedly happy. For no one would call a person blessedly happy who has no shred of courage, temperance, justice or practical

---

1   Translated by Reeve, pp. 191-97, with some modifications.

wisdom, but is afraid of the flies buzzing around him, stops at nothing to gratify his appetite for food and drink, betrays his dearest friends for a pittance, and has a mind as foolish and prone to error as a child's or a madman's. But while almost all accept these claims, they disagree about quantity and relative superiority. For they consider any amount of virtue, however small, to be sufficient, but seek an unlimitedly excessive amount of wealth, possessions, power, reputation, and the like.

We, however, will say to them that it is easy to reach a reliable conclusion on these matters even from the facts themselves. For we see that the virtues are not acquired and preserved by means of external goods, but the other way around, and we see that a happy life for human beings, whether it consists in pleasure or virtue or both, is possessed more often by those who have cultivated their characters and minds to an extreme degree, but have been moderate in their acquisition of external goods, than by those who have acquired more of the latter than they can possibly use, but are deficient in the former. Moreover, if we investigate the matter on the basis of argument, it is plain to see; for external goods have a limit, as does any tool, and all useful things are useful for something; so excessive amounts of them must harm or bring no benefit to their possessors. In the case of each of the goods of the soul, however, the more extreme it is the more useful it is (if these goods too should be thought of as useful and not simply as noble).

It is generally clear too, we shall say, that the relation of superiority holding between the best condition of each thing and that of others corresponds to that holding between the things whose conditions we say they are. So, since the soul is unqualifiedly more valuable, and also more valuable to us, than possessions or the body, its best states must be proportionally better than theirs. Besides, it is for the sake of the soul that these things are naturally choiceworthy, and every sensible person should choose them for its sake, not the soul for theirs.

We may take it as agreed, then, that each person has just as much happiness as he has virtue, practical wisdom, and the actions that express them. We may use god as evidence of this; for he is blessedly happy, not because of any external goods but because of himself and a certain quality in his nature. This is also the reason that good luck and happiness are necessarily different; for chance or luck produces goods external to the soul, but no one is just or temperate as a result of luck or because of luck.

The next point depends on the same arguments. The happy state is the one that is best and acts nobly. It is impossible for those who do not do noble deeds to act nobly; and no action, whether a person's or a state's, is noble when separate from virtue and practical wisdom. But the courage, justice, and practical wisdom of a state have the same capacity and are of the same kind as those possessed by each human being who is said to be just, practically wise, and moderate.

So much, then, for the preface to our discussion; for we cannot avoid talking about these issues altogether, but neither can we go through all the arguments pertaining to them, since that is a task for another type of study. But for now let us assume this much: that the best life, both for individuals separately and for states collectively, is a life of virtue sufficiently equipped with the resources needed to take part in virtuous actions. With regard to those who dispute this, if any happen not to be persuaded by what has been said, we must ignore them in our present study, but investigate them later.

FOR DISCUSSION:

Is it true that luck doesn't figure at all in being morally virtuous?

Aristotle seems comfortable with claiming that the happiness and virtues of an individual are the same as those of the state as a whole, i.e., in treating collective well-being and excellence with the same set of concepts he applies to the individual. This may not be as obvious as Aristotle seems to think it is. There is also mention of the purely theoretical activity of contemplation as a kind of excellence which the state might strive for. What would this mean in practical terms? But the greater part of the chapter is given over to a rejection of imperial rule as a proper end for a state. When it engages in this, the state becomes like a tyrant, the worst kind of ruler of all.

2. It remains to say whether the happiness of each individual human being is the same as that of a state or not. But here too the answer is evident, since everyone would agree that they are the same. For those who suppose that living well for an individual consists in wealth will also call a whole state blessedly happy if it happens to be wealthy. And those who honor the tyrannical life above all would claim that the state that rules the greatest number[1] is happiest. And if someone approves of an individual because of his excellence, he will also say that the more excellent state is happier.

Two questions need to be investigated, however. First, which life is more choice-worthy, the one that involves taking part in politics with other people and participating in a state, or the life of an alien cut off from the political community? Second, and regardless of whether participating in a state is more choiceworthy for everyone or for most but not for all, which constitution, which condition of the state is best? This second question, and not the one about what is choiceworthy for the individual, is a task for political thought or theory. And, since that is the investigation we are now

---

1   Probably Aristotle means the greatest number of other states.

engaged in, whereas the former is a further task, our task is the second question.

It is evident that the best constitution must be that organization in which anyone might do best and live a blessedly happy life. But the very people who agree that the most choiceworthy life is the life of excellence are the ones who dispute about whether it is the political life of action that is worthy of choice or rather the one released from external concerns, a contemplative life, for example, which some say is the only life for a philosopher. For it is evident that almost all of those, past or present, with the greatest love for the honor accorded to excellence have chosen between these two lives (I mean the political life and the philosophic one). And it makes no small difference on which side the truth lies, since anyone with sound practical wisdom must at least organize his affairs by looking to the better target; and this applies to human beings individually and to the constitution communally.

Some people think that ruling over one's neighbors like a master involves one of the greatest injustices, and that rule of a statesman, though it involves no injustice, does involve an impediment to one's own well-being. Others think almost the opposite; they say that an active, political life is the only one for a man, since the actions expressing each of the virtues are no more available to private individuals than to those engaged in communal affairs and politics. Some give this reply, then, but others claim that only a constitution that involves being a master or tyrant is happy.

For some people, indeed, the fundamental aim of the constitution and the laws is just to rule their neighbors like a master. That is why, even though most customs have been established pretty much at random in most cases, anywhere the laws have to some extent a single aim, it is always domination. So in Sparta and Crete the educational system and most of the laws are set up for war. Besides, all the nations that have the power to be acquisitive honor military power, for example, the Scythians, Persians, Thracians, and Celts. Indeed, some of them even have laws designed to foster military virtue. It is said that in Carthage, for example, they receive armlets[1] as decorations for each campaign in which they take part. There was once a law in Macedonia too that any man who had not killed an enemy must wear a halter[2] for a belt. Among the Scythians, when the cup passes around at a feast, those who have not killed an enemy are not permitted to drink from it. And among the Iberians, a warlike race, they place small obelisks in the earth around a man's tomb to show the number of enemies he has killed. And there are many other similar practices among other peoples, some prescribed by law, others by custom.

Yet to anyone willing to investigate the matter, it would perhaps seem quite absurd

---

1 A band worn on the upper arm.
2 The arrangement of straps that goes around the head of an animal.

if the task of a statesman involved being able to study ways to rule or master his neighbors, whether they are willing or not. For how could this be a political or legislative task, when it is not even lawful? Such rule whether carried out justly or unjustly is unlawful, and domination by force is not done justly. Certainly, this is not what we see in the other sciences; for it is not the doctor's or captain's task to use force on his patients or passengers if he cannot persuade them. Yet many seem to think that the political art is the same as mastership, and what they all say is unjust or nonbeneficial when it is done to them, they are not ashamed to do to others. For they seek just rule for themselves, but pay no attention to justice in their dealings with others. It is absurd to deny, however, that one thing is fit to be a master and another not fit to be a master. So, if indeed one is that way, one should not try to rule as a master over everyone, but only over those who are fit to be ruled by a master. Similarly, one should not hunt human beings for a feast or sacrifice, but only animals that are fit to be hunted for these purposes, and that is any wild animal that is edible.

Furthermore, it is possible for even a single state to be happy all by itself, provided it is well governed, since it is possible for a state to be settled somewhere by itself and to employ excellent laws. And *its* constitution will not be organized for the purposes of war or of dominating its enemies, for we are assuming that it has none.

It is clear, therefore, that all military practices are to be regarded as noble, not when they are pursued as the highest end of all, but only when they are pursued for the sake of the highest end. The task of an excellent legislator, then, is to study how a state, a race of people, or any other community can come to have a share in a good life and in the happiness that is possible for them. There will be differences, of course, in some of the laws that are instituted; and, if there are neighboring peoples, it belongs to legislative science to consider what sort of policies are needed in relation to which sorts of people and which measures are to be used in relation to each.

But the question of which end the best constitution should aim at will receive a proper investigation later.

In this next chapter Aristotle defends a life of activity, and he has in mind mainly political activity, although mention is made of the activity of contemplative thought. Freedom from having to rule is not really superior to ruling, because the rule of a master over a slave is not the only kind of ruling that exists. There is also the rule of one free person over other free people for the latter's benefit, and this is an opportunity for virtue.

3. We must now reply to the two sides who agree that the life of excellence is most choiceworthy, but disagree about how to practice it. For some rule out the holding of

political office and consider that the life of a free person is both different from that of a statesman and the most choiceworthy one of all. But others consider that the political life is best, since it is impossible for someone inactive to do or act well, and that doing well and happiness are the same. We must reply that they are both partly right and partly wrong. On the one hand, it is true to say that the life of a free person is better than that of a master. For there is certainly nothing grand about using a slave as a slave, since ordering people to do necessary tasks is in no way noble. Nonetheless, it is wrong to consider that every kind of rule is rule by a master. For the difference between rule over free people and over slaves is no smaller than the difference between being naturally free and being a natural slave. We have adequately distinguished them in our first discussions. On the other hand, to praise inaction more than action is not correct either. For happiness is action, and many noble things reach their end in the actions of those who are just and moderate.

Perhaps someone will take these conclusions to imply, however, that having authority over everyone is what is best. For in that way one would have authority over the greatest number of the very noblest actions. It would follow that someone who has the power to rule should not surrender it to his neighbor but take it away from him, and that a father should disregard his children, a child his father, a friend his friend, and pay no attention to anything except ruling. For what is best is most choiceworthy, and doing well is best.

What they say is perhaps true, if indeed those who use force and commit robbery will come to possess the most choiceworthy thing there is. But perhaps they cannot come to possess it, and the underlying assumption here is false. For a ruler [who rules all the time] cannot do noble actions unless he is as superior to those he rules as a husband is to his wife, a father to his children, or a master to his slaves. Therefore, a transgressor could never make up later for his deviation from virtue. For among those who are similar, ruling and being ruled in turn is just and noble, since this is equal or similar treatment. But unequal shares for equals or dissimilar ones for similar is contrary to nature; and nothing contrary to nature is noble. Hence, when someone else has superior virtue and his capacity to do the best things is also superior, it is noble to follow and just to obey him. But he should possess not virtue alone, but also the capacity he needs to do these things.

If these claims are correct, and we should assume that happiness is doing well, then the best life, whether for a whole state collectively or for an individual, would be a life of action. Yet it is not necessary, as some suppose, for a life of action to involve relations with other people, nor are those thoughts alone active which we engage in for the sake of action's consequences; the reflection and thought that are their own ends and are engaged in for their own sake are much more so. For to do or act well is the end, so that action of a sort is the end too. And even in the case of actions involving external objects, the one who does them most fully is, strictly speaking, the master artisan, who directs them by means of his thought.

Moreover, states situated by themselves, which have deliberately chosen to live that way, do not necessarily have to be inactive, since activity can take place even among their parts. For the parts of a state have many sorts of communal relationships with one another. Similarly, this holds for any human being taken singly; for otherwise god and the entire universe could hardly be in a fine condition, for they have no external actions, only the internal ones which are their very own.

It is evident, then, that the same life is necessarily best both for each human being and for states and human beings collectively.

FOR DISCUSSION:

Where participation in politics on the basis of equality of citizens with each other is possible, is it essential for living excellently?

(2) Chs. 13-14[1]

The *blessedly* happy state will have to have some goods which depend on luck, for example material resources. But external goods are not what is crucial for a state to be happy, any more than the physical instrument is what is crucial to being a good musician. Rather, just as in the case of music what is of prime importance is the mastery of an art that the person possesses in his or her soul, so too in happiness it is the possession of excellences.

13. But we must now discuss the constitution itself, and from which and what sorts of people a state should be constituted if it is to be a blessedly happy and well governed one. In all cases, well-being consists in two things: setting up the aim and end of action correctly and discovering the actions that bear on it. These factors can be in harmony with one another or in disharmony. For people sometimes set up the end well but fail to achieve it in action; and sometimes they achieve everything that promotes the end, but the end they set up is a bad one. Sometimes they make both mistakes. For example, in medicine it sometimes happens that doctors are neither correct in their judgment about what condition a healthy body should be in, nor successful in producing the condition they have set up as their end. In the arts and sciences both of these have to be under control, the end and the actions directed toward it. It is evident that everyone aims at living well and at happiness. But while some can achieve these ends,

---

1 Translated by Reeve, pp. 212-18, with some modifications.

others, whether because of luck or because of something in their nature, cannot. For we also need resources in order to live a good life, although we need fewer of them if we are in a better condition, more if we are in a worse one. Others, though they could achieve happiness, search for it in the wrong place from the outset. But since we are proposing to look at the best constitution, and this is one under which a state will be best governed, and since a state is best governed under a constitution that would above all make it possible for the state to be happy, it is clear that we should not overlook the question of what happiness actually is.

We say, and we have given this definition in our ethical works (if anything in those discussions is of service), that happiness is a complete actualization or use of excellence, and not a qualified use but an unqualified one. By 'qualified uses' I mean those that are necessary; by 'unqualified' I mean those that are noble. For example, in the case of just actions, just retributions and punishments spring from virtue, but are necessary uses of it, and are noble only in a necessary way, since it would be more choiceworthy if no individual or state needed such things. On the other hand, just actions that aim at honors and prosperity are unqualifiedly noblest. The former involve choosing something that is somehow bad, whereas the latter are the opposite: they construct and generate goods. To be sure, a good man will deal with poverty, disease, and other sorts of bad luck in a noble way. But blessed happiness requires their opposites. For according to the definition established in our ethical works, a good person is the sort whose excellence makes *unqualifiedly* good things good *for him*. Clearly, then, his use of them must also be unqualifiedly good and noble. That is why people think that external goods are the causes of happiness. Yet we might as well hold that a lyre is the cause of fine and brilliant lyre playing, and not the performer's art. It follows, then, from what has been said, that some goods must be there to start with, whereas others must be provided by the legislator. That is why we pray that our state will be ideally equipped with the goods that luck controls (for we assume that luck does control them). When we come to making the state excellent, however, that is no longer a task for luck but one for scientific knowledge and deliberate choice. A state is excellent, however, because the citizens who participate in the constitution are excellent; and in our state all the citizens participate in the constitution. The matter we have to investigate, therefore, is how a man becomes excellent. For even if it is possible for all the citizens to be collectively excellent without being so individually, the latter is still more choiceworthy, since, if each is excellent, all are. But surely people become good and excellent because of three things. The three are nature, habit, and reason. For first one must possess a certain nature from birth, namely, that of a human being, and not that of some other animal. Similarly, one's body and soul must be of a certain sort. But in the case of some of these qualities, there is no benefit in just being born with them, because they are altered by our habits; for some qualities are naturally capable of being developed by habit either in a better direction or in a worse one. The other animals mostly live under the guidance of nature alone, although some are guided a little by habit. But human beings live under the guidance of reason as well, since they alone have reason. Consequently, all three of these factors need to be harmonized with one another. For people often act contrary to their habits and their nature because of reason, if they happen to be persuaded that some other course of action is better.

We have already determined[1] the sorts of natures people should have if it is to be easy for the legislator to take them in hand. Everything thereafter is a task for education. For some things are learned by habituation, others by instruction.

Two topics arise here: (1) whether the same people should rule throughout their lives, or whether rule should be shared around among all the citizens; (2) what ends the legislator should get the best sort of state to pursue. On the first, Aristotle thinks it is virtually impossible to find men whom we should want to rule over us permanently; in just about all cases the ruling has to be shared. On the second question, Aristotle inveighs against the old practice of the Spartans in taking warfare as the main goal of the state. War is for the sake of achieving peace, and the citizens should be educated more in the activities open to them in peacetime than in military prowess. Similarly, in the best state, leisure activities are more valued than those of work, since the latter are undertaken to attain the necessities of life and for the sake of having leisure; work is not properly an end in itself.

14. Since every political community is composed of rulers and ruled, we must investigate whether rulers and ruled should be the same or different throughout life; for clearly their education must correspond to this division. Now, if they differed from one another as much as gods and heroes are believed to differ from human beings, if the former were so greatly superior, first in body and then in soul, that their superiority was indisputable and manifest to those they ruled, it would clearly be altogether better if the same people always ruled and the others were always ruled. But this is not easy to achieve, and there are not, as Scylax[2] says there are in India, kings that are so superior to the ruled. Evidently, then, and for many different reasons, it is necessary for all to share alike in ruling and being ruled in turn; for equality consists in giving

---

1 In ch.7; not included in these selections.
2 A geographer of the late sixth century BCE, mentioned by Herodotus.

the same to those who are alike, and it is difficult for a constitution to last if its organization is contrary to justice, for the citizens being ruled will be joined by those in the surrounding territory who want to stir up change, and those in the government cannot possibly be numerous enough to be more powerful than all of them.

Surely it is indisputable, however, that the rulers should be different from the ruled. Hence the legislator should investigate the question of how this is to be achieved, and how they should share with one another. We discussed this earlier,[1] for nature itself settled the choice by making part of the same species younger and part older, the former fit to be ruled and the latter to rule. For young people do not object to being ruled, or think themselves better than their rulers, particularly when they are going to be compensated for their contribution when they reach the proper age. We must conclude, therefore, that rulers and ruled are in one way the same and in another different. Consequently, their education too must be in one way the same and in another different; for, if someone is going to rule well, as the saying goes, he should first have been ruled.

As we said in our first discussions,[2] however, there is a kind of rule that is for the sake of the ruler and a kind that is for the sake of the ruled. The former, we say, is rule by a master; the latter, rule over free people. Now some commands differ not with respect to the tasks they assign but with respect to that for the sake of which they are done. That is why it is noble even for free young men to perform many of the tasks that are held to be appropriate for slaves; for the difference between noble and shameful actions does not lie so much in the acts themselves as in their ends, on that for the sake of which they are performed. Since we say that the virtue of a citizen or ruler is the same as that of the best man, and that the same man should be ruled first and a ruler later, the legislator should make it his business to determine how and through what practices men become good, and what the end of the best life is.

The soul is divided into two parts, one of which has reason intrinsically, whereas the other does not, but is capable of listening to it, and we say that the virtues of the latter entitle a man to be called in a certain sense good. As to the question of which of these parts the end is more particularly found in, to those who make the distinction we mentioned it is not unclear what must be said. For the worse part is always for the sake of the better, and this is as evident in the products of the arts as it is in those of nature. But the part that has reason is better; and it, in accordance with our usual way of dividing, is divided in two: for there is practical reason and theoretical reason. So it is clear that the rational part of the soul must also be divided in the same manner. Ac-

---

1   In ch.9; not included in these selections.
2   In Bk.iii, 4 and 6; see selection **B.6.c** above.

tions, too, we will say, are divided analogously, and those that belong to the naturally better part must be more choiceworthy to anyone who can carry out all or only two of them. For what is most choiceworthy for each individual is always this: to attain what is highest. But the whole of life too is divided into work and leisure, war and peace, and of actions some are necessary or useful, others noble. And the same choice must be made among these as among the parts of the soul and their actions. War must be chosen for the sake of peace, work for the sake of leisure, necessary and useful things for the sake of noble ones.

A statesman must, therefore, look to all these things, particularly to those that are better and those that are ends, and legislate in a way that suits the parts of the soul and their actions. And he should legislate in the same way where life and the divisions of actions are concerned. For one should be able to work or go to war, but even better able to remain at peace and leisure; able to perform necessary or useful actions, but better able to perform noble ones. These then are the aims that should be kept in view when educating citizens, both when they are still children and whenever else they need education.

It is evident, however, that those Greeks who are currently held to be best governed, and the legislators who established their constitutions, did not organize the various aspects of their constitutions to promote the best end. Nor did they organize their laws and educational system to promote all the excellences, but instead were vulgarly inclined to promote the ones held to be more useful and more conducive to acquisition. Some later writers have expressed the same opinion in the same spirit; for they praise the Spartan constitution and express admiration for the aim of its legislator, because his entire legislation was intended to promote conquest and war. What they say is easy to refute by argument, and has now been refuted by the facts too. For most human beings are eager to rule as masters over many because it provides a ready supply of the goods of luck. And Thibron and all these other writers are no different: they admire the Spartan legislator because by training the Spartans to face danger he enabled them to rule over many. And yet it is clear, now that their empire is no longer in their hands at any rate, that the Spartans are not a happy people, and that their legislator is not a good one. Moreover, it is absurd if it was by keeping to his laws and putting them into practice without impediment that they lost their fine way of life. They are also incorrect in their conception of the sort of rule a legislator should be seen to honor; for rule over free people is nobler and more virtuous than rule by a master. Besides, one should not consider a state happy or praise its legislator because he trained it to conquer and rule its neighbors, since such things involve great harm; for clearly any citizen who is able to should also try to acquire the power to rule his own state, yet this is precisely what the Spartans accused their king, Pausanias, of doing, even though he held so high an office.

Arguments and laws of this sort are not worthy of a statesman, then, nor are they beneficial or true. For the same things are best both for individuals and for communities, and it is these that a legislator should implant in the souls of human beings. Training in war should not be undertaken for the sake of reducing those who do not deserve it to slavery, but, first, to avoid becoming enslaved to others; second, to pursue a position of dominance in order to benefit the ruled, not to be masters of all of them; and, third, to be masters of those who deserve to be slaves.

Both facts and arguments testify, then, that the legislator should give more serious attention to how to organize his legislation, both the part that deals with military affairs and the part that deals with other matters, for the sake of peace and leisure. For most states of the sort described remain secure while they are at war, but come to ruin once they have acquired empire. Like an iron sword they lose their edge when they remain at peace. But the one responsible is their legislator, who did not educate them to be able to be at leisure.

FOR DISCUSSION:

Should education of the young be mainly directed at enabling the students to engage well in leisure activities rather than in ones necessary for making a living?

DIOGENES LAERTIUS, FROM *LIVES:* ABOUT ARISTOTLE:[1]

Being asked how the educated differ from the uneducated, "As much," he said, "as the living from the dead." He used to declare education to be an ornament in prosperity and a refuge in adversity. Teachers who educated children deserved, he said, more honour than parents who merely gave them birth; for bare life is furnished by the one, the other ensures a good life.

---

1   *Lives*, V, 19. Translated by Hicks, vol. 1, p. 463.

C: HELLENISTIC AND ROMAN PERIOD

P olitical theory after Aristotle divides sharply between those who view society and its laws as basically a matter of agreements and conventions and those who think both are strongly rooted in a reality (nature) that precedes all such artificial creations. The Epicureans argue for the former position and the Stoics for the latter, both being unequivocal about where their sympathies lie. This dispute seems to be one that has continued, in one form or another, to the present day. Those who caution strongly against expecting different societies and cultures to agree on values, ethics, and political arrangements, are in the Epicurean tradition. Those who claim that cultural differences are relatively superficial compared to the common values that cut across all societies inherit the Stoic tradition of universalism. The attitude we take toward proposals for world government, for example, will be very strongly affected by which of these schools of thought we align with. Or is it possible to find some coherent middle position between the Epicurean and Stoic extremes?

C.1: EPICUREANS

The Epicurean[1] school was founded by Epicurus in the late fourth century BCE and remained devoted to the memory and ideas of its founder throughout its long existence in the ancient world. The Epicurean approach to both the formation of societies and the institution of rules of justice is to see them as making life for human beings safer and easier. Human beings are afflicted with emotions like envy which easily lead them into conflict; people must agree on rules which limit this and establish some way of punishing violators. Society and justice are, then, artificial constructs justified by their utility; and, since different forms of society and different laws of justice suit different peoples and different situations, we can expect to find significant differences in both across various peoples and at diverse times. Clearly, when it comes to the ancient dispute between the supporters of "convention" (*nomos*) on the one hand and those of "nature" (*phusis*) on the other, the Epicureans are in the former group. The rules of justice and the proper form of government for society are not writ into the fabric of objective reality.

FRANS B.M. DE WAAL, FROM "HOW ANIMALS DO BUSINESS":[2]

As 17th-century English philosopher Thomas Hobbes put it, "Every man is presumed to seek what is good for himselfe naturally, and what is just, only for Peaces sake, and accidentally." In this still prevailing view, sociality is but an afterthought, a "social contract" that our

---

1 In later non-philosophical use, the word 'epicurean' has come to denote devotion to the sensual pleasures of unusual culinary delights, instead of to the pleasures attendant on simply living without pain and stress, which were the ones Epicurus in fact espoused.
2 *Scientific American*, April 2005, pp. 73-74.

ancestors entered into because of its benefits, not because they are attracted to one another. For the biologist, this imaginary history falls as wide off the mark as can be. We descend from a long line of group-living primates, meaning that we are naturally equipped with a strong desire to fit in and find partners to live and work with.

C.1.a: EPICURUS, *KEY DOCTRINES*

31-37[1]

Born around 341 BCE Epicurus is reported to have started as a follower of the atomist philosophy of Democritus, and indeed that doctrine is preserved in his extant writings. He came to Athens in 306 and established a school in his "Garden" where he and his followers could practice a life of simple enjoyments, a result merely of eliminating pain and stress from life. He died in 271.

Epicurus' view was that justice arises only from contracts between people in which they agree not to harm each other in order to preserve the benefits of social relationships. The ways in which people arrange to minimize conflict vary from society to society, but the general nature of justice is the same for all.

31. Nature's justice is a guarantee of benefit with a view to not harming one another and not being harmed.

32. Nothing is just or unjust in relation to those creatures which were unable to make contracts over not harming one another and not being harmed; so too with all peoples who were unable or unwilling to make contracts over not harming and not being harmed.

33. Justice was never anything in itself but a contract, regularly arising at some place or other in people's dealings with one another, over not harming or being harmed.

34. Injustice is something bad not in itself but in the fear that arises from the suspicion that one will not escape the notice of those who have the authority to punish such things.

---

1   Translated by Long and Sedley, vol.1, p. 125, with some modifications.

35. No one who secretly infringes any of the terms of a mutual contract made with a view to not harming and not being harmed can be confident that he will escape detection even if he does so countless times. For right up to his death it is unclear whether he will actually escape.

36. Taken generally, justice is the same for all, since it is something beneficial in people's social relationships with each other. But in the light of what is peculiar to a region and to the whole range of causal factors, the same thing does not turn out to be just for all.

37. What is legally deemed to be just has its existence in the domain of justice whenever it is attested to be beneficial in fulfilling what is required for social relationships, whether or not it turns out to be the same for all. But if someone makes a law and it does not happen to accord with the benefits of social relationships, it no longer has the nature of justice. And even if what is beneficial in the sphere of justice changes but fits the preconception for some time, it was no less just throughout that time for those who do not confuse themselves with empty utterances but simply look at the facts.

FOR DISCUSSION:

When according to Epicurus would a contract regarding harming and not being harmed be unjust?

Why on Epicurus' view does what is just differ from place to place and time to time?

DIOGENES LAERTIUS, FROM *LIVES*: ABOUT EPICURUS:[1]

Friends indeed came to him from all parts and lived with him in his garden. This is stated by Apollodorus, who also says that he purchased the garden for eighty minae; and to the same effect Diocles in the third book of his *Epitome* speaks of them as living a very simple and frugal life; at all events they were content with half a pint of thin wine and were, for the rest, thoroughgoing water drinkers.

---

1 *Lives*, X, 10-11. Translated by Hicks, vol. 2, p. 539.

C.1.b: LUCRETIUS, *DE RERUM NATURA* (*ON THE NATURE OF THINGS*)

Bk.V. 1010-1027, 1105-1157[1]

L ucretius wrote in the first century BCE, but his dates of birth and
death are unknown, as is where he lived. Cicero makes mention of
him in a letter written in 54, but it is not clear that Lucretius was still
alive at that time. His great poem, *De rerum natura*, was rediscovered in the
renaissance and came to have an influence then that probably exceeded
what it had had in ancient times. The work is an attempt to popularize the
doctrines of Epicurus, but Lucretius adds many embellishments for which
he is no doubt responsible.

Lucretius sees both friendships and constitutions arising from the need
to curtail violence of people against one another. He presents this theory
in the form of a history of human development over time from primitive
unions through the rise of cities ruled by kings and ending with constitutions and laws that put limits on people's self-aggrandizing tendencies.

As time went by, men began to build huts and to use skins and fire. Male and female learned to live together in a stable union and to watch over their joint progeny.
Then it was that humanity first began to mellow. Thanks to fire their chilly bodies
could no longer so easily endure the cold under the canopy of heaven. Venus subdued
brute strength. Children by their wheedling easily broke down their parents' stubborn temper. Then neighbors began to form *mutual alliances*, wishing neither to do

---

1 Translated by Latham, pp. 202, 205-06.

nor to suffer violence among themselves. They appealed on behalf of their children and womenfolk, pointing out with gestures and inarticulate cries[1] that it is right for everyone to pity the weak. It was not possible to achieve perfect unity of purpose; yet a substantial majority kept faith honestly. Otherwise, the entire human race would have been wiped out there and then instead of being propagated, generation after generation, down to the present day.

As time went by, men learned to change their old way of life by means of fire and other new inventions, instructed by those of outstanding ability and mental energy. *Kings began to found cities* and establish citadels for their own safeguard and refuge. They parceled out cattle and lands, giving to each according to his looks, his strength and his ability; for good looks were highly prized and strength counted for much. Later came the invention of property and the discovery of gold, which speedily robbed the strong and the handsome of their pre-eminence. The man of greater riches finds no lack of stalwart frames and comely faces to follow in his train. And yet, if a man would guide his life by true philosophy, he will find ample riches in a modest livelihood enjoyed with a tranquil mind. Of that little he need never be beggared. Men craved for fame and power so that their fortune might rest on a firm foundation and they might live out a peaceful life in the enjoyment of plenty. An idle dream. In struggling to gain the pinnacle of power they beset their own road with perils. And then from the very peak, as though by a thunderbolt, they are cast down by envy into a foul abyss of ignominy. For envy, like the thunderbolt, most often strikes the highest and all that stands out above the common level. Far better to lead a quiet life in subjection than to long for sovereign authority and lordship over kingdoms. So leave them to the blood and sweat of their wearisome, unprofitable struggle along the narrow pathway of ambition. Since they savor life through another's mouth and choose their target rather by hearsay than by the evidence of their own senses, it avails them now, and will avail them, no more than it has ever done.

So the kings were killed. Down in the dust lay the ancient majesty of thrones, the haughty scepters. The illustrious emblem of the sovereign head, dabbled in gore and trampled under the feet of the rabble, mourned its high estate. What once was feared too much is now as passionately downtrodden. So the conduct of affairs sank back into the turbid depths of mob rule, with each man struggling to win dominance and supremacy for himself. Then some people showed how to form a constitution, based on fixed rights and recognized laws. Mankind, worn out by a life of violence and enfeebled by feuds, was the more ready to submit of its own free will to the bondage of laws and institutions. This distaste for a life of violence came naturally to a society

---

1   Lucretius thinks that these "alliances" preceded the development of human language.

in which every individual was ready to gratify his anger by a harsher vengeance than is now tolerated by equitable laws. Ever since then the enjoyment of life's prizes has been tempered by the fear of punishment. A man is enmeshed by their own violence and wrong-doing, which commonly recoil upon their author. It is not easy for one who breaks by his acts the mutual compact of social peace to lead a peaceful and untroubled life. Even if he hides his guilt from gods and man, he must feel a secret misgiving that it will not rest hidden forever. He cannot forget those oft-told tales of people betraying themselves by words spoken in dreams or delirium that drag out long-buried crimes into the daylight.

FOR DISCUSSION:

Is it Lucretius' view that our whole sense of right and wrong come from the need to live together without violence?

Is the origin of the state and laws due mostly to the need to contrive some way of keeping people from harming one another on account of their envy and ambition?

C.2: Stoicism

Stoicism itself was founded in the fourth century BCE by Zeno of Citium, and the school, located in Athens, was brought to its greatest sophistication in the third century BCE by Cleanthes and Chrysippus. Unfortunately hardly any of their work remains in existence. Its doctrines evolved over time but it was still a very important force in the thought of the educated when the Roman statesman and orator, Marcus Tullius Cicero, studied for a while in Athens in the first century. He is now our chief witness to Stoic political theory, and his writings show that in this area of inquiry he was an advocate for the Stoic position in political theory as he knew it in the first century BCE. In contrast to the Epicureans, the Stoics emphasized the naturalness of human society as well as of the basic laws which establish justice in society. This view they tie back to their theology in which a supreme god, elsewhere called the "designing fire" or "*logos*", constructs the world in such a way that it is suitable for human flourishing. Humans themselves differ from the rest of the creatures in that they have a share in the divine reason which governs all things, and thus they are capable of knowing the laws which the divine lawgiver intends human societies to abide by. Here is the source for the distinction between "eternal" law and human law which was to become so important in the western medieval tradition of political thought.

Stoicism downplays the differences between different peoples, claiming that on the basics of what constitutes justice all people are agreed. Thus it is possible to formulate laws which should apply to all people no matter what cultural differences they may exhibit. In this they laid a foundation for the idea of a worldwide commonwealth and government that would draw all peoples together in a single society. Perhaps it was intended that such unification would go along with a gradual spread of each individual's concern for others from the narrow sphere of his own countrymen to all human beings everywhere.

DIOGENES LAERTIUS, FROM *LIVES*: ABOUT ZENO OF CITIUM:[1]
Nothing, he declared, was more unbecoming than arrogance, especially in the young.

---

1   *Lives*, VII, 22. Translated by Hicks, vol. 2, p. 133.

C.2.a: CICERO, *DE FINIBUS BONORUM ET MALORUM* (*ON THE ULTIMATES IN GOODS AND EVILS*)

Cicero was born in 106 BCE in the town of Arpinum located in the foothills of the Appenines about 100 km southeast of Rome. He came from an aristocratic lineage, but Cicero was the first of his family to hold public office in Rome itself. He had a distinguished career in law and in the senate, ultimately becoming consul in 63. His oratorical skills were unparalleled, but he also had interests in Greek philosophy. When the Republic came to an end with the rise of Julius Caesar, Cicero was no longer able to function in government, and he turned back to philosophy, writing, in effect, a compendium of the philosophy of the main Greek schools at the time. He ended up being assassinated in December of 43 by agents of the government of the time.

III, SECTIONS 62-68[1]

The excerpt below comes from a letter to Brutus who a few months later (in 44 BCE) was to be one of the assassins of Julius Caesar and who would have received the letter in the summer of 45. It is part of a series of works on philosophy that Cicero wrote after he had been forced out of the political arena and consists of three dialogues, each of which expounds the ethical doctrine of one of the three main schools of philosophy in Cicero's day: Epicureanism, Stoicism, and Academic Skepticism. The title of the work indicates that under review are the varying positions these schools take

---

1 Translated by Woolf (*On Moral Ends*), pp. 84-87.

on what are the ultimate things to be sought in life and what are the worst things to be avoided. It is not to be assumed that Cicero himself entirely agreed with any of these doctrines.

In the passage below, Cicero has Cato the younger presenting the Stoic position. It is clear that even more than Aristotle, the Stoics emphasize the naturalness of human unions of all sorts, including political unions.

[62] "Now the Stoics consider it important to realize that parents' love for their children arises naturally. From this starting-point we trace the development of all human society. It should be immediately obvious from the shape and the parts of the human body that procreation is part of nature's plan. And it would hardly be consistent for nature to wish us to procreate yet be indifferent as to whether we love our offspring. Even among non-human animals the power of nature is evident. When we observe the effort they devote to breeding and rearing, it is as if we hear nature's very own voice. Thus our impulse to love what we have generated is given by nature herself as manifestly as our aversion to pain.

[63] "This is also the source of the mutual and natural sympathy between humans, so that the very fact of being human requires that no human be considered a stranger to any other. Some of our bodily parts—for example our eyes and ears—are as it were created just for themselves. Others—for example legs and hands—also enhance the utility of the other parts. In the same way, certain animals of great size are created merely for themselves. But take the so-called 'sea-pine', with its broad shell, and the creature known as the 'pine-guard', because it watches over the sea-pine, swimming out of the latter's shell and being shut up inside it when it retreats, as if apparently having warned the sea-pine to beware.[1] Or take ants, bees and storks—they too act altruistically. Yet the ties between human beings are far closer. Hence we are fitted by nature to form associations, assemblies and states.

[64] "The Stoics hold that the universe is ruled by divine will, and that it is virtually a single city and state shared by humans and gods. Each one of us is a part of this universe. It follows naturally from this that we value the common good more than our own. Laws value the welfare of all above the welfare of individuals. In the same way one who is good and wise, law-abiding and mindful of civic duty, considers the good of all more than that of any particular person including oneself. Even to betray one's country is no more despicable than to neglect common advantage and

---

1　The pinna is a Mediterranean mussel; the pinna-guard is a small crab which is often entangled in the mussel's beard. The ancients thought they were in a symbiotic relationship, with the little crab protected by living inside the mussel's shell, and warning it to close in case of danger.

welfare for the sake of one's own. That is why preparedness to die for one's country is so laudable—it is right and proper that we love our homeland more than our very selves. It is thought wicked and inhuman to profess indifference about whether the world will go up in flames once one is dead (the sentiment is usually articulated in a familiar Greek verse[1]). And so it is undoubtedly true that we must consider on their own account the interests of those who will one day come after us.

[65] "This human affection is the reason why people make wills and appoint guardians for their children when dying. And the fact that no one would choose to live in splendid isolation, however well supplied with pleasures, shows that we are born to join together and associate with one another and form natural communities. Indeed we are naturally driven to want to help as many people as possible, especially by teaching and handing on the principles of practical reason. [66] It is hard to find anyone who does not pass on what they know to someone else. Thus we have a propensity for teaching as much as for learning. Nature has given bulls the instinct to defend their calves against lions with immense passion and force. In the same way, those with great talent and the capacity for achievement, as is said of Hercules and Liber,[2] have a natural inclination to help the human race.

"Now we also give Jupiter the names of 'Greatest' and 'Highest'; we call him our Saviour, our Shelter, our Defender. By this we mean that our security as humans rests on his protection. But it is hardly consistent to ask for the care and love of the immortal gods while despising and neglecting each other! We use the parts of our body before we have learned the actual reasons why we have them. In the same way it is by nature that we have gathered together and formed ourselves in civil societies. If things were not that way, there would be no place for justice or benevolence.

[67] "But though they hold that there is a code of law which binds humans together, the Stoics do not consider that any such code exists between humans and other animals. Chrysippus made the famous remark that all other things were created for the sake of humans and gods, but that humans and gods were created for the sake of their own community and society; and so humans can use animals for their own benefit with impunity. He added that human nature is such that a kind of civil code mediates the individual and the human race: whoever abides by this code will be just, whoever breaches it unjust.

"Now although a theatre is communal, it can still rightly be said that the seat which one occupies is one's own. So, too, in city or universe, though these are communal, there is no breach of law in an individual owning property. [68] Also, since we

---

1 The Greek line alluded to says: "Once I'm dead, let the earth be consumed by fire."
2 Liber was an ancient Roman fertility god.

observe that humans are born to protect and defend one another, it is consistent with human nature for the wise person to want to take part in the business of government, and, in living by nature, to take a spouse and to wish to have children. Not even sexual passion, so long as it is pure, is considered to be incompatible with being wise. Some Stoics say that the Cynics' philosophy and way of life is suitable for the wise person, should circumstances arise conducive to its practice. But others rule this out altogether.[1]

FOR DISCUSSION:

Do you think that people have a natural inclination to consider the welfare of others, even of future generations? Would the existence of such a natural inclination show that we *ought* to care about others, even those unborn?

---

1   The Cynics were known for their asceticism and withdrawal from political and family life.

C.2.b: CICERO, *DE RE PUBLICA* (*ON THE COMMONWEALTH*) I

33, 38-43, 54-55, 65, 68-69[1]

C icero wrote *On the Commonwealth* between 55 and 51 BCE, but he has situated the dramatic date of the dialogue in 129, a time of political turmoil in Rome in which the main character, Scipio, was involved in trying to overturn the agrarian reforms of the Gracchi. In fact Scipio died only a few days after this conversation was imagined to have taken place. Scipio, i.e., Publius Cornelius Scipio Aemilianus Africanus, was the same Scipio who destroyed Carthage at the end of the Third Punic War, and was admired by Cicero as combining the virtues of both an educated mind and a dedication to the public good. The views he espouses in this selection combine those of Stoic and Peripatetic thinkers, whom Cicero himself favoured in this area of inquiry. Scipio had in real life been a friend of the Stoic philosopher Panaetius, one of Cicero's own teachers. The conversation here is started by Gaius Laelius, who was in fact a very close friend of Scipio's.

[33] ... *LAELIUS*: The skills that make us useful to the state: that, I think, is the most outstanding task of philosophy and the greatest evidence and function of virtue. Therefore, so that we may devote this holiday to conversations that will be most useful to the commonwealth, we should ask Scipio to explain to us what he thinks the best organization of the state to be. After that, we will investigate other subjects, and when we have learned about them I hope that we will arrive directly at these present circumstances and will unravel the significance of the current situation....

---

1 Translated by Zetzel, pp. 15-31.

[**38**] *SCIPIO*: I will do what you want to the best of my ability, and I will begin my discussion with this proviso—something that speakers on every subject need to use to avoid mistakes—namely that we agree on the name of the subject under discussion and then explain what is signified by that name; and when that is agreed on, only then is it right to begin to speak. We will never be able to understand what sort of thing we are talking about unless we understand first just what it is. And since we are looking into the commonwealth, let us first see what it is that we are looking into.

When Laelius agreed, *SCIPIO* said: In talking about such a well-known and important subject, I will not begin by going back to the origins which learned men generally cite in these matters, starting from the first intercourse of male and female and then from their offspring and family relationships; nor will I give frequent verbal definitions of what each thing is and how many ways it can be named. In speaking to knowledgeable men who have earned great glory through participation in the public life, both military and domestic, of a great commonwealth, I will not make the mistake of letting the subject of my speech be clearer than the speech itself. I have not undertaken this like some schoolteacher explaining everything, and I make no promises that no tiny details will be left out.

LAELIUS: The kind of speech you promise is just what I am waiting for.

[**39a**] *SCIPIO*: Well, then: the commonwealth is the concern of a people,[1] but a people is not any group of persons assembled in any way, but an assemblage of some size associated with one another through agreement on law and community of interest. The first cause of its assembly is not so much weakness as a kind of natural herding together of people; this species is not isolated or prone to wandering alone, but it is so created that not even in an abundance of everything <do people wish to live a solitary existence....> [a portion of the text is missing here] ... [**41**] ... These assemblages, then, were instituted for the reason that I explained, and their first act was to establish a settlement in a fixed location for their homes. Once they had protected it by both natural and constructed fortifications, they called this combination of buildings a town or a city, marked out by shrines and common spaces. Now every people (which is the kind of large assemblage I have described), every state (which is the organization of the people), every commonwealth (which is as I said the concern of the people) needs to be ruled by some sort of deliberation in order to be long lived. The deliberative function, moreover, must always be connected to the original cause which engendered the state; [**42**] and it must also either be assigned to one person or to selected individuals or be taken up by the entire population. And so, when the

---

1   The *res publica* is the *res populi*. '*Res publica*' is Cicero's Latin translation of the Greek term '*politeia*' found in both Plato and Aristotle where it means either the state itself or the constitution or mode of government of a state.

control of everything is in the hands of one person, we call that one person a king and that type of commonwealth a monarchy. When it is in the control of chosen persons, then a state is said to be ruled by the will of the aristocracy. And that in which everything is in the hands of the people is a "popular" state—which is what they call it. And of these three types any one, even though it may not be perfect or in my opinion the best possible, still is tolerable as long as it holds to the bond which first bound men together in the association of a commonwealth; and any one might be better than another. A fair and wise king, or selected leading citizens, or the people itself, although that is the least desirable, if injustice and greed do not get in the way, may exist in a stable condition.

[43] But in monarchies no one else has sufficient access to shared justice or to deliberative responsibility; and in the rule of an aristocracy the people have hardly any share in liberty, since they lack any role in common deliberation and power; and when everything is done by the people itself, no matter how just and moderate it may be, that very equality is itself inequitable in that it recognizes no degrees of status....

[54] *LAELIUS*: What do you think, Scipio? Which one of these three forms do you most approve?

SCIPIO: You are right to ask which one of the three I most approve, since I approve of none of them by itself, separately. I prefer to the individual forms the type that is an alloy of all three. But if I had to express approval of one of the simple forms, then I would choose monarchy....

[55] Here are the aristocrats, who claim that they can do this same job better and say that there is more judgment in the deliberations of several people than of one, but the same equity and honor. And here is the populace shouting loudly that they will not obey one person or a few; that even for wild animals there is nothing sweeter than liberty, and that everyone is deprived of it, whether it is a king or aristocrats to whom they are enslaved. And so kings captivate us by their affection, aristocrats by their judgment, and the people by its liberty, so that in comparing them it is hard to pick the most desirable....

[65] *SCIPIO*: When I have said what I think about the type of commonwealth I most admire, I must speak with greater precision about the transformations of commonwealths, even though I think that they will not take place easily in the best type. But the alteration of the monarchic form is the first and the most certain: when a king begins to be unjust, the form is immediately destroyed, and that same person is a tyrant, the worst form, but closest to the best. If the aristocracy gets rid of him (which generally happens), the commonwealth has the second of the three forms; it is almost monarchic, that is, a senatorial council of leaders taking good care of the people. If the people themselves kill or expel the tyrant, the government is reasonably restrained,

so long as it is intelligent and perceptive: they rejoice in their accomplishment, and want to protect the commonwealth that they have set up. But when either the people bring force to bear on a just king and deprive him of his throne or even (as happens more frequently) have tasted the blood of the aristocracy and subordinated the entire commonwealth to their own desires, do not make the mistake of thinking that any huge ocean or fire is harder to calm than the violence of a mob out of control....[1]

[68] ... For just as the excessive power of the aristocracy causes their fall, so too liberty itself makes slaves out of this excessively free populace. Anything that is too successful—in weather, or harvests, or human bodies—generally turns into its opposite, and that is particularly true of commonwealths: extreme liberty, both of the people at large and of particular individuals, results in extreme slavery. From this pure liberty arises a tyrant, the most unjust and harshest form of slavery. For from this unruly, or rather monstrous, populace some leader is usually chosen against those aristocrats who have already been beaten down and driven from their place: someone bold, corrupt, vigorous in attacking people who have often served the commonwealth well; someone who buys the people's good will using others' property as well as his own. As a private citizen he fears for his safety, and so he is given power which is renewed; he is protected by bodyguards, like Pisistratus[2] in Athens; and finally he emerges as tyrant over those very people who promoted him. If, as often happens, a tyrant is overthrown by respectable people, the state is restored; if by men of daring, it becomes an oligarchy, which is just another form of tyranny. The same type of regime can often emerge from a good aristocratic government, when corruption turns the leaders themselves from the right path. In this way, they snatch the government from one another as if it were a ball; tyrants from kings, aristocrats or the people from them, and from them oligarchies or tyrants. No form of commonwealth is ever maintained for very long.

[69] Since that is the case, of the three primary forms my own preference is for monarchy; but monarchy itself is surpassed by a government which is balanced and compounded from the three primary forms of commonwealth. I approve of having something outstanding and monarchic in a commonwealth; of there being something else assigned to the authority of aristocrats; of some things being set aside for the judgment and wishes of the people. This structure has, in the first place, a certain degree of equality, which free people cannot do without for very long; it also has solidity, in that those primary forms are easily turned into the opposite vices, so that a master arises in place of a king, a faction in place of an aristocracy, a confused mob in place

---

1 What follows here is a translation into Latin of a portion of Plato's *Republic* VIII, viz. 562c-563e. See selection **B.5.h.** above pp. 242-43.
2 A tyrant who ruled Athens on several occasions in the sixth century BCE.

of the people; and these types are often replaced by new ones. That does not occur in this combined and moderately blended form of commonwealth unless there are great flaws in its leaders. There is no reason for revolution when each person is firmly set in his own rank, without the possibility of sudden collapse.

FOR DISCUSSION:

How might Scipio's proposal that the three basic forms of government be combined in a fourth be instituted? Can you think of any modern governments which have something like what he proposes?

C.2.c: CICERO, *DE LEGIBUS* (*ON THE LAWS*)

*O*n the Laws consists of a conversation between Cicero (whose full name was Marcus Tullius Cicero), his brother Quintus, and his close friend, Titus Pomponius Atticus. In these selections Cicero enunciates the basic Stoic ideas behind his doctrine of a law that is not a mere matter of conventional regulations enforced by human authorities.

(1) I, 17-33[1]

[17] ... *MARCUS*: The object of inquiry in this conversation, Atticus, is not how to write legal documents or how to answer legal questions. Granted, that is a great task, which used to be performed by many famous men and is now done by one man of the greatest authority and wisdom;[2] but in this discussion we must embrace the whole subject of universal justice and law, so that what we call "civil law"[3] will be limited to a small and narrow area. We must explain the nature of law, and that needs to be looked for in human nature; we must consider the legislation through which states ought to be governed; and then we must deal with the laws of decrees of peoples as they are composed and written, in which the so-called civil laws of our people will not be left out.

[18] *QUINTUS*: You are looking deep, and (as is right) to the source of what we seek; people who teach civil law differently are teaching not so much the way of justice as of the courtroom.

MARCUS: That isn't true, Quintus, and in fact ignorance of law leads to more

---

1 Translated by Zetzel, pp. 111-17.
2 The reference is to Servius Sulpicius Rufus, who was consul in 51 BCE and the last great jurist of the republican period.
3 I.e., the law of some particular state, for example Rome.

lawsuits than knowledge of it. But that comes later; now we should consider the origins of law.

Philosophers have taken their starting point from law; and they are probably right to do so if, as these same people define it, law is the highest reason, rooted in nature, which commands things that must be done and prohibits the opposite. When this same reason is secured and established in the human mind, it is law. [19] And, therefore, they think that law is judgment, the effect of which is such as to order people to behave rightly and forbid them to do wrong; they think that its name in Greek[1] is derived from giving to each his own, while I think that in Latin[2] it is derived from choosing. They put the essence of law in equity, while we place it in choice; both are attributes of law. I think that these ideas are generally right; and, if so, then the beginning of justice is to be sought in law: law is a power of nature, it is the mind and reason of the prudent man, it distinguishes justice and injustice. But since all our speech is based on popular conceptions, we must sometimes speak in popular terms and call that a law (in the language of the common people) which prescribes in writing what it wants by ordering or forbidding. But in establishing the nature of justice, let us begin from that highest law, which was born aeons before any law was written or indeed before any state was established.

[20] *QUINTUS*: That is certainly more convenient and appropriate to the manner of the conversation we have begun.

MARCUS: Then shall we go back to the beginning, to the source of justice itself? Once we have found it, there will be no doubt about how to judge what we are seeking.

QUINTUS: In my opinion that is what we should do.

ATTICUS: I subscribe to your brother's opinion.

MARCUS: Then, since we want to preserve and protect that form of commonwealth which Scipio showed was the best in the six books of *On the Commonwealth*,[3] and since all the laws must be fitted to that type of state, and since morals must be planted and we should not rely on the sanctions of written laws, I will seek the roots of justice in nature, under whose leadership our entire discussion must unfold.

ATTICUS: Absolutely, and with nature's leadership there will be no possibility of getting lost.

[21] *MARCUS*: Then, Atticus, will you grant me this (I know Quintus' opinion), that all nature is ruled by the force or nature or reason or power or mind or will—or whatever other word there is that will indicate more plainly what I mean—of the

---

1   'nomos' which the Stoics thought derived from 'nemō' meaning to divide.
2   'lex' from 'lego' meaning to select.
3   Some of Scipio's remarks can be found in selection **C.2.b** above.

immortal gods? If you don't accept this, then I will have to start by making a case for that.

ATTICUS: Of course, I will grant it, if you wish; the singing of the birds and the noise of the river give me reason not to fear that any of my fellow students will hear me.[1]

MARCUS: But you need to be careful; they can become very angry, as good men do, and they will not take it lightly if they hear that you have betrayed the opening sentence of the best of men,[2] in which he wrote that god is not troubled by his own affairs or those of others.

[22] *ATTICUS*: Go on, please. I am waiting to hear the relevance of what I have conceded to you.

MARCUS: You don't have long to wait. This is its relevance: this animal—provident, perceptive, versatile, sharp, capable of memory, and filled with reason and judgment—which we call a human being, was endowed by the supreme god with a grand status at the time of its creation. It alone of all types and varieties of animate creatures has a share in reason and thought, which all the others lack. What is there, not just in humans, but in all heaven and earth, more divine than reason? When it has matured and come to perfection, it is properly named wisdom. [23] And, therefore, since there is nothing better than reason, and it is found both in humans and in god, reason forms the first bond between human and god. And those who share reason also share right reason; and, since that is law, we humans must be considered to be closely allied to gods by law. Furthermore, those who share law also share the procedures of justice; and those who have these things in common must be considered members of the same state, all the more so if they obey the same commands and authorities. Moreover, they do obey this celestial order, the divine mind and the all-powerful god, so that this whole cosmos must be considered to be the common state of gods and humans. And, as in states distinctions in the legal condition of individuals are made in accordance with family relationships (according to a kind of system with which I will deal at the proper time), it is all the more grand and glorious in nature at large that humans should be a part of the family and race of gods.

[24] For, when people consider the nature of human beings, it is usual to argue (and I think that the argument is right) that in the constant motions and revolutions of the heavens a proper season came for planting the seeds of the human race; when it was scattered and sown over the earth, it was enhanced by the divine gift of souls. And, although all the other things of which humans are composed came from mortal stock

---

1   Atticus is an Epicurean and would not have accepted as literally true the rule of the gods over the world.

2   He refers to Epicurus himself.

and were fragile and bound to perish, the soul was implanted in us by god. Hence there is in truth a family relationship between us and the gods, what can be called a common stock or origin. And thus out of so many species there is no animal besides the human being that has any knowledge of god, and among humans themselves there is no tribe, either civilized or savage, which does not know that it must recognize a god, even though it may not know what kind of god it should recognize. [25] The result is that they acknowledge god as a sort of recollection and acknowledgement of their origin. Furthermore, virtue is the same in human and god, and it is found in no other species besides; and virtue is nothing else than nature perfected and taken to its highest level. There is, therefore, a similarity between human and god. And since that is so, what closer or more certain relationship can there possibly be? That is why nature has bestowed such an abundance of things for human convenience and use, such that those things which exist seem to have been deliberately given to us, not randomly created; and this applies not only to the earth's profusion in bringing forth crops and fruits, but even to animals, some of which were created for human use, some for enjoyment, and some for food. [26] Countless branches of knowledge have been discovered under the tutelage of nature, which reason imitated in order skillfully to achieve things necessary for life.

Nature also not only adorned the human being with swiftness of mind, but also gave him the senses as servants and messengers; she supplied the latent and not completely formed conceptions of many things as the basis of knowledge, and she gave bodily shape that is both adaptable and suited to the nature of human beings. For, although she made all other animate creatures face the earth for grazing, she made the human alone upright and roused him to look on the sky, as if on his family and former home; and she shaped the appearance of his face so as to mould in it the character hidden within. [27] For the eyes most expressively say how we feel in our minds, and what is called the expression, which cannot exist in any other creature besides the human, indicates character (the Greeks know the idea, but they have no equivalent word[1]). I leave out the capacities and abilities of the rest of the body, the modulation of the voice and the power of speech, which is the greatest force in promoting bonds among humans. Not everything is appropriate to this discussion and this moment, and it seems to me that Scipio deals sufficiently with this subject in the book[2] that you have read.

Now, since god produced and equipped the human being in this way, desiring humans to have the first place among all other things, it is clear (to be selective in my

---

1 Greek uses 'prosōpon' to mean both face and expression.
2 I.e., On the Commonwealth.

discussion) that human nature itself has gone further: with no instruction, and taking as a starting point the knowledge of those things whose characteristics she knew from the first inchoate conceptions, she herself has strengthened reason and perfected it.

[28] *ATTICUS*: Good lord! What a distant starting point you take for the origins of justice! But you do it in such a way that I am not only not in a hurry to hear what I was waiting for from you on the civil law, but I could happily spend the whole day in this conversation. What you are discussing now, perhaps for the sake of other subjects, is more important than the things to which it serves as a preface.

MARCUS: Important they are, however briefly I am mentioning them now. But of all the things which are a subject of philosophical debate there is nothing more worthwhile than clearly to understand that we are born for justice and that justice is established not by opinion but by nature. That will be clear if you examine the common bonds among human beings. [29] There is no similarity, no likeness of one thing to another, so great as the likeness we all share. If distorted habits and false opinions did not twist weak minds and bend them in any direction, no one would be so like himself as all people would be like all others. Thus, whatever definition of a human being one adopts is equally valid for all humans. [30] That, in turn, is a sufficient proof that there is no dissimilarity within the species; if there were, then no one definition would apply to all. In particular, reason, the one thing by which we stand above the beasts, through which we are capable of drawing inferences, making arguments, refuting others, conducting discussions and demonstrations, reason is shared by all, and, though it differs in the particulars of knowledge, it is the same in the capacity to learn. All the same things are grasped by the senses; and the things that are impressed upon the mind, the rudiments of understanding which I mentioned before, are impressed similarly on all humans, and language, the interpreter of the mind, may differ in words but is identical in ideas. There is no person of any nation who cannot reach virtue with the aid of a guide.

[31] The similarity of the human race is as remarkable in perversities as it is in proper behavior. All people are ensnared by pleasure; and, even if it is an enticement to bad conduct, it still has some similarity to natural goodness: it gives delight through its fickle sweetness. Thus through a mental error it is adopted as something salutary; by a similar sort of ignorance death is avoided as a dissolution of nature, life is sought because it keeps us in the state in which we were born, and pain is considered one of the greatest evils both because of its own harshness and because the destruction of our nature seems to follow from it. [32] Because of similarity between honor and glory, people who have been honored seem blessed, and those who have no glory seem wretched. Trouble, happiness, desires and fears pass equally through the minds of all, and if different peoples have different beliefs, that does not mean that the superstition

that affects people who worship dogs and cats is not the same as that which besets other races. What nation is there that does not cherish affability, generosity, a grateful mind and one that remembers good deeds? What nation does not scorn and hate people who are proud, or evildoers, or cruel, or ungrateful? From all these things it may be understood that the whole human race is bound together; and the final result is that the understanding of the right way of life makes all people better. If you agree with all this, then we can go on to the rest; if you think anything is left out, then we should discuss that first.

ATTICUS: We are quite satisfied, if I may answer for both of us.

[**33**] *MARCUS*: It follows, then, that we have been made by nature to receive the knowledge of justice one from another and share it among all people. And I want it to be understood in this whole discussion that the justice of which I speak is natural, but that such is the corruption of bad habits that it extinguishes what I may call the sparks given by nature, and that contrary vices arise and become established. But if human judgment corresponded to what is true by nature and people thought nothing human alien to them (to use the poet's phrase[1]), then justice would be cultivated equally by all. Those who have been given reason by nature have also been given right reason, and therefore law too, which is right reason in commands and prohibitions; and if they have been given law, then they have been given justice too. All people have reason, and therefore justice has been given to all; so that Socrates rightly used to curse the person who was first to separate benefit from justice, and to complain that that was the source of all ills.

FOR DISCUSSION:

Is the thesis that justice is natural to humans necessarily tied to the view Cicero subscribes to here, that humans are created by god and are similar to god in their rational capacity?

Are various peoples really as similar to each other as Cicero claims? Is this thesis necessary to defend the naturalness of justice?

(2) II, 8-13[2]

Cicero here enunciates in no uncertain terms the doctrine that the divine and totally rational ruler of the world has designed laws that humans are to obey, that humans have an innate sense of what these laws are, and that no humanly constructed law has any force if it contradicts that divine law.

---

1 Terence, *Heautontimorumenos* 77.
2 Translated by Zetzel, pp. 132-34.

[8] *MARCUS*: Then before we get to particular laws, let us consider again the meaning and nature of law, so that—since everything else in our discussion rests on this—we don't slip from time to time in the misuse of language and make mistakes about the meaning of the [word]¹ by which our laws are to be defined.

QUINTUS: Fair enough; that's the right course of instruction.

MARCUS: This has, I know, been the opinion of the wisest men: that law was not thought up by human minds; that it is not some piece of legislation by popular assemblies; but it is something eternal which rules the entire universe through the wisdom of its commands and prohibitions. Therefore, they said, that first and final law is the mind of the god who compels or forbids all things by reason. From that cause, the law which the gods have given to the human race has rightly been praised: it is the reason and mind of a wise being, suited to command and prohibition.

[9] *QUINTUS*: You have dealt with that subject several times already, but before you come to legislation enacted by popular vote, please explain the meaning of that heavenly law, so that we may not be sucked in by the tide of habit and drawn to the customs of everyday language.

MARCUS: From the time we were small, Quintus, we were taught to call "if there is a summons to court"² and other things of that sort "laws". But in fact it should be understood that both this and other commands and prohibitions of peoples have a force for summoning to proper behavior and deterring from crime, a force which is not only older than the age of peoples and states but coeval with the god who protects and steers heaven and earth. [10] It is not possible for there to be a divine mind without reason, nor does divine reason lack this force in sanctioning right and wrong. The fact that it was not written down anywhere that one man should stand on the bridge against all the forces of the enemy and order the bridge to be cut down behind him does not mean that we should not believe that the famous Horatius Cocles performed his great deed in accordance with the law and command of bravery; nor does the absence of a written law on sexual assault during the reign of Lucius Tarquinius mean that the violence which Sextus Tarquinius brought against Lucretia the daughter of Tricipitinus was not contrary to the eternal law. Reason existed, derived from nature, directing people to good conduct and away from crime; it did not begin to be a law only at that moment when it was written down, but when it came into being; and it came into being at the same time as the divine mind. And therefore that true and original law suitable for commands and prohibitions, is the right reason of Jupiter, the supreme god.

---

1   The text is corrupt at this point.
2   The opening clause of the Twelve Tables, the ancient law of Rome.

[11] *QUINTUS*: I agree, brother, that what is right and true is also eternal and neither rises nor falls with the texts in which legislation is written.

MARCUS: Therefore, just as that divine mind is the highest law, so too when in a human being it is brought to maturity, [it resides]¹ in the mind of wise persons. The legislation that has been written down for nations in different ways and for particular occasions has the name of law more as a matter of courtesy than as a fact; for they teach that every law that deserves that name is praiseworthy, using arguments such as these: it is generally agreed that laws were invented for the well-being of citizens, the safety of states, and the calm and happy life of humans; and that those who first ordained legislation of this sort demonstrated to their peoples that they would write and carry such legislation the adoption of which would make their lives honorable and happy; and that what was so composed and ordained they would call laws. From this it should be understood that those who wrote decrees that were destructive and unjust to their peoples, since they did the opposite of what they had promised and claimed, produced something utterly different from laws; so that it should be clear that in the interpretation of the word 'law' itself there is the significance and intention of choosing something just and right.

[12] So I ask you, Quintus, as they generally do: if the lack of something causes a state to be worthless, is that something to be considered a good thing?

QUINTUS: Among the very best.

MARCUS: Then should not a state lacking law be considered as nothing for that very reason?

QUINTUS: No other conclusion is possible.

MARCUS: Then it is necessary that law be considered one of the best things.

QUINTUS: I agree completely.

[13] *MARCUS*: What of the fact that many things are approved by peoples that are damaging and destructive, which no more approach the name of law than whatever bandits have agreed upon among themselves? The instructions of doctors cannot truly be so called if in ignorance and inexperience they prescribe poisons in place of medicine; nor, even if the people approve of it, will something harmful in a nation be a law of any kind. Law, therefore, is the distinction between just and unjust things, produced in accordance with nature, the most ancient and first of all things, in accordance with which human laws are constructed which punish the wicked while defending and protecting the good.

QUINTUS: I understand entirely, and I now think that any other law should not only not be accepted, but should not even be given the name of law.

---

1 There is another gap in the text here.

FOR DISCUSSION:

Does one have to believe in a divine lawgiver in order consistently to claim that there is a law of right and wrong that precedes all laws humans make?

Can a regulation be enacted by properly constituted authorities but not have the force of genuine law?

Could the "dictates of conscience" be considered something of a substitute for the divine law?

JEAN-JACQUES ROUSSEAU, FROM *THE SOCIAL CONTRACT*:[1]

Good laws lead men to make better ones; bad laws lead to worse. As soon as someone says of the business of the state, "What does it matter to me?"—then the state must be reckoned lost.

---

1 First published in 1762 as *Du contrat social ou Principes du droit politique*. Widely available in contemporary editions. This translation by Maurice Cranston (Harmondsworth: Penguin Classics, 1968).

C.2.d: CICERO, *DE RE PUBLICA* (*ON THE COMMONWEALTH*) III

33[1]

Book three of *On the Commonwealth* exists only in fragmented form. The following short selection reveals Cicero's adoption of the Stoic conception of a law binding on all people and nations.

[**33**] True law is right reason, consonant with nature, spread through all people. It is constant and eternal; it summons to duty by its orders, it deters from crime by its prohibitions. Its orders and prohibitions to good people are never given in vain; but it does not move the wicked by these orders or prohibitions. It is wrong to pass laws obviating this law; it is not permitted to abrogate any of it; it cannot be totally repealed. We cannot be released from this law by the senate or the people, and it needs no exegete or interpreter like Sextus Aelius.[2] There will not be one law at Rome and another at Athens, one now and another later; but all nations at all times will be bound by this one eternal and unchangeable law, and the god will be the one common master and general (so to speak) of all people. He is the author, expounder, and mover of this law; and the person who does not obey it will be in exile from himself. Insofar as he scorns his nature as a human being, by this very fact he will pay the greatest penalty, even if he escapes all the other things that are generally recognized as punishments.

FOR DISCUSSION:

Is the above view at all compatible with holding that different peoples have somewhat different views about what is right and what is wrong conduct?

---

1 Translated by Zetzel, pp. 71-72.
2 Sextus Aelius Paetus Catus, who was consul in 198 BCE and censor in 194. He was famous for his legal commentaries on the Twelve Tables, the ancient foundation of Roman law.

C.2.e: STOBAEUS ON THE DOCTRINE OF HIEROCLES[1]

S tobaeus compiled an anthology of earlier thought probably in the fifth century CE. Here he reports some ideas of the Stoic philosopher Hierocles who would have been working around 100 CE.

Part of the Stoic doctrine of "appropriation" involved making people "one's very own" starting with one's immediate family. But, as the doctrine presented below of ever larger concentric circles implies, the drawing in of people to the area of one's concern extended ultimately to the whole human race.

Each one of us is as it were entirely encompassed by many circles, some smaller, others larger, the latter enclosing the former on the basis of their different and unequal dispositions relative to each other. The first and closest circle is the one which a person has drawn as though around a centre, his own mind. This circle encloses the body and anything taken for the sake of the body. For it is virtually the smallest circle, and almost touches the centre itself. Next, the second one further removed from the centre but enclosing the first circle; this contains parents, siblings, wife, and children. The third one has in it uncles and aunts, grandparents, nephews, nieces, and cousins. The next circle includes the other relatives, and this is followed by the circle of local residents, then the circle of fellow-tribesmen, next that of fellow citizens, and then in the same way the circle of people from neighboring towns, and the circle of fellow-countrymen. The outermost and largest circle, which encompasses all the rest, is that of the whole human race. Once these have all been surveyed, it is the task of a well-tempered person, in his proper treatment of each group, to draw the circles somehow towards the centre, and to keep zealously transferring those from the enclosing circles

---

1 Translated by Long and Sedley, pp. 349-50, with some modifications.

into the enclosed ones ... It is incumbent on us to respect people from the third circle as if they were those from the second, and again to respect our other relatives as if they were those from the third circle. For although the greater distance in blood will remove some affection, we must still try hard to assimilate them. The right point will be reached if, through our own initiative, we reduce the distance of the relationship with each person. The main procedure for this has been stated. But we should do more, in the terms of address we use, calling cousins brothers, and uncles and aunts fathers and mothers ... For this mode of address would be no slight mark of our affection for them all, and it would also stimulate and intensify the indicated contraction of the circles.

FOR DISCUSSION:

Should we in fact try to exercise the same care and concern for people in distant lands as we do for our own countrymen, or for our own family?

C.3: POLYBIUS, *HISTORIES* VI

3-9[1]

B orn in 208 BCE to an aristocratic family in Megalopolis, an important city in the Peloponnesus, Polybius had a distinguished political and military career which brought him into close relationship with the Romans, who achieved dominance over Greece after defeating the Macedonians in 168. He had long been an advocate of the Greek cities' acquiescing to Roman hegemony while retaining a degree of autonomy, but, nevertheless, the Romans took him prisoner and brought him to Rome. In 151 he was given his liberty, but chose to remain in Rome where he was welcome in the highest echelons of the Roman ruling class. Out of this came his great project of writing a history and defense of Rome's rise to dominance. The result was *The Histories*, in forty books, of which only the first five survive in complete versions; the others are known only from excerpts quoted in other works. Polybius died at the age of 82 from an accident while riding a horse.

Polybius wrote just as Rome was establishing its empire in the Greek speaking lands of the eastern Mediterranean. The following selection serves as a preface to his analysis of the form of government Rome had before it slid into autocracy under the Caesars. Particularly noteworthy is his belief in a cycle of forms of government that states inevitably pass through. The whole theory makes for an interesting contrast with both Plato and Aristotle.

3. In the case of those Greek states which have often risen to greatness and have often experienced a complete change of fortune, it is an easy matter both to describe their

---

1 Translated by Paton, vol. iii, pp. 271-89, with some changes.

past and to pronounce as to their future. For there is no difficulty in reporting the known facts, and it is not hard to foretell the future by inference from the past. But about the Roman state it is neither at all easy to explain the present situation owing to the complicated character of the constitution, nor to foretell the future owing to our ignorance of the peculiar features of public and private life at Rome in the past. Particular attention and study are therefore required if one wishes to attain a clear general view of the distinctive qualities of their constitution.

Most of those whose object it has been to instruct us methodically concerning such matters, distinguish three kinds of constitutions, which they call kingship, aristocracy, and democracy. Now we should, I think, be quite justified in asking them to enlighten us as to whether they represent these three to be the sole varieties or rather to be the best; for in either case my opinion is that they are wrong. For it is evident that we must regard as the best constitution a combination of all these three varieties, since we have had proof of this not only theoretically but by actual experience, Lycurgus having been the first to draw up a constitution—that of Sparta—on this principle. Nor, on the other hand, can we admit that these are the only three varieties; for we have witnessed monarchical and tyrannical governments, which, while they differ very widely from kingship, yet bear a certain resemblance to it, this being the reason why monarchs in general falsely assume and use, as far as they can, the regal title. There have also been several oligarchical constitutions which seem to bear some likeness to aristocratic ones, though the divergence is, generally, as wide as possible. The same holds good for democracies.

4. The truth of what I say is evident from the following considerations. It is by no means every monarchy which we can call straight off a kingship, but only that which is voluntarily accepted by the subjects and where they are governed rather by an appeal to their reason than by fear and force. Now again can we style every oligarchy an aristocracy, but only that where the government is in the hands of a selected body of the justest and fairest men. Similarly that is no true democracy in which the whole crowd of citizens is free to do whatever they wish or purpose, but when, in a community where it is traditional and customary to reverence the gods, to honor our parents, to respect our elders, and to obey the laws, the will of the greater number prevails, this is to be called a democracy. We should, therefore, assert that there are six kinds of constitutions, the three above mentioned which are in everyone's mouth and the three which are naturally allied to them, I mean monarchy, oligarchy, and mob-rule. Now the first of these to come into being is monarchy, its growth being natural and unaided; and next arises kingship derived from monarchy by the aid of art and by the correction of defects. This then changes into its related bad form, tyranny; and next, the abolishment of both gives birth to aristocracy. Aristocracy by its very nature

degenerates into oligarchy; and when the commons inflamed by anger take vengeance on this government for its unjust rule, democracy comes into being; and in due course the license and lawlessness of this form of government produces mob-rule to complete the series.

The truth of what I have just said will be quite clear to anyone who pays due attention to such beginnings, origins, and changes as are in each case natural. For that person alone who has seen how each form naturally arises and develops will be able to see when, how and where the growth, perfection, change, and end of each are likely to occur again. And it is to the Roman constitution above all that this method, I think, may be successfully applied, since from the outset its formation and growth have been due to natural causes.

5. Perhaps this theory of the natural transformations into each other of the different forms of government is more elaborately set forth by Plato and certain other philosophers; but, as the arguments are subtle and are stated at great length, they are beyond the reach of all but a few. I, therefore, will attempt to give a short summary of the theory as far as I consider it to apply to the history of what actually goes on and to appeal to the common intelligence of mankind. For if there appear to be certain omissions in my general exposition of it, the detailed discussion which follows will afford the reader ample compensation for any difficulties now left unresolved.

What, then, are the beginnings I speak of and what is the first origin of political arrangements? When owing to floods, famines, failure of crops or other such causes there occurs such a destruction of the human race as tradition tells us has more than once happened, and as we must believe will often happen again, all arts and crafts perishing at the same time, then in the course of time, when springing from the survivors as from seeds people have again increased in numbers and just like other animals form herds (it being a matter of course that they too should herd together with those of their kind owing to their natural weakness), it is a necessary consequence that the person who excels in bodily strength and in courage will lead and rule over the rest. We observe and should regard as a most genuine work of nature this very phenomenon in the case of the other animals which act purely by instinct and among whom the strongest are always indisputably the masters; I speak of bulls, boars, cocks, and the like. It is probable, then, that at the beginning people lived like this, herding together like animals and following the lead of the strongest and bravest, the ruler's strength being here the sole limit to his power and the name we should give his rule being 'monarchy'.

But, when in time feelings of sociability and companionship begin to grow in such gatherings of people, then kingship has struck root, and the notions of goodness, justice, and their opposites, begin to arise in people.

6. The manner in which these notions come into being is as follows. Since people are all naturally inclined to sexual intercourse, and the consequence of this is the birth of children, whenever any of these who have been reared do not on growing up show gratitude to those who reared them or defend them, but on the contrary take to speaking ill of them or ill treating them, it is evident that they will displease and offend those who have been familiar with their parents and have witnessed the care and pains they spent on attending to and feeding their children. For seeing that humans are distinguished from the other animals by possessing mind and rational thought, it is obviously improbable that such a difference of conduct should escape them, as it escapes other animals; they will notice the thing and be displeased at what is going on, looking to the future and reflecting that they may all meet with the same treatment.

Again, when a person who has been helped or assisted when in danger by another does not show gratitude to his preserver, but even goes to the length of attempting to do him injury, it is clear that those who become aware of it will naturally be displeased and offended by such conduct, sharing the resentment of their injured neighbor and imagining themselves in the same situation. From all this there arises in everyone a notion of the meaning and theory of what is one's due, the very thing which is the beginning and end of justice. Similarly, again, when anyone is foremost in defending his fellows from danger, and braves and awaits the onslaught of the most powerful beasts, it is natural that this person should receive marks of favor and honor from the people, while the person who acts in the opposite manner will meet with reprobation and dislike. From this again some idea of what is base and what is noble and of what constitutes the difference is likely to arise among the people; and noble conduct will be admired and imitated because it is advantageous, while base conduct will be avoided. Now, when the leading and most powerful person among the people always throws the weight of his authority on the side of the notions on such matters which generally prevail, and when in the opinion of his subjects he apportions rewards and penalties according to desert, they yield obedience to him no longer because they fear his force, but rather because their judgement approves him; and they join in maintaining his rule even if he is quite enfeebled by age, defending him with one consent and battling against those who conspire to overthrow his rule. Thus by insensible degrees the monarch becomes a king, ferocity and force having yielded the supremacy to rational thought.

7. Thus is formed naturally among people the first notion of goodness and justice, as well as their opposites; this is the beginning and birth of true kingship. For the people maintain the supreme power not only in the hands of these persons themselves, but in those of their descendants, from the conviction that those born from and reared by such persons will also have principles like to theirs. And, if they ever are

displeased with the descendants, they now choose their kings and rulers no longer for their bodily strength and brute courage, but for the excellence of their judgement and rational thinking, as they have gained experience from actual deeds of the difference between the one class of qualities and the other.

In old times, then, those who had once been chosen to the royal office continued to hold it until they grew old, fortifying and enclosing fine strongholds with walls and acquiring lands, in the one case for the sake of the security of their subjects and in the other to provide them with abundance of the necessities of life. And, while pursuing these aims, they were exempt from all vituperation or jealousy, as neither in their dress nor in their food and drink did they make any great distinction, but lived very much like everyone else, not keeping apart from the people. But, when they received the office by hereditary succession and found their safety now provided for, and more than sufficient provision of food, they gave way to their appetites owing to this superabundance, and came to think that the rulers must be distinguished from their subjects by a peculiar dress, that there should be a peculiar luxury and variety in the dressing and serving of their meals, and that they should meet with no refusal in the pursuit of their amours, however lawless. These habits having given rise in the one case to envy and offence and in the other to an outburst of hatred and passionate resentment, the kingship changed into a tyranny; the first steps towards its overthrow were taken by the subjects, and conspiracies began to be formed. These conspiracies were not the work of the worst men but of the noblest, most high-spirited, and most courageous, because such men are least able to brook the insolence of princes.

8. The people, now having got leaders, would combine with them against the ruling powers for the reasons I stated above; kingship and monarchy would be utterly abolished, and in their place aristocracy would begin to grow. For the commons, as if bound to pay at once their debt of gratitude to the abolishers of monarchy, would make them their leaders and entrust their destinies to them. At first these chiefs gladly assumed this charge and regarded nothing as of greater importance than the common interest, administering the private and public affairs of the people with paternal solicitude. But here again, when children inherited this position of authority from their fathers, having no experience of misfortune and none at all of civil equality and liberty of speech, having been brought up from the cradle amid the evidences of the power and high position of their fathers, they abandoned themselves, some to greed of gain and unscrupulous moneymaking, others to indulgence in wine and the convivial excess which accompanies it, and others again to the violation of women and the rape of boys; and thus converting the aristocracy into an oligarchy they aroused in the people feelings similar to those of which I just spoke, and in consequence met with the same disastrous end as the tyrant.

9. For, whenever anyone who has noticed the jealousy and hatred with which they are regarded by the citizens has the courage to speak or act against the chiefs of the state, he has the whole mass of the people ready to back him. Next, when they have either killed or banished the oligarchs, they no longer venture to set a king over them, as they still remember with terror the injustice they suffered from the former ones, nor can they entrust the government with confidence to a select few, with the evidence before them of their recent error in doing so. Thus the only hope still surviving unimpaired is in themselves, and to this they resort, making the state a democracy instead of an oligarchy and assuming the responsibility for the conduct of affairs. Then, as long as some of those survive who experienced the evils of oligarchical dominion, they are well pleased with the present form of government, and set a high value on equality and freedom of speech. But, when a new generation arises and the democracy falls into the hands of the grandchildren of its founders, they have become so accustomed to freedom and equality that they no longer value them, and begin to aim at preeminence; and it is chiefly those of ample fortune who fall into this error.

So, when they begin to lust for power and cannot attain it through themselves or their own good qualities, they ruin their estates, tempting and corrupting the people in every possible way. And hence, when by their foolish thirst for reputation they have created among the masses an appetite for gifts and the habit of receiving them, democracy in its turn is abolished and changes into a rule of force and violence. For the people, having grown accustomed to feed at the expense of others and to depend for their livelihood on the property of others, as soon as they find a leader who is enterprising but is excluded from the honors of office by his penury, institute the rule of violence; and now uniting their forces massacre, banish, and plunder, until they degenerate again into perfect savages and find once more a master and monarch.

Such is the cycle of political revolution, the course appointed by nature in which constitutions change, disappear, and finally return to the point from which they started. Anyone who clearly perceived this may indeed in speaking of the future of any state be wrong in his estimate of the time the process will take, but if his judgement is not tainted by animosity or jealousy, he will very seldom be mistaken as to the stage of growth or decline it has reached, and as to the form into which it will change. And especially in the case of the Roman constitution will this method enable us to arrive at a knowledge of its formation, growth, and greatest perfection, and likewise of the change for the worse which is sure to follow some day. For, as I said, this state, more than any other, has been formed and has grown naturally, and will undergo a natural decline and change to its contrary. The reader will be able to judge the truth of this from the subsequent parts of this work.

FOR DISCUSSION:

Do you agree that each form of government creates the conditions which eventually undermine it?

Acknowledgements

Aeschylus. *The Oresteian Trilogy: Agamemnon, the Choephori, the Eumenides*, translated by Philip Vellacott (Penguin Classics, 1956, Revised edition 1959). Copyright © Philip Vellacott, 1956, 1959. Reproduced by permission of Penguin Books Ltd.

Emily Katz Anhalt. Excerpt from *Solon the Singer: Politics and Poetics*, translated by Emily Katz Anhalt. Lanham, MD: Rowman & Littlefield, 1993. Reprinted with the permission of Emily Katz Anhalt.

Aristophanes. *Aristophanes: Lysistrata and Other Plays*, translated with an introduction and notes by Alan H. Sommerstein (Penguin Books, 2002). Copyright © Allan H. Sommerstein, 2002. Reproduced by permission of Penguin Books Ltd.

Aristophanes. Volume IV, *Frogs, Assemblywomen, Wealth*. Loeb Classical Library Volume 180, translated by Jeffrey Henderson, pp. 267-73. Cambridge, MA: Harvard University Press, copyright © 2002 by the President and Fellows of Harvard College. Loeb Classical Library ® is a registered trademark of the President and Fellows of Harvard College. Reprinted by permission of the publishers and the Trustees of the Loeb Classical Library.

Aristotle. "Ethics Nichomachea," translated by W.D. Ross from *Ethics* from *The Oxford Translation of Aristotle*, edited by W.D. Ross (Volume 9, 1925). Reprinted by permission of Oxford University Press.

Aristotle. *Politics*, translated by C.D.C. Reeve. Indianapolis and Cambridge: Hackett, 1998. Reprinted by permission of Hackett Publishing Company, Inc. All rights reserved.

Marcus Tullius Cicero. *On Moral Ends*, edited by Julia Annas and translated by Raphael Woolf. Cambridge and New York: Cambridge University Press. Copyright © 2001 Cambridge University Press. Reprinted with the permission of Cambridge University Press.

Marcus Tullius Cicero. *On the Commonwealth* and *On the Laws*, edited and translated by James E.G. Zetzel. Cambridge and New York: Cambridge University Press. Copyright © 1999 Cambridge University Press in the editorial matter, selection, and English translation.

Diogenes Laertius. Volume I, *Lives of Eminent Philosophers*, Books I-IV, Loeb Classical

INDEX

Academic Skepticism, 325
Academy, 2, 133, 203
action
  goals, 98-99, 262, 310
  happiness, 308
  leisure, 309, 311
  property, 272
  punishment, 110-11, 262
  types of, 310-11
  virtue, 262
Admetus, 24
Aegeus, 22
Aeschylus, 5, 13-31, 243
Agamemnon, 13
age
  athletics, 182
  breeding, 191
  procreation, 193
  rulers, 161-62, 212, 310
alliances, 282-83, 319-20
altruism, 326-27
Amazons, 22
anarchy, 47, 242-43
Andronicus of Rhodes, 255
animals
  breeding, 191
  democracy, 243
  domestic animals, 273
  guard dogs, 158-59
  nature, 309
  self-sufficiency, 270, 326
  Stoicism, 327
Antigone (Sophocles), 39-50
Aphrodite, 67, 72

Apollo, 13, 14, 16, 19-25
appropriation, 347-48
Areopagus, 14, 22
arguments, 119, 129, 131, 262-63
aristocracy
  defined, 279, 294, 331, 350, 353
  degradation, 221-22, 223, 331
  feasibility of, 296-97, 300
  freedom, 331
  friendship, 261
  ideal state, 219
  justice, 220
  marriage, 260, 261
  oligarchy, 350-51, 353
  superiority, 293-94
  virtue, 294
  See also government forms
Aristophanes, 37, 61-81, 83
Aristotle
  about, 255-56
  constitutions, 262
  education, 312
  government forms, 37
  Lyceum, 2, 255-56
  Nicomachean Ethics, 256-66
  Plato, 255
  Politics I, 267-76
  Politics III, 277-92
  Politics IV, 293-300
  Politics VII, 301-12
  timocracy, 219n2
arrogance, 7, 18, 43, 297
Artemis, 13